Creativity and Democracy in Education

The struggle to establish more democratic education pedagogies has a long history in the politics of mainstream education. This book argues for the significance of the creative arts in the establishment of social justice in education, using examples drawn from a selection of contemporary case studies including Japanese applied drama, Palestinian teacher education and Room 13 children's contemporary art.

Jeff Adams and Allan Owens use their research in practice to explore creativity conceptually, historically and metaphorically within a variety of UK and international contexts, which are analysed using political and social theories of democratic and relational education. Each chapter discusses the relationship between models of democratic creativity and the cultural conditions in which they are practised, with a focus on new critical pedagogies that have developed in response to neoliberalism and marketisation in education. The book is structured throughout by the theories, practices and ideals of democratic citizenship and equality that were once considered to be foundational for education.

Creativity and Democracy in Education will be of key interest to postgraduate students, researchers and academics in the field of education, especially those interested in the arts and creativity, democratic learning, teacher education, cultural and organisational studies and political theories of education.

Jeff Adams is Professor of Education at the University of Chester, UK. His current research explores contemporary arts in education and the professional development of teachers through creative practices.

Allan Owens is Professor in Drama Education at the University of Chester, UK, and a National Teaching Fellow. His practice and research are concerned with the professional and social applications of drama and theatre.

Adams and **Owens** are both co-Directors of RECAP, the international centre for Research into Education, Creativity and the Arts through Practice.

Routledge Research in Education Policy and Politics

The Routledge Research in Education Policy and Politics series aims to enhance our understanding of key challenges and facilitate ongoing academic debate within the influential and growing field of Education Policy and Politics.
Books in the series include:

Teacher Education through Active Engagement
Raising the professional voice
Edited by Lori Beckett

Health Education
Critical perspectives
Edited by Katie Fitzpatrick and Richard Tinning

US Education in a World of Migration
Implications for Policy and Practice
Edited by Jill Koyama and Mathangi Subramanian

Student Voices on Inequalities in European Higher Education
Challenges for theory, policy and practice
Edited by Fergal Finnegan, Barbara Merrill and Camilla Thunborg

Social Context Reform
A Pedagogy of Equity and Opportunity
Edited by P.L. Thomas, Brad Porfilio, Julie Gorlewski, and Paul R. Carr

Narrowing the Achievement Gap for Native American Students
Paying the Educational Debt
Edited by Peggy McCardle and Virginia Berninger

Demythologizing Educational Reforms
Responses to the Political and Corporate Takeover of Education
Edited by Arthur T. Costigan and Leslee Grey

The Politics of Compulsive Education
Racism and learner-citizenship
Karl Kitching

Educational Binds of Poverty
The lives of school children
Ceri Brown

Pedagogy, Praxis and Purpose in Education
C.M. Mulcahy, D.E. Mulcahy, and D.G. Mulcahy

Creativity and Democracy in Education
Practices and politics of education through the arts
Jeff Adams and Allan Owens

Creativity and Democracy in Education

Practices and politics of learning through the arts

Jeff Adams and Allan Owens

Routledge
Taylor & Francis Group
LONDON AND NEW YORK

First published 2016
by Routledge

2 Park Square, Milton Park, Abingdon, Oxon OX14 4RN
711 Third Avenue, New York, NY 10017, USA

Routledge is an imprint of the Taylor & Francis Group, an informa business

First issued in paperback 2017

Copyright © 2016 J. Adams and A. Owens

The right of J. Adams and A. Owens to be identified as authors of this work has been asserted by them in accordance with sections 77 and 78 of the Copyright, Designs and Patents Act 1988.

All rights reserved. No part of this book may be reprinted or reproduced or utilised in any form or by any electronic, mechanical, or other means, now known or hereafter invented, including photocopying and recording, or in any information storage or retrieval system, without permission in writing from the publishers.

Notice:
Product or corporate names may be trademarks or registered trademarks, and are used only for identification and explanation without intent to infringe.

British Library Cataloguing in Publication Data
A catalogue record for this book is available from the British Library

Library of Congress Cataloging-in-Publication Data
Adams, Jeff, 1956–
  Creativity and democracy in education : practices and politics of learning through the arts / Jeff Adams and Allan Owens.
     pages cm
  Includes bibliographical references and index.
  1. Art in education—Social aspects. 2. Arts—Study and teaching—Social aspects. 3. Social justice—Study and teaching. 4. Creative ability—Study and teaching. 5. Creative teaching. 6. Democracy and education. I. Owens, Allan, 1957– II. Title.
  LC192.2.A43 2016
  707'.1—dc23
  2015007313

ISBN: 978-0-415-74121-7 (hbk)
ISBN: 978-1-138-10391-7 (pbk)

Typeset in Galliard
by Apex CoVantage, LLC

Figure 0.1 'Solar Girl' by Marly Falconer of Room 13, Caol Primary School, Scotland; reproduced with the kind permission of Room 13 International.

Contents

	Acknowledgements	x
	Introduction	1
1	Theories of creativity and democratic education	5
2	Relational and critical creativity	22
3	Creative pedagogies: Palestine	41
4	Independent and democratic learning	62
5	Contemporary creative pedagogies: Japan	81
6	Creative interventions	97
7	Democratic trends in the politics of creativity and innovation	109
	Conclusion: creative acts, democratic acts	135
	References	141
	Index	155

Acknowledgements

Our grateful thanks to

Hala Al Yamani and colleagues at Bethlehem University, An-Najah University, Al Quds University, Abdelfattah Abu Srour, Al Rowwad/Beautiful Resistance Cultural and Theatre Society, Aida Camp, Bethlehem, and British Council Occupied Palestinian Territories; Anne Pässilä, Tuija Oikarinen, Vesa Harmmkorpi, Helinä Melkas, Laura Mellanen and colleagues at Lappeenranta University of Technology, School of Business and Management, (LUT Lahti), Finland; Kai Lehikoinen and Pekka Korhonen, Theatre Academy University of Arts, Helsinki; Raija Airaksinen-Björklund, Draamatayo; Raquel Benmergui, Cultural Co-operative Kiito and University of Tampere, Finland; John Freeman, Falmouth University, UK; Naomi Green, Tomoki Yoshimura NEC, Tokyo University of Technology, Yosuke Ohashi and Taichi Kikaku Theatre, Tokyo, Japan; Eva Österlind, Stockholm University, Sweden; Elisabet Aznar and David Martinez, La Nave Va-Teatro Catalunya; Jordi and Montse Forcadas, Forn de Teatre Pa'tothom, Barcelona, Catalunya, Spain; Dave Kellman, Western Edge Youth Arts, Melbourne, Australia; Joseph Valenta, Hana Kasíková, Jaroslav Provazník, Radek Marušák, Charles University, Bohuslava Bradbrook, Prague, Czech Republic; Katrin Nielsen, Aurika Komsaare, Viljandi Culture Academy, University of Tartu, Estonia; Heinrik Sproedt, SPIRE, University of Southern Denmark; Holger Jahnke, University of Flensburg, Germany; Mick, Susie and Leeroy Darling, Yorkshire, UK; Claire Gibb, Rob Fairley and the Room 13 children at Caol and Lochyside Primary Schools, Fort William, Scotland; Dennis Atkinson, Paul Dash, Tara Page, Steve Herne and colleagues at Goldsmiths, University of London; Kelly Worwood, Juliet Morris and teachers in London and Liverpool on the 'Teaching Though Contemporary Art' project; Deborah Riding at Tate Liverpool; jan jagodzinski, University of Alberta; Luca Hughes-Piper; the editorial team of the *International Journal of Art and Design Education*: Claire Penketh, Wendy Hyde, Maddy Sclater, Deborah Riding and Sandra Hiett; Lesley Butterworth and Sophie Leach at the National Society for Education in Art and Design; Clive Holtham, Cass Business School, City University, London; Giovanni Schiuma, University of Arts London/ Università della

Basilicata Italy; Elena Antonocopoulu, Management School, University of Liverpool; Jonothan Neelands, WBS Create, University of Warwick; Rod Hyde, RSA North West; Kate Dodgson Frodsham Foundation; the late John Doona, North West Drama Services; Tony Pickford, Barbara Pickford, Traveller Education CWAC; Hyung-Sook Kim, Jeong-Ae Park and colleagues, Korean Society for Education through Art.

Much of our research has been under the auspices of the Centre for Research into Creativity, Education, and the Arts through Practice (RECAP, http://www.chester.ac.uk/recap), and we would like to give special thanks to our researchers Emma Ayra-Manesh (née Godding) and Rachel Merriman and all members of RECAP and its networks; Anna Sutton, Rob Hulme, Dean Garratt, Darren Sproston, and all our friends and colleagues in the Faculty of Education and Children's Services and the Faculty of and Arts & Media at the University of Chester for their patience and support.

Last, but not least, of course, we would like to give our thanks to our families, especially Wendy Hyde; Clare, April, Jasmine, Arthur and Sheila Owens; Mary and Frank Philbin for their patience and unstinting support throughout.

Many of the projects discussed in this book been supported by research councils, businesses, educational societies, learned societies and charities, and we would like to acknowledge funding from the British Academy; British Council; World Bank; EU Comenius and Grundtvig Schemes; Cheshire West and Chester Council; Race Hate Crime UK; Society for the Advancement of Management Studies; Royal Society of Arts (North West Venture Fund); Japan Foundation, Santander; Higher Education Academy; Higher Education Funding Council; National Endowment for Science, Technology and the Arts; Esmée Fairbairn Foundation; Korean Society for Education through Art; National Society for Education in Art and Design, and Tate.

Introduction

In many ways this is an ambitious book about huge themes – democracy, creativity and education – and we are keen throughout to keep sight of the bigger picture, the overarching context in which our practices occur. The book is also about little accomplishments and momentary events, in the belief that greater social changes are constituted from numerous small ways of doing things, and many of the social and political issues here are explored through the idiosyncrasies of everyday, localised creative practices.

It is not the purpose of this book to try to establish more definitive or enduring meanings of creativity or even a model with distinctive features that we could coin as our own. The practices that we discuss in this book take many different forms and models of creativity; the similarities between them are more to do with the specific social relations established in each case, and the cultural and political contexts within which the practices occur. We are interested in arts' and creative practices' relationship to democracy and pedagogy and in the conditions by which this affiliation is established. In the realm of the arts, rethinking or reimagining ways of being constitute the practices to which we give our attention. Creativity in this scenario is a means to perceive differently, just as much as it is a means to do things differently. The type and means of creativity vary from practice to practice and from culture to culture, so much so that discovering what creativity can or might be, and how it might function, has become an integral part of many of our projects.

All of our research, in many different international and educational contexts over many years, has been concerned with social learning through the arts, whether it be performance or artistic activities in community settings, with students in schools and colleges, or creative practices with businesses: in each case it is intersubjective imaginings, the ways in which people might interact creatively, and in so doing construct ideas about others and culture that interests us. Our preoccupation with the social means of politics is ever present in our work in education through the arts, for when people come together to learn, to make, to express and to think creatively, and, therefore, *de facto*, to think differently, tensions inevitably emerge; this is a feature of democratic education and something we attempt to embrace and explore throughout our work.

In Williams's (1961) theory of the long revolutions – democratic, industrial, and cultural – in which our societies have been embedded for generations, he argues that the very large scale of the changes and the many generations affected over time make it difficult to have any adequate perspective on the scale, depth and complexity of the transformations that we nonetheless experience. The democratic revolution, the progress towards people governing themselves, has had a turbulent history and has been subject to fierce opposition, sometimes in the form of violent authoritarianism. Similarly, the cultural, communicative revolution evokes hostility, and the tussle between progressivism and reaction finds its way into our everyday lives and our ways of learning. These long-term social changes and conflicts are inevitably manifest in short-term, contingent, and local ways: ways of thinking and practising are continually changing and in so doing mirror or amplify the deeper currents of social change.

Change is determined by agency on the ground; although it seems as if we are in an ocean pulled by currents of such depth and strength that it exceeds our imagination, it is also true that these changes are composed of a myriad of micro events, and the ways we create things, the ways that we collaborate, in turn constitute the larger movement: we may not be able to resist the current, but we can swim in imaginative ways, we can keep each other afloat, and in doing so we contribute to the greater social project and become an integral part of the long revolution.

The struggles to establish more democratic education pedagogies have a long history in the politics of mainstream education, in parallel with the struggle to establish democracy itself in the greater polity. Prominent interventions by radical education theorists into this conflict, such as Dewey and Rancière, have been well documented over the years, and often the ascendancy of ethics and social justice in education have been accompanied by the expansion and status of creative arts disciplines and their practices in mainstream and higher education. The history of this symbiotic relationship is often referenced in this book to provide a framework for the exploration of the political significance of contemporary creative practices and their place in the enduring project of democratic emancipation.

The ideological dominance of neoliberalism in many Western governments' educational policies, as evidenced by the proliferation of market-based models of practice, have debased and marginalised formerly well-established democratic pedagogies and, with them, their signature creative practices. This book seeks to explore how democratic educational models survive under neoliberal hegemony and how new pedagogical practices in the arts respond to corporatisation and marketisation.

The locus of creativity in practice, however, is an enduring theme throughout this book; practice with all its specificities and cultural nuances, its implication of agency and collaboration, is a medium through which creativity is not only produced but which determines the forms of practice and, sometimes, its distortions and elaborations. Practice is an important concept here, because much of our research, our theoretical explorations, our creative experiences, occur in and through practice; moreover, practices that arise from social interactions and collaborations are our main concern.

We use practice to mean the ways in which ideas are manifest in the world, and creative arts practices are the most important of these for our discussions. Practice means more than the physical putting into effect of an idea; it goes beyond this to constitute the idea itself: thinking through practice to the point where thinking *is* the practice and vice versa. Many of the examples and case studies that we discuss are situated on the boundary between imagining and doing, so that the practice of making an artwork may arise from the routines of domestic activity for example, before it is extended into its physical manifestation as a painting or a performance. This is more than saying that practice encompasses thinking before the act; it is to suggest that the practice is indistinguishable from either thinking or from material production: it paradoxically precedes an idea as it is simultaneously the result of one. We have chosen to conceptualise practice in this extended way as it permits a dynamic analysis of the politics of the arts, allowing us to attempt to equate democratic thinking with democratic practices. We focus in our case studies on our first-hand encounters and engagements with others' practices, in which we share questions about the nature and conditions of creativity, education and democracy.

A brief outline of the contents of the book

In Chapter 1 we discuss and situate theories of creativity and democratic practices that have emerged in an increasingly globalised world. Through theories of dissensus and agonism developed by Rancière and Mouffe we explore the ascendancy of neoliberalism in educational practices and policies, and the ways in which this is contested through critical creative practices. Chapter 2 considers the emergence of relational practices and their increasing popularity in contemporary arts over recent decades before turning to relational arts in practice, relational creativity in education, and the politics of these practices. Chapter 3 is the first of five case-study chapters and focuses on creative practice in Palestinian schools, the dangerous and domesticated nature of creativity and democracy in education in a state under occupation; Chapter 4 discusses Dewey's theories of democratic and independent experiential learning, exploring their application to examples of children's creative practices such as those of Room 13; Chapter 5 considers a response to contemporary creative pedagogy in Japan through a case study informed by the relationship between the imaginaries of Western individualism and Eastern collectivity; Chapter 6 is concerned with the concepts of identity, translation and understanding applied in the context of developing understandings about Gypsy, Roma and Traveller culture in England; Chapter 7 moves beyond formal education institutions to look at the place of creativity in organisations and business in a wider community context with the democratic vision of lifelong learning.

We conclude by turning to recent developments in social and artistic media, discussing how these may affect creativity and democratic practices in education in the future. These developments are contextualised historically, as we continually look backwards as well as forwards, considering the ways in which our predecessors struggled to establish democratic education, and what implications this might have for our future.

Chapter 1

Theories of creativity and democratic education

Themes of creativity and democracy

Concepts of creativity are always historically contingent, arising from social conditions and configurations of power at specific moments, and are therefore always politically and culturally constructed (Fannes, 2013; Nelson, 2013). In the many and varied constructions of creativity that we have available to us there are many commonalities as well as divergences, and there exist deep contradictions that are instructive when analysed in relation to the wider political struggles embedded in global capitalism.

The idea of creativity can be as amorphous as it is ubiquitous, and its history and etymology only confirm the ambiguity and contradictions of the concept. Williams (1976/1984) in his definitions of creativity traces the biblical origins of the word – creativity as the original moment, the genesis – before he goes on to look at the 18th-century development of the concept, where it begins to encompass creativity as an individual practice and as an intellectual faculty and its subsequent association with the arts and philosophy. As he notes, a tension emerges during this transformative period of the concept, as creativity began to be applied to everyday practices while still retaining an emphasis on originality derived from its older meanings. The proliferation of the term has accelerated under the hegemony of neoliberal thought and has become ubiquitous to the point where it has a diminished currency.

The fabric of creativity has been worn threadbare by adorning a multitude of ideological conceptualisations. Craft (2001) has tried to make sense of the many configurations and transformations of creativity that have arisen during the post-war period, and has provided us with a taxonomy of the many, occasionally competing traditions. The variety of types and definitions, and the differing purposes to which these have been used, remind us of the dangers of loosely using this term; creativity signifies many things and has done so with great variety in many cultures and contexts around the world, from the psychological powers of the individual 'genius' to the problem-solving capacities of young children. Craft also alerts us to the myriad uses of creativity in governmental policies and to what this might tell us about the political attitudes of the governments and the populace towards the arts and creative practices at any given time.

One important distinction that has frequently been identified (e.g. Vygotsky, 1930/2014; Craft, 2001; Jones, 2009) is that between high and popular or democratic creativity. This is important for us in our text because the former is associated with elitism and notions of the exceptional and the gifted, notions that we reject and have no place in our conception of democracy or education. Democratic creativity, on the other hand, is clearly the domain that we wish to explore; this is the concept of creativity that includes the imaginative events and productions of ordinary people, the masses of the populace. Jones's (2009) survey of intellectual thought around creativity discusses its recuperation in school curricula in England, noting the transformations that had to be made in some cases to detach it from prior notions that would have linked creativity to equality and criticality, offering instead technical and instrumental conceptions of the idea, more easily assimilated into a performance-based curriculum.

Given this expansion of use, it is necessary to conceptualise *creativity* as a heterogeneous term, plural and multivalent, with many varieties contingent on an infinite number of specific and local contexts. Nevertheless, new emerging themes of creativity can be identified, some of which have distinctive political features. Most significantly, one can detect forms of creative practice that have an antithetical relationship to global capitalism and neoliberalism in particular. For example, in the Republic of Korea, the intense and competitive curriculum has many casualties manifest in the very high teenage suicide rate (Al Jazeera, 2011); in this case opportunities to be creative in education are seen as a possible panacea for these ills of intense competition, as a protection from the excesses of extreme performativity in education.

As jagodzinski (2010) has observed, innovation frequently crops up as acquiescence, a cynical appropriation of creativity, which is instead a reinforcement of existing orthodoxies. Deleuze, as jagodzinski (2010) has pointed out, argues that 'creativity proper' should be distinguished from innovation, the former being a significant event and the latter being what passes for creativity in the routine activity of global capitalism.

This appropriation of creativity for innovation is most obvious in the work of 'creatives' in the design and media industry, an example that serves to sustain and mobilise forces of capitalism and to maintain the status quo (jagodzinski, 2010, pp. 160–163). The case of the 'shockvertising' precipitated by the Benetton adverts in the 1980s being a case in point; these had the guise of a creative disruption to traditional order but were little more than the novel peddling of goods, which sustained rather than challenged existing orthodoxies and inequalities. On the other hand, the creative activities of Palestinian demonstrators occupying West Bank hilltops in a pastiche of settlers' land-grabs (e.g. the creation of Bab al Shams), or the creative organisation of protests in Turkey's Taksim Square, may offer a radical critique of global capitalism as, Zizek (2013) suggests.

The content of creativity, of the creative act, and of creative agency, are all of significance in our work. There are many thorough studies of the typographies of creativity, models in which the content is later added, or analyses of features or characteristics of creative events to which a formula is applied (e.g. Cropley and Cropley, 2008; National Advisory Committee on Creative and Cultural Education [NACCCE], 1999). However, the case studies of which this book comprises are principally concerned with the way that content shapes the form of creativity: content is always conceived and understood through practice. The practice of creativity brings about its forms, and the retrospective application of particular models is of secondary importance for us. This is significant for understanding the way that neoliberalism hollows out and colonises creative acts and events, because this is dependent on a mutable, reproducible and eventually dispensable content. For our purposes here, however, the content of the creative event is the antithesis of this conception: it is highly specific, context dependent, and socially engaged. This high degree of specificity determines the form of the creative act or event; in other words the creative form is a manifestation of a particular practice that may be neither transferable nor even replicable, existing only in the moment of the event in which it is identified. Content that is constructed through a specific practice, and governed by the proclivities and politics of a given social situation, is most certainly not amenable to the kind of flexible creativity favoured by corporate, neoliberal advocacy. On the contrary it may be singular, inflexible, immutable and even profound within the micro-culture that produced it. For example Palestinian student teachers' improvisations in a drama pretext about their situation under occupation are very far from being readily assimilated into formulaic and adaptable notions of creativity. This is not say that creative phenomena should not be subjected to theoretical analysis and classification retrospectively but, rather, that a focus on specific practices that produce equally singular creative events are better understood through the thick cultural narratives from which they arose.

Democracy and equality in education

The conditions for creative practices to flourish in education are largely determined by the extent to which democratic principles are established. Rancière (1991) argues that equality should be the fundamental principle around which education, particularly education by the state, should be founded and function (1991;). This echoes Williams's (1961) argument that participation is the most fundamental component – and a goal – of democracy, and that the institutions of state, including education, should be seen as enabling in this respect. Equality for Williams is a necessary condition for full participation, and *de facto* for democracy. Yet for Rancière the means of achieving equality runs contrary to many accepted notions of what education might mean, the 'ignorant schoolmaster' polemic being a case in point. In his narrative ignorance is cast as a virtue on the part of the teacher, as a prerequisite for learning to occur.

This is because equality disrupts traditional power relations in education in Rancière's thesis; the teacher is equal to the learner in ignorance, and both refer – and defer – to the object of study as the source of knowledge. The teacher is no longer the explicator or the arbiter of understanding on the part of the student, which Rancière argues is a disabling process, an additional layering of meaning to the original object of study, over which the teacher has absolute control and thereby institutes an unequal and permanent power relation between teacher and student. As Rancière elaborates this model it becomes apparent that he sees this laying as a deliberately obstructive process, which not only ensures that access to knowledge is governed and mediated by the teacher, but that it also structures the student, creating a dependency – which Rancière argues is the real learning that is taking place – learning to be dependent upon the teacher. This disabling of the student, the removal of the belief that the student can learn independently, is a key power formulation that is replicated in western state education systems, and ensures that inequalities are perpetuated, as articulated by class reproduction theorists such as Bourdieu and Passeron (1990). Rancière (1991) makes clear the relations that these cultural structures in schools and universities exist to ensure that the unequal social relations that occur in the wider society are replicated and perpetuated throughout an education system.

In creating this argument Rancière problematises several key terms that are normally associated with learning, most notably *understanding*. Through the maintenance of inequality, understanding becomes constantly subject to validation by assessment, and this is under the absolute control of the explicator. The determination of understanding is wholly based on the mediation and packaging of knowledge that is presented to the student, and ignores any new, original, idiosyncratic or personal interpretation that the student might bring to the study, because this may deviate from the 'correct' understanding provided, and potentially render it invalid. Assessment is then, for Rancière, a validation of the explicator and the controlled mediation of knowledge, rather than a measure of any actual understanding of the original object of study. In this way the determination of understanding is also supported by the acquiescence of the learner, who has internalised the erroneous belief that understanding cannot occur beyond the structures of explication and its subsequent validation. If these arbiters of understanding are also embedded in an unequal society, then it must follow that the consequent form of education will also be entrenched in inequality. Rancière exposes the contradictions of progressive education, especially where it is construed as a panacea for social disadvantage; for while education is purported to, as Rancière puts it, make 'inequality visible', as a means to make tangible its egalitarian project, it simultaneously functions as a means to endlessly defer the attainment of equality. As he explains, '[s]cholarly progression is the art of limiting the transmission of knowledge, of organising delay, of deferring equality' (2010b, p. 8).

Disruptive democracy

Giroux (2014b) argues that one way of challenging this new authoritarianism is 'to reclaim the relationship between critical education and social change'. The problem he identifies is that democracy has been sullied as a concept and no longer offers the promise of emancipation. The solution for this, Giroux argues, is to institute a critical education as a means to revitalise democracy by encouraging and enabling people to engage with issues of citizenship and emancipation, and, as he puts it, 'reclaiming a kind of humanity that should inspire and inform our collective willingness to imagine what a real democracy might look like' (para. 42). As Giroux argues, it is not only participation in education that is important but also the way that education provides the means towards governance. Crucial to this idea is critical thinking, but 'critical thinking divorced from action is often as sterile as action divorced from critical theory' as Giroux explains it (2014b, para. 45). Critical education for Giroux is one that is not subservient to corporations or business interests but, rather, one that is designed in the form of democracy and from which democracy is produced and enabled.

Mouffe (2005, 2009) has argued that democracy is a contest, and on a global scale. She emphasises that capitalism is not integrated with democracy, and therefore, the spread of the former does not necessarily mean the spread of the latter. What it does mean, however, is the spread of conflict as capitalist enterprises colonise new territories and appropriate local powers and means of control. Mouffe analyses this in terms of the articulation of neoliberalism and democracy (2009, pp. 6–7); in this dynamic engagement neoliberalism is frequently the dominant ideology, and democracy is weakened or even negated by the partnership. The casualties of the neoliberal dominance are, according to Mouffe, invariably democratic governance and social justice; the struggle for equality is abandoned and replaced with the deception of liberal freedom. This is a catastrophic mistake because political rights for the majority have always had to be won by political struggle, a contest that continues despite neoliberal assurances to the contrary. Mouffe points out that, historically, the ruling classes have never freely given away their privileges; moreover, those democratic rights that have already been won are constantly being eroded by powerful groups in the maintenance or restoration of their particular interests.

Carr and Hartnett (2010) concur with Mouffe on this concept of democracy being an enduring struggle, a series of rights that are never bestowed on the masses but, rather, have to be won through assertion; they also argue that democratic rights are in a perpetual state of fragility and vulnerability, and therefore have to be protected by constant vigilance. They focus on the free access to high-quality education as the touchstone for the well-being of a democratic society and describe the struggles that have taken place in the establishment of the notion of 'education for all' in Western nations. They look at the political shaping of policies for mass secondary education in the UK to demonstrate the resistance to this idea, and the uneven progress towards its establishment as a widely accepted feature of the political landscape. Going on to look at subsequent developments in the education system through the lens of the interests of powerful groups, they warn of education's susceptibility to policies of privatisation and special interests, which have a corrosive effect on democratic access by the populace. This is exacerbated by fundamental weaknesses present in the structures of a comprehensive education system, whereby privileged interests are preserved in the very foundation of the system – as witnessed by the continued and uninterrupted existence of high-status private schools throughout the period of comprehensive school reforms and reorganisation. The consequent further segregation and division of education into types of schooling, when seen from this perspective, can only exacerbate the erosion of democratic education and create hierarchies of schools.

Ken Jones (2012, using the work on democracy of Canfora), looks at the events of 1945 and after, that is to stay the establishment of secondary education for all in the UK and the growth of teacher control of both the content and methods of delivery of the curriculum in the period running up to the reactionary clampdowns of the 1980s. He argues that the growth of teacher influence was indicative of the wresting of power away from traditional authorities and further that this was also indicative of the progress of democracy itself. Democracy, in Jones's view, should be seen as a disruptive strategy for redistributing power and wealth. Moreover, it is a contingent and momentary occurrence that has to be constantly reinvigorated. Thus, the events of 1945 in the UK, the nationalisation of health and education, whilst having an important and enduring effect on policy and attitudes to education, were nonetheless limited and proscribed by traditional orthodoxies, which continue to try to re-establish their authority. For Jones, however, the key point is that teachers and educators have managed in the past to collectively establish authority over the content and methods of their teaching and the conditions under which they work and that this can still be reclaimed despite the advances of neoliberalism.

For Mouffe, the critical aspect of democracy is to be located in the idea of antagonism, or agonsim, as Mouffe (2009) would describe it. This is the idea that politics proper can only occur when it is an expression of the deep social divisions within a society. Mouffe explains that the problem with 'third-way' politics is that it attempts to remove conflict or antagonisms in order to achieve consensus and, in doing so, weakens rather than strengthens politics proper. In her arguments against 'aggregative' models of democracy, which discourage active participation and foster the privatisation, she develops her model of agonism. In this theory, informed by Wittgenstein and his critique of rationalism, she offers an analysis of the limits of consensus. She quotes from his *Philosophical Investigations*, where he critiques the ideal of rational consensus in politics, on the grounds that politics cannot escape from the practices of life with all its inherent contradictions:

> We have got to the slippery ice where there is no friction and so in a certain sense the conditions are ideal, but also, just because of that, we are unable to walk: so we need friction. Back to the rough ground.
> (Wittgenstein, quoted in Mouffe, 2009, p. 98)

The politics that results from so-called consensus or dialogic politics, she argues is impoverished to the point of redundancy as a social action. The vacuum that is created by this absence of antagonism is filled with other expressions of conflict, such as the rise of nationalist, religious or ethnic fundamentalism, which are entrenched and sit outside the democratic political process; this marks the end of politics proper and therefore should be resisted. For Mouffe the only way that this crisis of democracy can successfully be avoided is by reinstituting adversarialism into the political process. Agonism attempts to do this, by acknowledging the impediments and impossibility of 'unconstrained public deliberation' (Mouffe, 2009, p. 98). Using Schmitt she introduces the idea that power must be thought of as constituting identity, rather than being an external relation:

> Since any political order is the expression of a hegemony, of a specific pattern of power relations, political practice cannot be envisaged as simply representing the interests of pre-constituted identities, but as constituting those identities themselves in a precarious and always vulnerable terrain.
> (Mouffe, 2009, p. 100)

Legitimising claims to power within the democratic process, rather than outside of it, even when those claims may be hotly contested or even beyond rational argument, is one of the features of Mouffe's agonistic pluralism. In this way Mouffe (2009) brings conflict back into politics and into democracy. She distinguishes between politics and the political, whereby the former is the institutions and practices, and the latter is the 'the dimension of antagonism that is inherent in human relations' (p. 101). Democracy then is not the elimination of antagonism or conflict, but rather its 'domestication' within a pluralist democracy, converting the 'enemy' into the 'adversary', into the legitimate opponent (p. 102). Importantly, in this model of agonism, Mouffe retains the idea that conflicting ideals cannot necessarily be resolved through rational discussion, which means that the antagonism may remain unresolved and may even be a permanent condition. The difference that agonism makes is that it permits 'a struggle between adversaries' to persist within the democratic process,

> providing channels through which collective passions will be given ways to express themselves over issues which, while allowing enough possibility for identification, do not construct the opponent as an enemy but as an

adversary ... The prime task of democratic politics is not to eliminate passions from the sphere of the public, in order to render a rational consensus possible, but to mobilise those passions towards democratic designs ... Well functioning democracy calls for a vibrant clash of democratic political positions. ... Too much emphasis on consensus and the refusal of confrontation leads to apathy and disaffection with political participation ... It is for that reason that the ideal of a pluralist democracy cannot be to reach a rational consensus in the public sphere. Such a consensus cannot exist.

(Mouffe, 2009, pp. 103–104)

This model of democracy, Mouffe argues, is more able to accommodate the many different voices of a diverse and multicultural society.

McDonnell (2014) has demonstrated, using the work of Rancière, that the relationship between art, democracy and education is significant in terms of the way that art enables 'political subjectification'; by this she means that Rancière sees parallels between models of democracy and models of art, whereby art is able to disrupt normalising societal roles and practices. This is important for McDonnell, because, like Rancière and Mouffe, she sees democracy as perpetually challenging, critical and disruptive. Therefore, art provides a means to enable this critical social engagement with the distribution of power. McDonnell points out that the arts and democracy are both collaborative and collective projects, dismissing the more conventional view that the arts are singular and individual. In this common ground the arts are fundamental to the democratic and educational process, especially given their propensity for disruption and critical questioning. Democratic subjectivity can be constructed through creative practices, especially those in which a context for collective democratic action is created.

McDonnell's reading of this relationship occurs at a time when the field of contemporary art has opened up spaces for social engagement and collective action. This context is important because in the present day the whole field of the arts is characterised by diversity, in part as a manifestation of social media and globalisation, and this plurality of means and content makes contemporary creative practices especially amenable to collective and collaborative action across geographic and cultural divisions.

Creativity under the global governance of education

One of the most striking features of education in terms of globalisation is the emergence of the indiscriminate standardisation of testing, embraced by governments of diverse cultures and nations. Global media has permitted the instant sharing of results in the form of league tables (a metaphor not coincidently drawn from competitive sport), which has effectively enabled a very powerful – and extremely reductive – form of global governance of education. The form that this international calibration has taken, PISA (Programme for International

Student Assessment) is run by the OECD (Organisation for Economic Cooperation and Development), an organisation designed to impose and enforce economic markets. As Meyer and Benavot (2013) point out, the contradictions of PISA are as manifest as its power and influence: the OECD is an economic, not an educational organisation; it is largely unaccountable, although it demands accountability of governments, schools and teachers across the world; it is historically rooted in US capitalist models of education and masquerades as a culturally neutral standard benchmark. Most importantly for education and its social democratic functions, its tests are narrow and take no account of creative, expressive, social or collaborative aspects of education, which are therefore relegated to occupy superficial and dispensable positions in the minds of governments across the world.

When the OECD does turn to creativity and arts education, the discussion is usually framed uncritically in relation to innovation and economic growth. In *Art for Arts Sake: the Impact of Arts Education* (Winner, Goldstein, and Vincent–Lacrin, 2013) the OECD Centre for Educational Research reports on a systematic overview undertaken of all extant empirical research since 1980 in arts education concerned with 'skills for innovation', which are defined as 'technical', 'thinking and creative' and 'behavioural and social' and are presented as being 'beyond and above artistic skills and cultural sensitivity' (p. 3); these are taken to be the traditional ground of arts education unquestioningly conceptualised in consensual, domesticated terms as means of valuing the 'human experience'. The focus is on 'transfer' from the arts fostering individual skills in other subjects and domains that contribute to innovation and economic growth, the endgame being better performance in a competitive world market. The proposed agenda for future research and policy with regard to the impact of arts education continues to centre on transfer but with increased emphasis on the measurement of its contribution to individual skills for innovation.

Measuring, calibrating and segregating

Lemov provides us with a dramatic example of the new world of the globalised and homogenised education system and its proponents' desire to audit, classify and calibrate and, thereby, reduce people – particularly children – to metrics: 'In the last ten years we've been able to measure the annual progress of kids systematically. If there's one thing that would improve the UK education system it's data' (Lemov, quoted in Weale, 2014). This remarkable statement is perfectly indicative of the neoliberal, instrumentalist vision of education. All the more poignant and disturbing because it emerges from an almost idealistic vision of education that might have, in the past, been thought of as progressive. It is plausible, and in one sense at least, practicable and workable in the classroom. The taxonomy of features that Lemov has developed are packed with high-energy, no-nonsense, direct instructions for teachers that are expected to produce predictable responses from children. Teachers are exhorted to succeed by following these examples (our selection):

> set a high standard of correctness in your classroom; to succeed students must take their knowledge and express it in the language of opportunity; a great lesson objective and therefore a great lesson should be Manageable, Measurable, Made first, and Most important on the path to knowledge; it's as important to plan for what students will be doing during each phase of a lesson as it is to plan for what you will be doing and saying.
>
> (selected from Lemov, 2010)

Lemov may be well meaning, but the assumption that all that is meaningful and important in education is amenable to measurement, or that the translation of experience and performance into data is unproblematic, or that such a process will have nothing but positive effects on its subjects, all these are commonly recurring features of the neoliberal mind-set that have been successfully established as 'common sense', despite their obvious and blatant shortcomings. The dominance of measuring and auditing in education is a good example of the ideological legitimation and the naturalisation of a formerly subsidiary concept and its rehabilitation as a central and indispensable core of education. Its effects on people in education are striking and are everywhere to be seen, despite its destructiveness and pointlessness being equally apparent; it is difficult have a conversation with a serving educator who is not likely at some point to complain about the time, thought and energy that used to be devoted to teaching and care that now have to be diverted to bureaucratic tasks, most of which are orientated towards the metrics of performance, of both student and teacher. Tomlinson and Lipsitz (2013) have no doubts about the reasons for this contradictory state of affairs:

> Neoliberalism is not just an economic system. Unimpeded capital accumulation requires extensive ideological legitimation. Neoliberal practices seek to produce neoliberal subjects through a social pedagogy that aims to naturalize hierarchy and exploitation by promoting internalized preferences for profits over the needs of people, relentless individuation of collective social processes, cultivation of hostile privatism and defensive localism based on exaggerated fears of difference, and mobilization of anger and resentment against vulnerable populations to render them disposable, displaceable, deportable, and docile.
>
> (p. 4)

For Tomlinson and Lipsitz these contradictions that are apparent enough in theory, and even more so in practice, are a necessary part of neoliberal strategy. Because the aim is the reduction of democratic practices and the accumulation of wealth and power in an ever-reducing percentage of the population, the intensifying of a burgeoning and authoritarian bureaucracy, most commonly expressed in performance metrics, to which the great majority of public-service educators must conform, begins to make sense. That this way of thinking should be adopted willingly and uncritically by its agents, in this case teachers and educators, is testament to the ideological hegemony of neoliberalism. Apple (2013) is more nuanced in his analysis, distinguishing between the different factions that constitute this ideology, and arguing that 'audit culture' is a phenomenon that has grown with middle managerialism, a new social class of people that seek to control entirely through measurement and evaluation of performance, 'the tail of tests wagging the dog of teachers' (p. 42). However, Tomlinson and Lipsitz recognise that, despite its success, when this ideology is expressed in practice its deleterious effects are obvious enough:

> The grandiose aspirations of neoliberal pedagogy, however, are often undermined by the system's ruinous effects. Neoliberalism promises prosperity but delivers austerity. It confuses consumer choice with human agency and reduces justice to revenge and punishment. It produces resistance among the very populations it hopes to suppress and control.
> (Tomlinson and Lipsitz, 2013, p. 4)

The diminished conception of education as obedient behaviour expressed as data, as promulgated by the likes of Lemov, has nonetheless dominated much political debate. This is reminiscent of Gielen's (2013) metaphor for a globalised, neoliberal and mass-media-dominated world, determined by an undiscerning and undifferentiated relativism, which he refers to as the 'horizontal or flat world'. In such a world, measurement and calibration are key: to be of use an entity must be measured, and the act of measuring is itself of paramount importance. As Gielen puts it, in the flat world number is king, and creativity in its random, non sequitur, haphazard modes, fares badly (2013, p. 42). The forms that education takes are fundamentally affected as a consequence of this: all components or features that can be readily measured are valued highly, those that cannot are marginalised or eliminated altogether. This is a thin disguise for a system that is determined principally by economics. This has further consequences for education: if the cultural and emancipatory dimensional is diminished, and the qualitative, performative aspects are amplified, the system acquires commensurate features such as constant reorganisation and change. This is necessary in order to continually defer difficult questions such as the purpose and value of education for the majority of people for whom an economic model is disadvantageous, because only a minority can never prosper in such a system. The underlying democratic ground upon which mass education in many Western states was founded is increasingly absent; the resulting vacuum must be filled, and attention diverted away from any suspicion that there have been, and might still be, more equitable and just systems. Change for the sake of change, reorganisation and the relentless tide of auditing and calibration must dominate in order that attention is drawn elsewhere.

The cult of managerialism is an important manifestation of the fetishisation of endless change and plays an important part in the camouflage of the democratic recession; Western systems of education are increasingly prey to this, and often the main victims are creative educators. As Gielen acerbically explains,

> [t]hat many organisational restructurings seemed pointless and later turn out to be so, and that the endless chain of 'creative' changes often results in a status quo on the work floor, is a fact that many employees are by now wise to. The rank and file have long since figured out that this neophilia primarily serves to keep the neo-managers themselves firmly in the saddle, as every newly announced change legitimises their own survival. Whereas creative individuals come and go, anyone who is good at measuring and counting stays on. After all, creativity must be flexibly deployable, devoid of any ardent belief, ideology or conviction. The creative deed must be depoliticised, in other words.
>
> (2013, p. 52)

This brings us to the heart of the problem of creativity: if creativity is conceptualised as infinitely variable and adaptable, and creative individuals thought of likewise, its appropriation and manipulation must also follow. Given the context of the all-consuming force of neoliberalism allied to mass and social media, it is unsurprising that creativity is readily appropriated, and with it creative practitioners and educators. On the other hand, this susceptibility to be adapted for whatever purpose, irrespective of content, also proves to be an advantage especially when considered in terms of political resistance and opposition, as we shall explore in the subsequent chapters of this book.

Creativity producing tensions in conformist education systems

Creativity has a long history of being viewed with suspicion by forms of education aligned with traditions other than democracy and the consequence of this is that schools with a focus on 'traditional' values, which are currently encouraged by the government in England, tend to opt for prescriptive and easily audited curricula content, often at the expense of creative subjects or approaches. The reduction and loss of autonomous creative content in the curriculum, or in teacher education, are indicative of the overarching loss of a democratic and civic ethos (Hall, 2011), and this can be seen as a symptom of the neoliberalisation of education (Adams, 2013). However, it is possible to find, through the same globalising mechanisms subsumed into neoliberalism, creative networks and alliances brought together through mutual resistance to neoliberal commodification and authoritarianism in education, as some of our case studies demonstrate.

If free, secular mass education, high status and well funded (relative to gross domestic product), is a fundamental component of the egalitarian and democratic ideal and directly commensurate with a thriving democratic society, then what part does creative education play in this democratic project? We argue that creativity is to education what education is to democracy: fundamental and essential, so much so that one cannot truly function without the other. Far from the popular notion that creative education is an added extra, an additional spice added to the education recipe, creativity can be seen as basic or as 'core' as numeracy or literacy, in that creative practices potentially comprise increased awareness: perceptually, socially, criticality, materially and politically. This integration of the social and the critical with the material and the sensible has the potential to catalyse the whole education project, to make the world relevant and comprehensible to the individual subject.

Taken in the context of the struggle for democracy described earlier, there must be – and is – a price to be paid for creativity in a state education system. Creativity can be seen as an expression of the tension produced within the social orders that underpin the orthodox configurations of education. Creativity, in the institutional setting of the school, begins to take on risky and potentially disruptive qualities, as jagodzinski, (2010) makes us aware. These risks arise from the nature of the creative act in the context of the school. They may take the form of a teacher developing a pedagogy that is underpinned by the principles of spontaneity and responsiveness, and that confers a pronounced form of responsibility on students as they are inaugurated as active agents in the education process rather than as merely its recipients, or the risk may be ignoring pre-planned outcomes and all the usual characteristics of performativity that focus on predetermined learning goals, productivity, individualism and competition. In doing so there is a perceptible and significant – and risky – shift away from the notion of the teacher as instructor or explicator, and there is a significant erosion of the teacher as the ruling authority. The rather idealistic notion of a community of creative agents – artists or creative teachers, for instance – nonetheless does carry the extremely potent idea of equality; this cannot be sanctioned by the institution, and at best it is ignored or ameliorated by being disguised or, at worst, punished.

It should come as no surprise that creative subjects and creative acts are commonly marginalised in state schools throughout the industrialised world. Teachers associated with creativity accrue fewer funds and frequently have less power. The hierarchical managers within schools put creativity low down in their priorities, and they are normally vigilant to ensure that the ethos of the institution remains conformist and obedient. This reflects the wider global interface between local communities and global capitalism, where the latter is in the ascendency at the cost of democracy. As Zizek (2013) argues,

> Global capitalism is a complex process that affects different countries in different ways. What unites the protests, for all their multifariousness, is that

they are all reactions against different facets of capitalist globalisation. The general tendency of today's global capitalism is towards further expansion of the market, creeping enclosure of public space, reduction of public services (healthcare, education, culture), and increasingly authoritarian political power.

(p. 11)

If we take Zizek's point here, we can see that certain conceptions of creativity take on an added resonance: creativity that champions the unorthodox, is antagonistic to conformism, is disobedient and imaginative, and offers insights into the political machinations of the institution in which it is housed. These are ideals, mythological and imaginary in themselves, but they nonetheless provide an alternative to the oppressive conformism of the market ideology and its authoritarianism. The potency of creativity in education can be measured by the efforts made by authorities in schools to suppress its acts and subjugate its agents, creative teachers.

The creative activities of Al Rowwad (Theatre of the Beautiful Resistance) in Bethlehem's Aida refugee camp, for instance, is an example of imaginative peaceful and creative resistance flourishing in an education context, where children, using contemporary drama methods, re-enact the Nakba (the initial expulsion of Palestinians, which led to the creation of the refugee camps in which they still live), the teaching of which is largely forbidden in the territories of the occupying administration. (Abdel-Fattah, 2013). This appears to be a good example of what Edward Said (1993) describes as 'speaking truth to power', where creative acts are directly responsive to oppressive practices, revealing and disseminating the truth of a situation. Zizek (2007) is sceptical of this tactic, however, arguing that the slogan 'speak truth to power' is limited; (quoting Safouan) he explains: 'The trouble with this slogan is that it ignores the fact that power will not listen' (para. 42). To overcome this impasse, creative acts need to be dynamic, perpetually adaptable, and critical.

As Carr and Hartnett (2010) have explained, state education is about the struggle for emancipatory democracy itself, played out in contemporary schools (cf. K. Jones, 2009). Seen in this way, creative pedagogies, subjects and events in schools acquire prescience: they at once anticipate the attainment of an ideal, a socially equitable society, just as they disrupt the structures of conformity and performativity. Bureaucratic marginalisation is probably the most effective means to neutralise this potential disruption to authority. Creative acts, whether they be the imaginative organisation of a teacher's pedagogy in the face of a highly restrictive curriculum, or refugee camp children preserving the memory of their confiscated homes in a play, are humble but significant indicators of democracy in education. It may be that their very creative nonconformity highlights the deeper ills of democracy that obeisance to neoliberalisation brings about.

Figure 1.1 Entrance to Aida Refugee Camp, Bethlehem, Palestine

Critical creativity

Our idea of a critical creativity is derived from the notion of competing voices in a diverse cultural context. The kind of creativity that concerns us here is not so much a type, as a configuration. It is the juxtaposition of creativity with democracy, a dynamic engagement, an intersection between the imaginary and the political. It is the point at which the notion of imagination is combined with and embedded in the corresponding notion of citizenship. Critical creativity is in many ways similar to Gielen's (2013) concept of 'vertical creation', in which he articulates the idea of creativity which contains within it the potency of criticism.

Gielen laments at length the loss of critical analysis within creative activity, brought about by neoliberalism and mass media, whereby creativity is reduced to replicable and ubiquitous forms of pastiche, often posturing as 'avant-garde'. For Gielen, criticism in the form of artistic and social critique is perhaps the single most important feature of the concept, because it enables creative acts and events to be fully engaged with the society and culture within which they are formed, a dialectic in which new political, social and artistic ideas may emerge. Without this fundamental component creativity can only ever be a pastiche of itself, anodyne and decorative and devoid of political potency. Creativity without its critical edge is little more than a decorative social activity that can be colonised and utilised for any political or ideological ends. Gielen refers to this as capitalist or neoliberal creativity, which is the antithesis of vertical or critical creativity:

> The type of creation that we have been calling 'art' since the modern age depends to a large degree on the possibility of taking a critical stance in one's own society and culture. Only when creative individuals can rise above their own world for a while . . . can they actually make a difference in their culture. Criticism is indeed a form of verticalization. It starts with self-reflection and self-criticism rising above one's own ego and seeing oneself from some distance.
>
> (2013: 72)

We use the term critical creativity to indicate that agency, imagination and political action are the fundamental constituents in this process. Just as Mouffe (2009) argues, in her model of agonism, this process accommodates, but does not attempt to settle, the conflicting voices from which it is constituted. In this model of creativity engagement is key: resolution is not the aim. That diverse or opposing participants in a collaborative process can give voice to their imaginative conjectures is a sufficient goal in itself.

It is this critical stance or formulation of creativity that makes it so indispensable to democratic education, just as the reintroduction of conflict or antagonism in its proper place is to the political process. What this means, in effect, is that the ideals, concepts, and the practices of democracy are opened up and laid bare, subjected to critical appraisal. This is not an occasional or superficial questioning of a process; rather, it is the regular, daily, and perpetual, re-evaluating and contesting of the practices that constitute the polity. The critical, in this conception of politics, is the norm. Criticism in the context of creativity is a vital and fundamental constituent. It enables the imaginative, innovative impulse to be located socially in such a way that it offers a reflection of the social processes that gave rise to the concept in the first instance. This is not simply mirroring, but rather a questioning or probing of that context; this is exemplified in many of the practices that we have come to associate with relational arts, whereby the practice is not only specifically located socially but is also an irritant to the otherwise 'consensual' and superficial political practices.

If democracy is to be regarded as a struggle, an ongoing and enduring conflict that can never achieve consensus, but that can hope to encompass politics and debate rather than violence, and extend participation, then this prompts many questions about the nature of education, especially if we believe, as progressive educationalists like Dewey (1916/1966; 1938/1969) did, that education should resemble democracy. Williams (1983) goes to the heart of this matter when he argues that democracy, when boiled down to its most fundamental components, comprises participation and education, and Rancière (1991) goes further when he insists that none of this can be achieved unless equality is both a prerequisite and an outcome of education. He argues that the arts can resemble democracy through their critical disruption and that this unsettling and continually questioning process is indicative of the forms that creativity might take in education. Importantly, these arguments can be used to make the case that a critical creativity is a vital and necessary part of any educational system if it is to form part of a functioning democracy.

Chapter 2

Relational and critical creativity

The arts and democracy can both be collaborative or collective projects, especially if we dismiss the more conventional view that the arts are singular and individual. In this common ground the arts can be fundamental to the democratic educational process, given their propensity for reconceptualising and critical questioning, and democratic subjectivity can be constructed through arts practices, especially those in which a context for collective democratic action exists or is created. Relational education has become a significant mode in the contemporary arts and education world, synonymous with social interaction and intersubjectivity, and has had a great influence on social learning; in our context here it is discussed in relation to creativity and the arts: 'The laws of the world are not laws of things themselves but instead laws between the relationships of things' (Badiou, 2009)

There are a number of movements and projects that lay claim to this notion of the 'relational', such those characterised by appreciative inquiry and social constructionist theory (Gergen, 2009). However, in our experience few lean towards collaborative and collective practices, still less towards the critical and creative aspects of the relational that interest us. More common are the competitive models derived from sport studies, in which the reductive idea that good social relations lead to enhanced team performances and that the vested interests of stakeholders and shareholders will benefit economically; such arguments are readily applied to schools. These economic notions of the relational rely on the belief that capitalism, and therefore society, can be transformed by successful individuals contributing to a team, especially if backed by powerful corporations. Many of the theories and practices that we discuss problematise this equation, and explore how critical, relational arts can produce practices that have a much more nuanced and ambivalent relation to the dominant neoliberal ideology.

Bourriaud's (2002) theory of contemporary arts is one of the most significant relational theories applicable to creative education. Contemporary creative practices, that is conceptual, performance and installation, could all be thought of in terms of social relations, as opposed to the modernist notion of individual genius, and within this broad configuration these social/relational practices have specific features that have developed in relation to contemporary social conditions, such as digital technologies, social media and globalisation (especially migration/diasporas), for the creative exploration of subjectivity in the postmodern globalised context of uncertainty and cultural instabilities.

The emergence of relational practices

Relational practices have become increasingly popular in the contemporary arts over recent decades and it is possible to view these as an expression of the simultaneous rise of relativism in western secular cultures. They can also be seen as an expression of multiculturalism, and the relational phenomenon may be the inevitable consequence of far greater cultural engagement in a globalised and technologically networked world. As with all new movements in the arts it brings with it possibilities for new insights into the ways we live and conceive the world, although it also closes down older ways of thinking and practising creatively, especially those organised around aesthetics; one of the characteristics of relational creativity is that it endlessly defers aesthetic value and gives short shrift to connoisseurship and the hierarchies of taste. From an egalitarian point of view such practices provide the ground for a more just and equitable creativity in which multiple voices may be heard, especially those that in more traditional configurations would be marginalised or silenced.

In relational creative practices, social engagement is the dominant feature, and it is possible to view this as above all a means to enable encounters and interactions at the expense of more traditional, modernist concerns with formal and aesthetic qualities. Aesthetics and formalism continue to play an important role in creative practices but to be relational the practice must provide a vehicle for social encounters, real or imagined. The relational artistic encounter, with a reconceptualisation of aesthetic value, can be situated as a postmodern reaction to modernism, and in this context it is about as far from a modernist aesthetic, where a preoccupation with material and form dominated, that creativity can travel. This binary opposition is crude and does not acknowledge the many contemporary hybrids that retain a concern with form and yet are still organised around relational encounters, yet it serves to highlight the shift in the ground of contemporary arts just prior to the turn of the 21st century.

Whilst the individual is central to the history of modernism it is still replete with accounts of tense but creative relations, for example in visual art between artists, as well as those between artists and patrons. New art forms are often considered the result of such tensions, where the social and political frictions generate creative ingenuity to either confront, or accommodate, the controlling power relations, or, in the case of competition between artists, unorthodox means of creative production may be set as a challenge to existing orthodoxies. Theatre is noticeable by its absence in much modernist discourse mainly because of the Eurocentric conceptualisation of theatre as text rather than as theatrical performance. However, even within the theatre as text tradition there are many examples of profound intercultural encounters and relations between individual playwrights, dramaturgs, and performers working in radically different performance traditions that have also challenged existing orthodoxies.

In the realm of the visual arts Clement Greenberg's (1960) essay epitomises the modernist view of the values inherent in 'great' art, and is often quoted as such, and he provides many examples of these tensions brought about by patronage. In this history and critique of modernist painting, he uses the notion of 'self-criticism' to illustrate aesthetic engagements between artists as they corresponded with each other through innovations in their artwork, referencing across time and culture in order to establish, as Greenberg puts it, 'all that was unique to the nature of its [painting] medium' (1960, p. 755). For Greenberg, in the case of painting, the resulting 'purity' could be calibrated according to its recognition and celebration of the abandonment of the illusion of pictorial space; a development in painting famously coined by Greenberg as 'flatness'. What is important for our purposes here is this sense that, even at the height of modernist formalism, there was still a vital and essential relational frisson resulting from the creative dialogic reflexivity in the correspondence between artistic agents, which Greenberg identifies as 'self-criticism' (1960, p. 1).

This relational dimension has, in recent decades, not only been acknowledged but established as the essential grounding for contemporary creative production in some important theoretical instances. Bourriaud is one of the chief theorists and proposers of relational art practices, a thesis that he has developed over a number of texts, notably *Relational Aesthetics* (2002), and which culminated in the exhibition and accompanying text 'Altermodern' (2009). Relational art for Bourriaud can be summed up thus:

> Each particular artwork is a proposal to live in a shared world, and the work of every artist is a bundle of relations with the world, giving rise to other relations, and so on and so forth, ad infinitum.
>
> (Bourriaud, 2002, p. 22)

The idea of the relational is based on multiculturalism and globalism, particularly in the light of postcolonial theory. Bourriaud (2009, p. 42n) distances himself from what he describes as 'essentialist' multiculturalism and from the standardising and homogenising tendencies of globalism but nonetheless recognises that they are the essential ground from which relational practices arise:

> numerous contemporary artistic practices indicate, however, that we are on the verge of a leap, out of the postmodern period and the (essentialist) multicultural model from which it is indivisible, a leap that would give rise to a synthesis between modernism and post-colonialism. Let us call this synthesis 'altermodern'.
>
> (2009, p. 42n)

The social encounter at the core of relational art practices is a distinctive feature that has many implications for more traditional practices, not least the potential for the complete loss of material form in favour of performance, or the abandonment of aesthetics based on formalism, for instance. Works of art can look very different if their principal characteristics are to do with an encounter or social exchange rather than a material form that is readily commodified and given an economic value. This is not to say that creative acts and performances are beyond commodification within the realm of the relational, and indeed, capitalism is adept at colonising and normalising almost any avant-garde practice, and the history of Western arts is full of examples of revolutionary and disruptive practices being appropriated and subsequently sanitised. What relational practices do offer, however, is a means of liberating the creative practice from the confines of a class-based and privileged environment and of providing a voice for hitherto marginalised cultures, away from the private and exclusive production of arts into the realm of the public, in terms of both space and participation.

The popularity of relational practices corresponds to the major social upheavals that have occurred in the cultural shifts brought about through migration and diaspora, which have become a feature of the economically globalised world and through the technological revolution that has accompanied the development of the networked universe. It was inevitable that contemporary artistic practices would reflect these seismic social changes, and we should not be surprised that the forms that artworks now commonly take bear little resemblance to their ancestry in the canonised arts world.

One of the noticeable effects of these changes in the contemporary art world is the promotion of the importance and status of the curator or the director who now often replaces the formerly pivotal role of the artist as the author of the art event (Bourriaud himself rose to prominence as a curator of the 2009 'Altermodern' exhibition at Tate Britain). Because so many manifestations of contemporary relational practices involve the orchestration of many component parts it should come as no surprise to us that the role of author and that of director become conflated, or even the latter effacing the former. This creates its own tensions, with those advances in a greater democracy in the field of art being to some extent curtailed by the growth of the phenomenon of the artist as director, which is arguably simply replacing the former modernist hierarchy that privileged the author/artist with a new one celebrating the director/producer who has dominion over the artists/workers and their labour that produces the work or the event.

In the world of contemporary performance and the academy one of the noticeable effects of these changes is the reconfiguration of the distinctions and relationship between creator, performer and spectator in the field of 'Teatro sociale'. This umbrella term used by Schechner and Thompson (2004) denotes the many substantial forms of 'applied' theatre practice taking place outside designated theatre buildings in other professional and public spaces such as prisons, refugee camps, and hospitals. Bourriaud's restricted conceptualisation of theatre based on the orthodox aesthetic led him to draw the conclusion that theatre only allows for the bringing together of 'small groups . . . before specific unmistakable images . . . with no opportunity for live comment "until after the show"' (2002, p. 42), whereas in Teatro Sociale discussion takes place throughout the event and the traditional division of labour between roles is deliberately reconfigured and blurred.

This is captured in Boal's conceptualisation of the 'spect-actor', the participant who actively participates, interacts and creates; collaborates to perform; watches; and engages in critical dialogue. The term is now common currency in the world of contemporary theatre but was originally part of 'the arsenal' of 'Theatre of the Oppressed' which grew out of Boal's experimental work in São Paulo at the Arena Theatre during the 1950s and 1960s. Tired of commercial success without any political progress he sought ways of translating Freire's (1970/1996) radical form of emancipatory pedagogy into new theatrical forms as he created work in urban and rural settings with workers throughout Brazil, at first staging plays around their experiences in factories and on farms, and then shifting to increasingly relational, participatory, co-constructed forms. Boal conceptualised theatre primarily as dialogue, an opportunity to rehearse political change. In the move to Europe it was social and cultural rather than political oppression that provided the context for further experimentation in ways of 'democratising the means of production' (2005) rather than providing the gift of an artistic product.

Bishop (2004) argues that relational artworks are not necessarily more democratic, however, and takes issue with Bourriaud's claim that the dialogues that they produce are limited by the composition and interests of the audience and the framing of the work, despite its removal from the museum, gallery or theatre context. She points out, marshalling Alhussar, Mouffe and Lacau in support, that if democracy is conceived as a constant redrawing of the frontiers of conflict, as a strategy to avoid authoritarianism masquerading as consensus, then to be democratic, a work must engage in this political arena. Its role, in relational and cultural terms, is to produce the subject by transformative process that is inherently political. Too often, Bishop argues, relational works produce a dialogue that is socially affirmative, for example art collectors and critics meeting up and participating in a work, thereby reinforcing the status quo rather than questioning or challenging it; or a theatre company working with a public organisation to ensure that service targets are 'delivered', focusing on the 'when', 'how' and 'where' rather than the more challenging 'what' and 'why' questions. Hence, a distance between the relational work and the political work of democracy may be created and maintained, rather than bridged.

With this caveat in mind we can still look to relational practices as offering forms of contemporary creative practice that at least have the potential for democratic engagement and to evoke the democratic worlds that we might inhabit. Relational works can comprise the intersubjective engagements and narratives that form the fabric of the contemporary social world and, in this sense, provide an opportunity the transformative and critical engagements.

Relational arts in practice

With the turn in recent years towards a more conservative polity in the West, increasingly dominated by neoliberalism, relational practices sometimes meet with hostility and suspicion. Migration and diasporas, often the subject contemporary practices, are increasingly disparaged by politically right-leaning media that focuses on immigration pejoratively; the attendant multiculturalism is also denigrated, and relational works that derive from these may also be received with suspicion. Nonetheless, the inexorable flows of migration continue to generate creative forms that represent the myriad new cultural encounters to which they give rise. Similarly the networked urban societies that are expanding the world over, in correspondence with the economic pulse that gives life to them, shows no sign of abating, and their commensurate cultural manifestations, of which relational art is an important one, is set to continue.

An apposite example of relational practice is that of the 'Palestinian Embassy', produced by the Norwegian artists Toril Goksøyr and Camilla Martens, which was performed in 2009 in Oslo and in 2012 in Liverpool, the latter three-day performance occurring as part of the 2012 Liverpool Biennial festival of contemporary art. In this performance a hot-air balloon emblazoned with 'Palestinian Embassy' was flown over the city, upon which were staged discussions about the politics and state of the people of Palestine with the 'ambassador'. The discussions aboard this deeply ironic and poignant signifier of the statelessness of Palestinians were continually broadcast live to the audience in the city below. The relationships established during the performance occurred on at least three levels: first, those between the 'diplomats' that were onboard the balloon; second, those between the balloon participants and the constantly changing audience below; and, finally, the overarching visual and performed relationships created between Palestine and England/Norway.

Like many creative activities this work brings about a new perspective on an old problem; it forces the audience to see and think about things differently, in this case rethinking the Palestinian problem with its statelessness reimagined as a state. The notion of a state, with all its rituals and customs – and contradictions – encourages us to ask the question 'but what kind of state?' The relational aspect of this work takes this further by confronting us with this dilemma in the presence of others, and it is this intrinsically collaborative response which distinguishes the relational work from the more traditional private, solitary response that is more commonly elicited from the audience. For work of this kind, which arises from a political confrontation of the highest magnitude, the public forum nature and the arising relational qualities of Goksøyr and Martens' work are especially significant.

The public display of the hot air balloon floating over the cities of Oslo, and later Liverpool, make an imposing sight. It is no accident that Goksøyr and Martens choose one of the largest available airborne objects in which to stage their event, enabling them to emblazon this huge surface with the colours of the Palestinian flag as well as an embassy caption. The capturing of the events on film, and their large-scale reproduction in the galleries of the Liverpool Biennial (2012), further reinforce this effect.

The key pedagogical and political function of the work is to make us reflect and ask questions, ideally critical questions, of the artistic source of these manifestations, not in the usual bourgeois art-historical sense that has the origins of the idea rooted in the artists' biography, but rather the political and societal phenomena that compelled the artists and conditioned their responses. If we think of these as pedagogical as well as artistic events we can characterise them as a mixture of didacticism and constructivism; they are didactic in their political imperatives – the authors are driven to tell us something, and they are also constructivist because they also invite the participants, and us as spectators, to contribute to the meaning of the work as well as giving us the authority to appropriate and transform it. Thus, we become participant-learners, co-constructing meaning of the events and possessing them for our own use. In the case of the 'Palestinian Embassy', we are the recipients of an understanding of the situation politically: the statelessness of Palestinians, and what Goksøyr and Martens understand and feel about that; at the same time we are invited to compare those conditions were our own and, moreover, to voice those insights that have arisen from the specificity of the balloon event or its subsequent film screenings.

Vera Tamari's work 'Crushed Cars', produced in Ramallah in the occupied West Bank in 2002, is a similarly hybrid work: on one hand, it can be viewed as a sculptural installation, a conventional art object where the principal relationship is between the object and a solitary viewer; on the other hand, it can be thought of as a relational work, since the interactions of the participants (the military occupiers and the residents of Ramallah) arose from the work, and the events it provoked became its dominant feature. The installation comprised cars crushed gratuitously by the military's tanks, and the damaged vehicles were intended to symbolise the oppression and colonialism experienced by the residents of Ramallah. Cars can take on a poignant significance in the West Bank, as they are very expensive, essential for domestic travel in the absence of viable public transport and are frequently associated with domestic events such as weddings. People also have to spend a long time in their cars as they sit in the frequent traffic jams that occur in the West Bank, often precipitated by the military without warning or explanation and because long detours have to be taken to avoid the enormous and forbidden settlements with their settler-only roads. Consequently damage to, or destruction of, a vehicle has a great practical and emotional impact upon its owners. In our research in Palestine with undergraduate students studying education to become teachers, we noted that commuting around the West Bank was much more arduous given the potential for harassment by the military or by settlers. Since travel by car is the only option in most cases, having a car disabled or damaged whilst in transit as a real fear for the students, and this reminded us of the realities of attempting to carry on with a normal life on the West Bank. Work such as Tamari's has resonances with its audience in a context such as this which it could not have elsewhere. The specificity of its meaning does not however mean that it is without relevance for communities elsewhere.

As Tamari revealed in interview, she was well aware of the resonances and tensions that her work would produce:

> I had a road built in the middle of a football field – tarred and everything. It was a street that had no beginning and no end like all the streets in the West Bank. Every street leads you nowhere because you cannot move freely through towns and villages. I placed about six cars on the tarmac that were completely crushed, but very well polished – they looked like new cars except they were crushed. I put lights around them and there was music playing. On the opening day a lot of people came to the site where the installation [was]. That same evening there was another incursion in Ramallah, another curfew imposed. . . . After a few days, they went into the site and re-crushed the cars with tanks. I think the media oftentimes distorts the image of the Palestinians. Instead of showing that we resist because we want to survive, they simply paint everyone as terrorists. But not all resistance is terrorism.
>
> (Tamari, 2005)

Tamari makes clear in this interview that the subject of the work is the issue of free movement, as well as being an installation representing the wanton damage inflicted by the military. The free-movement issue gained more traction when the installation provoked a curfew, and subsequently another military intervention to destroy the artwork. Tamari concludes the interview by positioning herself and her work as a resistance to the occupation and it is the recognition of this work as an act of resistance which brings it into the realm of the relational, and in this respect it is truly transformational, because being part of the event transforms the Palestinian participants from audience to resistance.

A similar process was at play in the creation of a new Palestinian village, Bab al Shams, in area E1 between East Jerusalem and the West Bank in January 2013. Ordinarily, the frequent but illegal creation of settlements on the West Bank by armed settlers is supported and defended by the military. In a reversal of the normal chain of events, unarmed Palestinians created their own settlement, which followed the settlers' tactics of first claiming a patch of land by staking out fences and pitching tents, and then inviting more people and gradually making the temporary accommodation permanent. The 250 occupants were evicted within 48 hours by the military, but the creation of the village of Bab al Shams has become legendary, a peaceful act of resistance to settlement expansion that mimicked the tactics of the oppressors. Although the name comes from Elias Khoury's eponymous book, meaning 'gate of the sun', the event was never conceived as an artwork, and yet it has all the hallmarks of a relational event in much the same way as the Palestinian Embassy project of Goksøyr and Martens: a diverse group of people came together in solidarity over a common cause and in resistance to state-enforced injustice.

It is not unusual for contemporary theatre to be staged without material form other than the bodies of those who gather for reasons of community, professional interest and/or solidarity. For example 'Combatants for Peace' (CfP), founded in 2005, is a movement of activists using theatre to establish relationships between spectators and a targeted audience in order to open up discursive space in a pressing political context. In 2010 they staged a scene next to a roadblock set up by occupying forces in the West Bank of Palestine at Shufa village (CfP, 2010). The scene was devised to deliberately mirror an everyday life encounter that would be instantly recognised by the village audience who had come voluntarily with CfP to the road nearby. In the scene a Palestinian grandfather is trying to get back to his home in the village; he is ill but has been stopped and detained by occupying force soldiers. Before CfP performers act this out they announce that they will run it once, then play it again, and during the second run-though anyone watching can pause the action by shouting, 'Stop!' in order to say what they would 'do' at that moment or to step into the scene themselves to try out this new action.

The boundaries among creators, spectators and actors are deliberately blurred in such forum play (Boal, 2002). In this case there was also an added level of possible of intervention in that a group of actual occupying force soldiers were grouped around the road block and could not help watching and listening to the scene unfolding as the villagers offered suggestions for action and even stepped into the drama in order to take part. There was much laughter from the villagers at the suggestions made and the 'acting out' was triggered at times by playing between the reality of the theatre and that of everyday life. After a short while the soldiers ordered them to stop and move away. In this example a particular form of artistic and pedagogical practice created interactions between audience as participants and performers to open up discursive spaces as acts of political resistance.

The language used by CfP is grounded in the terms of resistance, stating, for example, that they have witnessed others 'mirroring how they look' in order to 'shoot embarrassment at them' (CfP, 2010). By comparison, Forn de Teatre Pa'tothom in Barcelona experiment with the same relational form but place more emphasis on the insistence of the right to challenge unquestioned assumptions and unchallenged inequalities, not only in political but also wider social and cultural contexts (Theatre Pa'tothom, 2015). The forum play 'Amina's Looking for a Job' was created at their base in the oven of a former bakery in the downtown Ravelas area of Barcelona and toured to Catalunya prisons. The spectactors step into the world of Amena as she searches for a job in Catalunya. Amina faces the triple discrimination of being old, an immigrant, and a woman. The fundamental nature of engagement in this work is not simply about greater integration of the audience in a meaning-making process created by a professional theatre group, but an interactive process created through participatory co-construction in which the means of production are shared and created in the specific context in which they are being staged.

By contrast, in England in 2014 Grayson Perry developed his project 'The Vanity of Small Differences'. The artworks he produced were a series of six tapestries which, on the face of it, are relatively conventional works: they are designed to be seen in a gallery as aesthetically interesting narratives, designed for contemplation by individuals in private reflection. However, the performances that Perry enacted as research for the tapestries, which formed the accompanying television series on taste (Perry, 2014), constituted a much more radical project, which at its best scratched at the open wound of inequality which permeates British society. Seen as a relational work, Perry's televised performances in drag on the streets of working-class, nightclubbing Sunderland, were indicative of Judith Butler's (1990) notion of gender trouble, where the performance of gender provoked a chain of reactions that not only indicated the instabilities of gender identity but also disturbed the more prejudicial concepts of class.

Perry's television and gallery events emphasised by his savvy manipulation of those particular platforms, particularly his use of television, where his dialogues with participants, often carried out through his simultaneous performance as a drag artist, sharpen his enactment of the idea and, in the process, transform it into theatre. This propels him into the role of protagonist orator, and as such he also becomes the pedagogue, bestowed with authority by his position, literally, at centre stage. His insistent oratory style, aided by careful editing, embellishes his conversations and interviews with a constant stream of interjections. Taken as a whole over the three television programs these provide us with a choreographed presentation of his views on the politics of taste in the UK.

Perry's audacity carries the performances, and this is perhaps what takes his whole project into the realm of the relational. People on the streets of Sunderland, unprepared for the spectacle of a man in drag, extremely carefully presented under the tutelage of his female companions for Friday night's entertainment, respond in unexpected ways. Here the artistic intervention elicits a new dynamic in social relations: people, in their surprise and incredulity at this anomalous spectacle, are momentarily precipitated into a realm of discourse with which they are unfamiliar and are therefore more inclined to disclose ideas normally protected from public view. Under the pretext of a television programme about taste, what actually happens is a provoked existential discourse about gendered identity. Young working-class men out for a night on the town who would normally be expected to protect their machismo find themselves discussing the finer points of Perry's sartorial choices and making judgements about the appropriateness of the colour or style of his dress for the occasion. In doing so they become reflexive, inadvertently, and the gendering of their own position becomes vulnerable to scrutiny; as Butler (1990) would say, gender is exposed for what it is: a performance, an artifice, rather than a natural condition.

Relational creativity in education

In relational, socially engaged artworks, like the examples cited above, the imperative to increase awareness and the desire to bring about political change, prompts the artists and participants assume a pedagogical imperative. These works, like many others in the contemporary relational genre, are created and executed in the public realm to directly engage with the public in order to most efficiently raise consciousness about the issues with which they are concerned. Bourriaud defines relational art as 'an art taking as its theoretical horizon the realm of human interactions and its social context rather than the assertion of an independent and private symbolic space' (2002, p. 14). Thought of in this way, the practice of education has many parallels with relational art practices. This is particularly the case when we examine its interactive nature in the social realm, and here creative relational practices are arguably most similar in character to education in the most fundamental sense of that term. This brings us to the question of what we might mean by 'fundamental' to education; just as the advent of relational art precipitated a questioning of contemporary art in the late 20th century, the advent of neoliberalism and its pervasive market ethos has generated much intellectual discussion about what we understand and value in education, and why the neoliberal turn is so corrosive to arts and creative education specifically.

At least part of the answer to this thorny question comes to light when we start to analyse education in terms of social interaction and social relations. Sennett (in Gielen and De Bruyne, 2012) proposes that innovative and creative work occurs principally through collaboration, and the instrument of creativity is 'dialogic conversation'. In doing so he alerts us to the dangers of adhering to the romantic idea of the individual genius, arguing instead that the driving force of creative activity is social interaction. The same can be said of creative education, predicated on interaction and 'conversation' – and by the latter we are referring to the whole gamut of relational interactions: variable, visual, aural and so on. This includes the interactions between all the participants in the learning environment: the teacher, the student, the carer, the assistant, the parent and members of the wider community and across all of these means of interaction. This is education as collective activity, just as relational art can be seen as collaborative or communalist in essence. Our argument here is that this collaborative activity is not merely an important aspect or element of education but is fundamental to it; this is most apparent when we turn to the creative aspects of education.

Practice: Teaching through contemporary art project

The 'Teaching through Contemporary Art' (TCA) project (Adams, Worwood, Atkinson, Dash, Herne and Page, 2008), which researched new art practices in primary and secondary schools in both London and Liverpool, England, found that one of the major difficulties with introducing contemporary practices into schools was the individualism upon which the curriculum was premised. In the context of national (and largely international) systems in which the tacit, and sometimes overt, assumption is that learning in schools is properly achieved through individual advancement in a competitive environment, assessment regimes are premised accordingly, leaving little scope for any pedagogical strategies that are based on collaboration. This meant that the relational activities of our project were severely curtailed and that practices that privileged social engagement were discarded whenever assessment came into play, which was frequently, especially in secondary education, and increasingly in primary. There was simply no accommodation within the tests, exams, and evaluations to which the pupils were routinely subjected in all disciplines for collaborative, relational activities to be credited. Many teachers took the view that collaboration, desirable though it may be, could have a negative effect on pupils' achievement, because it was hard to make it count within taxonomies of assessment criteria, all of which were geared to the individual production, not that of the group. Teasing out individual contributions within a group activity was not only difficult to do but also stole time from other focused activities based on individual performance, which paid off better for the pupils and therefore the teacher, when it came to assessment. This was the case even where the teachers were sympathetic to the idea of socially orientated work which privileged relational or issues based practices. Not only do these practices go against the grain of individualistic regimes; they can also expose ethical anomalies in the conceptual basis of learning and pedagogy in a school system. In an age where schools are increasingly dependent on reputation and performance through inter school competition, such exposures may be very unwelcome.

One TCA example that highlighted this dilemma was an experimental collaborative project carried out in a London secondary school in which a group of pupils decided to mimic the interventionist work of the artist Banksy (Adams, 2010; see Figure 2.1). In this work the pupils, with remarkable ingenuity, designed stencils and then graffitied images around the school buildings and in public areas

Figure 2.1 Students in masks and equipped with spray cans; Teaching through Contemporary Art project.

beyond the school. All of this was supported in principle by the teacher, on the understanding that all of the images were to be completely erased on completion of the project (Morris in Adams *et al.*, 2008). Consequently the pupils ensured that the inks used were non-staining and impermanent, and all were duly removed by them after the event. However, the pupils unexpectedly introduced a performance element into the work and widened its scope significantly in the process. This meant that not only was the graffiti apparent in many places in the greater environs of the school but that the act of administering it was itself also highly visible; the pupils emphasised this by wearing masks and choreographing the acts of graffiti and then filming the whole intervention. Both the images and the filming were designed, naïvely perhaps, to portray young people in a creative and positive light; although graffiti can be seen as defacement, by making positive images, elegantly performing their application, and then removing them entirely, the pupils wanted to make a public intervention that confronted negative expectations of young people's behaviour.

In relational terms this meant that the work moved beyond the aesthetics of graffiti and into the realm of public performance and still further into the realm of public participation. Ironically, given the mission of emphasising the acceptable face of graffiti that the pupils had set themselves, the project provoked some hostility from irate members of the public as they misconstrued what they saw as vandalism and complained to the pupils, to others around them and finally to the school. This misconception was not surprising and, to an extent, provoked and engineered by the pupils themselves, who conceived the performance not merely as an act of filmmaking but also as a polemical confrontation, and in this it exceeded their expectations, although perhaps not in the way they had imagined.

One of the features of the TCA project, that this example highlights, was the increased autonomy of the young people involved. As has just been demonstrated, this was not always to the liking of the school or the community, but where it occurred it did exemplify a corresponding amplification of the democratic process in a learning environment. As one of the TCA teachers commented,

> [T]his is very open ended project; there's no pressure on me at the end of it to have . . . this or have that . . . so I've taken a big step backwards, and I keep saying to them "Well its [*sic*] your work, you've got to decide, I can only point you in certain directions, you've got to do this." It's making them be more responsive and take a little bit more responsibility and control.
> (Adams *et al.*, 2008, p. 30)

The bestowing of responsibility and control to the learners that the teacher mentions necessitates a corresponding loss of control on the part of the teacher. A new relationship is established, which fundamentally changes the teacher/pupil configuration, in such a way that learning events are determined as much by the learner as by the teacher. Whilst the increase in democracy and the establishment of equality in the classroom may be desirable, it can be extremely difficult to manage. Management implies control, which in turn demands authority produced within a hierarchy. The creative practices that were produced within the TCA project were, however, not amenable to this more traditional model, and the imposition of a traditional teacher devised and managed project would have been antithetical to the idea of working with contemporary art.

This is one of the important findings of the TCA project: that the nature and the content of the work demand approaches that are not normally found in the classroom. The artists that were studied and their working practices were themselves often communal and democratic, and the materials and processes were unconventional in terms of school practices. Often it was the issue, idea or concept that precipitated the young people's work, which itself was unusual in being relational in conception and production. The models that the students chose from the contemporary art world, such as the work of Adrian Piper, for instance, inevitably led the pupils in the direction of social and relational modes of production: collaborative performances and events emerged in a number of cases. Piper's work is a good example of a practice that, when emulated, highlights many of the contradictions that occur in educational practices. Her artwork typically comprises events that have a political and moral principle to establish, and the means of establishing it is often through social confrontation. For example, her early work 'Catalysis III' (1971) involved performances that challenged racism, such as adorning herself in fresh white paint and moving amongst shopping crowds in a busy department store displaying the slogan 'Wet Paint', thereby establishing a new and tense relationship between herself and the public focused on race and colour.

One of the TCA groups that also addressed and challenged stereotyped thinking about race and culture produced an extensive collaborative broadcast, in which the video display screens around the school were commandeered. The broadcasts comprised a series of pupils presenting their personal family history as a cultural journey, genealogy of cultural hybridity. As they told stories of their national and cultural origins, relayed family tales and legends of how they or their families arrived in the UK, they overlaid semi-transparent geographic maps across their self-portraits, a powerful visual reminder of narratives derived from elsewhere, but nurtured and remembered in their school (Law in Adams *et al.*, 2008, p. 52). The normal information systems of the school became the vehicle for pupils' cultural histories that are ordinarily undisclosed: immigration was privileged rather than disguised or denigrated. As with Piper's performances the young people in this TCA project were reconfiguring the social relations among themselves, the population of the school, and the wider public who viewed the presentations.

Other TCA projects addressed social relations specifically. One, based in a state special school, was focused on interpersonal relations. The youngsters worked with artists through a gallery partnership where they were encouraged and enabled to create portraits. The children all had a diagnosis of autistic spectrum disorder, which is associated with difficulties in being able to read social situations, especially those with emotional content (Surtees-Smith in Adams *et al.*, 2008 p. 42). Using cameras the children made photographic portraits of staff and other children, after requesting them to adopt expressions that expressed particular emotions. The resulting images resembled those of Rineke Dijkstra or Cindy Sherman through their uneasy formality. These images were then enlarged and drawn by the children working in collaborative groups with staff. Throughout the process there was little regard to the ordinarily crucial requirements of school-based artwork, such as originality, aesthetics or assessment; work was readily copied, exchanged, duplicated and reused. What did prove to be essential for these children and the staff working with them was the idea of art being an investigation into subjectivity: together these groups were finding their way towards an understanding of themselves as being in a shared world. This was achieved through doing, their agency enhanced by their capability in producing work by and about themselves. It is difficult to quantify the worth and value of the project in any way except by having experience of it, and yet one could say that it was profound in its effects, because the participants were intensely concerned with themselves as relational beings for the duration of the project.

Practice: drama in education as a living process

As a social and collective art form, there has been much scope over the last 40 or so years in drama in education across many countries around the world for the development of pedagogical strategies based on collaborative learning, and this has extended to assessment regimes, with great variation over time and according to the particular country concerned. Whilst drama in education has traditionally placed an emphasis on 'de-centering the teachers power, negotiated learning and encouraging deeper contextual explorations of the bigger questions of life' (Neelands, 2009, p. 24), this is not always the case and varies considerably according to country, context and the impact of ongoing policy directives. In order to consider some of the implications surfacing from critical, creative, relational conceptualisations of practice, we draw here on three examples from North America, Australia and the UK.

Performed by 17- and 18-year-olds, 'Da Kink in My Hair' (2001), by Jamaican-Canadian playwright Trey Anthony, provided the context for two critical episodes in Gallagher and Rivieres's three-year ethnographic study of high school drama programs in four public urban schools in Toronto and New York (2007). The first was an exploration of power following a very heated whole class discussion about the idea of 'African History Month' in which it was proposed the class would stage scenes from the play alongside other events being held in high schools across Ontario. The school was very ethnically, culturally and linguistically diverse in a mostly 'poor/working-class' neighbourhood. The discussion included questions, for example, about who should and should not take part in this event and about the need for political leaders to apologise for past wrongs of the state.

Gallagher and Rivierre (2007) drew on the Boalian theatre technique of using inanimate objects to explore abstract concepts, in this case the related ones of privilege and racism that they identified as being implicit in the discussion. The students were asked 'to arrange a group of chairs in such a way that one would be more powerful than the others' (Gallagher and Rivierre, 2007, p. 10). From this they moved to a scene of a representative who was making his case for reparations for the descendants of slaves from someone who had benefitted from exploitation of a group, the president. One of the research assistants who was working in the school (white, male, American) took on the role of representative and a class student (Black, male, African-Canadian) stepped into the shoes of the president. The dialogue in this encounter played with and was shaped by unequal power relations switched around, which allowed the notion of any form of simple single truth to be challenged, and for the negotiation of 'a more nuanced meaning with the students' (Gallagher and Rivierre, 2007, p. 10).

The class went on to stage scenes from the play in both the school and beyond at a drama festival, so moving in relational terms beyond the aesthetics of Boalian theatre technique and into the realm of public performance. The three monologues performed 'told the story of three different black women, of varying ages and social positionings' (Gallagher and Rivierre, 2007, p. 42) and whilst it won the first level of competition at the public festival the backlash from a substantial number of the school students, teaching staff and administrators about the 'reverse racism' they felt governed the choice of text, shocked the class teacher. She 'began to notice just how deeply divided [the school] was in terms of race, and how all it took for those divisions to become clear was an abbreviated performance of "Da Kink in My Hair"' (Gallagher and Rivierre, 2007, p. 42). Gallagher and Rivierre argue that both of these critical episodes

> were catalysts for recognising how drama as a teaching practice . . ., is an ongoing quest, an ongoing set of complex relations, an upsetting of notions of authority and something which most certainly does not fit in to tidy positivist scientific/educational discourses.
>
> (2007, p. 42)

This example highlights something of the ongoing negotiation between leaners and teacher, teacher and school community, the challenges of engaging with learners attitudes, beliefs and values; of leaning against accepted norms, which as the example demonstrates is not always to the liking of the school community but which exemplifies an amplification of the democratic process in a learning environment. On the part of the teacher, relationships with students and colleagues shifted as changing existing invisible configurations were made visible through practice and the dialogue generated through it. Moves to democracy and the establishment of equality in the learning space questions the culture of relationships between teachers and students, and the challenge for both can be considerable. Bhabha draws on Fanon to argue that '[t]he time of liberation is . . . a time of cultural uncertainty' (1994, p. 35) when everything is called into question, and it is in relation to this that Bhabha elaborates his concept of the Third Space in terms that resist literal interpretation. The teacher and the students cannot 'un-see' what their actions have now made visible – they cannot, in other words, go back, nor are the ways forward always clear. Bhabha characterises this as a space of 'dis-ease' but as one that is profoundly hopeful.

Kellman (2009; Western Edge Youth Arts, Australia) frames his approach through third space theory and with a particular focus on how social meaning is constructed in young people's dramatised stories. Collaborating with teachers in Melbourne primary and secondary schools, the company run long-term programmes often starting with the aesthetics of process drama then shifting to the creation of performance for large community audiences. The work of the education programme of Western Edge is based on pedagogic processes that engage young people and explore complex ideas. The process is drama-based but incorporates dance, song, creative writing, poetry, digital media and visual arts. There is an explicit intention to develop 'complex, layered narratives that explore challenging content and young people's ownership of the work so they control their own learning' (Western Edge Youth Arts, 2008).

In the 'Government Project' Western Edge Youth Arts worked over a period of 14 weeks with a Melbourne primary school to dramatise stories in which far-reaching decisions were made by the Australian government that had a heavy impact on both Australians and people overseas. As with much drama education practice the extent to which the participants, in this case, young people at a primary school, controlled their own learning was framed and regulated by the teachers and artists, who, partly as a result of time and resource issues, made decisions prior to the start of the process. For example, it was the artist and teaching teams who selected the particular subjects for exploration of the material, part of the 'Civics and Citizenship' domain of the national curriculum, and who made the final selection of material for the performance. On the other hand, the negotiation, on both social and artistic levels, among the young people, teachers and artists in collaboratively devising the three 30-minute plays that constituted the final performance, was central to the process. It was through this negotiation that marginalised issues were foregrounded and validated (Western Edge Youth Arts, 2008).

In both of the examples from Canada and Australia, learners were encouraged through relational arts practices to make connections with their daily lives and the wider realities that informed and shaped these rather than compete with each other to acquire knowledge or social advantage. Neelands (2009) aligns the conceptualisation of the relational in drama even closer to democracy. An example of practice that he uses to situate his approach within the wider context of professional theatre is from his work in a school in Nottinghamshire, England, where he gave a workshop for 15-year-olds based on Shaun Tan's graphic novel *The Arrival*. The industry that gave birth to the town and which the school served had long since gone and had not been replaced. In the workshop participants explored the possible events that lead to migration, though the allegory of a mother's hand on a packed suitcase (Neelands, 2009). Neelands draws attention to, in his words, 'the serious intent of the work of discovering the meaning in action, conscious of the surrounding town and environments forcing people to leave' (2009, p. 42). He was present for one workshop, but what he came into contact with were young people who had formed significant relationships through 'being together' in drama, as they engaged collaboratively to explore ways of learning to live together as opposed to living 'against each other' (Neelands, 2009, p. 42). In his conviction that drama should be socially as well as artistically progressive, Neelands argues against prescribed subject knowledge to be learnt. He argues that the ensemble approach to drama, which is collaborative, and that involves co-creation and re-imagining the possibilities of how best to live together in a state of interdependence so providing a democratic model of living (Neelands 2009). In this approach to practice,

> [i]t is the participatory experience of being together in drama and how children are changed by that which is important rather than the form of drama work itself . . . it is the quality of the social and democratic 'being with' in the theatre that makes the distinctive difference to what is being learnt in drama.
> (Neelands, 2009, p. 42)

The politics of relational practices

These projects explored a variety of issues according to their participants' interests and their acquaintance with particular forms of contemporary arts. In each case a number of relationships were called into question, most profoundly those between the teacher and the learner but also those between the small creative community and the school institution or those between the school and the public. New relationships were established as old ones were disrupted, albeit temporarily in some cases. The arts practice was always the fulcrum over which the new balance was established. Balance may be a misleading term to use, however, because it implies an equilibrium or stasis, which had not necessarily occurred in these examples. Better to look again at the idea of agonism; viewed through this lens, the tensions that each of the projects encountered or provoked, whether it be between school, pupil, teacher or public, were in most cases never resolved or evened out as balance might imply. Instead, the creative event provided a space and a time where tensions and conflicts were permitted to surface without being exacerbated or causing further damage. This then is more akin to democracy in the polity, where it can be said to fulfil a similar social function; what the these projects revealed was the way in which these creative practices mimicked and replicated democratic practices. The equation between democracy and education, rooted in the forms of social relations, was emphasised; the forms that the arts take in education in instances like these may be thought of as a parallel with those of democracy: the space created by the arts in education is akin to the arena of democratic politics.

Rancière (2011) does not accept the idea that art is, or can be transformative, nor that it can go beyond itself into the realm of politics to become 'political art'. Rather, he argues that art is a process of reconfiguration, the idea that ordinary or common sense ways of conceiving the world are troubled and re-conceptualised. This occurs in ways that are not immediately obvious because these reconfigurations are embedded in our ideas of what is 'natural' (although our ways of conceiving the world are anything but). In this manner of functioning in the social world Rancière likens art to politics, for it is by this means of reimagining the ordinary and the everyday that both art and politics coincide:

> It is a practice [of the arts] that invents new trajectories between what can be seen, what can be said and what can be done. It is a practice that shakes up the distribution of places and competences, and which thereby works to blur the borders defining its own activity. Doing art means displacing art's borders, just as doing politics means displacing the borders of what is acknowledged as the political. Displacing art's borders does not mean leaving art, that is making the leap from 'fiction' (or 'representation') to reality. Practices of art do not provide forms of awareness or rebellious impulses for politics. Nor do they take leave of themselves to become forms of collective political action. They contribute to the constitution of a form of common sense that is 'polemical', to a new landscape of the visible, the sayable and the doable.
> (2011, p. 149)

In the terms of reconstituting the 'common sense' landscape that Rancière describes, the relational projects that we have discussed above are as political as they are creative. Often it is the realisation of the political, simultaneously emerging with the creative, that proved so unsettling for the institutions, sometimes for the participants too. Of course, many everyday projects that are unthinkingly sanctioned by institutions because they fall within the orthodoxies of practice are also deeply political, but because they occur within the realm of the 'ordinary', it seems like common sense to accept them as non-political. It is only when creative disturbances reconfigure or even reinvent the activity that its political content becomes more readily apparent. This transitional stage, before it too becomes normalised within a new orthodoxy, is the most unsettling and troubled period in the genealogy of a creative practice.

Chapter 3

Creative pedagogies: Palestine

Creativity الإبداع *khāliq*

This chapter is about testing and developing creative methods of teaching, and is drawn from our experience of our ongoing, long-term (20 years at the time of writing) work with teachers and teacher educators in mainstream education in Palestine. Our discussion about relational, creative pedagogical practices draws on the whole of the period since 1995, from the first project which ran in Gaza and West Bank, and examines the ways that these have subsequently played out in different forms and educational contexts. The specific examples of practice that we focus on have been chosen because of their significance in terms of the development of our thinking about creativity and democracy, in particular the concepts of self and other, the right to narrate, insistence and resistance. The initial locus of creativity is the primary schools and the Palestinian Ministry of Education, which are part of the wider network of practice of the Center for Research into Education, Creativity and the Arts through Practice (RECAP, based at the University of Chester), which also includes universities in West Bank and Gaza, a technical college and a grassroots cultural and theatre society centre. One specific focus is on the circumstances that gave rise to the subsequent development of a particular drama form, used initially in the in-service professional development of teachers, and Ministry of Education school supervisors. Before turning in detail to the social relations and forms of practice developed in this project with all their specificities, we first discuss the political context of the project in the Occupied Palestinian Territories.

Entry and exit points: the political context

To be an educator in Palestine is to work and live in a country under occupation, as named by the United Nations the Occupied Palestinian Territories (OPT). The political context is inextricably and overtly woven into almost every conversation and discourse including education. As we work, our individual political positions have been, and quite rightly continue to be, a live and troubling dimension of the collaborative process. When first trying to orientate ourselves we adopted a view, typical of a non-governmental organisations (NGOs), which aspired to neutrality while acknowledging that not to have an opinion would be naïve. In subsequent years, and in the light of our personal experiences, our reading and our reflections, we have largely abandoned the aspirations of neutrality yet, at the same time, attempted to resist the dogmatic orthodoxies prevalent in the country. How to realise this through the creative processes in our collaborative projects and programmes has been one of the challenges in which we have engaged with our Palestinian colleagues.

One of our ongoing tasks from the outset has been to make sense of the complex political geographic landscape of the OPT as we travel between schools, Ministry of Education buildings, universities and cultural centres. When looking at the maps we were, and still are, struck by the anomalies produced by the military occupation's impositions on geographical Palestine: first, that Palestine is split into two geographical areas, the West Bank (2.8 million) and Gaza strip (1.6 million people), and movement between them is prohibited for Palestinians (Tolan, 2006; Jewish Voice for Peace, 2015) and, second, the continually shrinking size of Palestine as it is steadily colonised by the conspicuous construction of enormous settlements, from which Palestinians are also excluded. Today in the West Bank the occupying forces continue to control not only the external borders but also all entry points along the hundreds of miles of the 'Separation' or 'Apartheid' Barrier (commenced in 2003; see Figure 3.1) – leading to the naming of Palestine

Figure 3.1 The Separation Barrier, Bethlehem

as '[t]he biggest prison on earth' (Pappe, 2015). We have repeatedly experienced teacher education students and staff spending lengthy periods and facing provocations at checkpoints when travelling to study and to return to their own homes. Their frustration and anxiety have been palpable on the occasions when they have been prevented from getting to their classes on time or have to miss days at college because of sudden curfews and roadblocks. We have listened to Palestinian colleagues talking of the psychological strength required to embark on a journey out of their own country, for example 'simply' to attend an academic conference. One result of the severity and arbitrariness of these controls has been the decline in recruitment of staff and students who are forced to pass through checkpoints to schools and universities, leading to a new localism and closing down of horizons.

The overwhelming visibility and proximity of occupation is also striking, which means that our attempts to work within the education system cannot help but be tempered by this intrusive environment (Segal and Weizman, 2003; see Figure 3.2). When we first worked in Gaza in the mid-1990s our

Figure 3.2 Banksy's work on a street wall in Bethlehem, Palestine

accommodation on the Mediterranean coastline was partly barbed-wired, looking out on gunboats patrolling, controlling all entry and exit by sea. Whilst resources were scarce, there was not the need then for the Palestinian people to dig tunnels out of their own country in order to ensure essential supplies, and whilst fighter planes flew low overhead every day, causing conversation in the classrooms to stop because of the deafening roar, there had not been the damage and destruction of homes, schools and university and other public buildings that have occurred since. Now in the West Bank, discrimination is a conspicuous visual backdrop to domestic and working life: cranes building the settlements fill most horizons; huge but prohibited fast roads bulldoze through the landscape, discriminatory colour-coded car number plates; and razor wire crosses pavements adjacent to school playgrounds.

Our political understandings of this context have been informed by the postcolonial approaches of Al Yamani, Pappe and Said. Pappe is committed to 'non-elite history', the theory and methodology of which focuses on the reclamation of social histories prior to their transformation and distortion by powerful interests (Pappe, 2014). In *The Ethnic Cleansing of Palestine* (2007) Pappe presents the case that the removal of Palestinians from their land has been achieved by systematically planned physical and economic colonial force. He focuses particularly on the period between 1947 and 1949, referencing the deliberate destruction of Palestinian villages, and the million people who were driven from their homes at gunpoint, or fled in fear of civilian massacres. In his forthcoming work *The Biggest Prison on Earth*, Pappe (2015) focuses on the annexation and occupation of Gaza and the West Bank looking in particular at the war of 1967 which drastically reshaped borders and lives.

A central theme in Pappe's argument is that war and neoliberalism are two faces of the same system of domination (Chomsky and Pappe, 2010), that occupation is achieved by means that are not only military but also legal and economic. Students and educators on their way to work not only face delays and abuse but are also aware that their homes, lands and their right to be there are not sacrosanct, nor even their lives. At the same time in the West Bank they face the economic blocks, dead ends and the structural injustices of neoliberalism that have permeated most areas of economic policy and social life. In the case of the West Bank these are characterised by high unemployment, lack of infrastructure, low wages and numerous strikes by academics and teachers struggling to live on their poor pay. In Gaza the situation is worse, with almost total reliance on international aid and donors.

The point is that occupation is brutalising and dehumanising in military, economic and social terms, and cannot be air-brushed out of any discussion about education in Palestine. As the Palestinian Ministry of Education states in the introduction to the 2014–2019 Education Strategy:

> Since the Palestinian education system is exposed to these political, financial, physical constraints and vulnerable to many variables that cannot be

controlled, uncertainty has become part of everyday life for a student, teacher, and administrative staff.

(Ministry of Education and
Higher Education Palestine (MoEHE; 2014)

In the face of such daily uncertainty in the Palestinian education system we sought to find, together with our Palestinian colleagues, appropriate pedagogical approaches with the most favourable conditions that we could create for learning.

Shaking off: the educational and cultural context

The Arabic word *Intifada* means 'to shake off' as a form resistance, of civil disobedience which can be non-violent or violent. The first intifada (1987–1991) was violent, and more than a thousand Palestinians died, Palestinian schools and universities were forcibly closed and the quality of education dropped significantly. Our entry point into Palestine's formal education system followed this in the aftermath of the signing of political agreements in 1993. These gave some autonomy to Palestinians, albeit very limited, in certain public sectors, one of which was education. The major source of funding to begin the task of rebuilding the education system was international, and the newly formed Palestinian National Authority Ministry of Education (PNAME) quickly started collaborative projects with a wide range of countries, including the Department for International Development (DfID) in the UK. Following work we had been doing in neighbouring Jordan we were funded by the DfID to run a project in collaboration with Palestinian colleagues focusing on the quality of learning experiences in primary schools and the relevance of the curriculum to young people.

The call from the PNAME to help develop 'new' approaches to teaching and learning has been repeated many times, albeit with different emphases, and we have partnered Palestinian teacher educators in a number of projects and programmes, funded by the PNAME and Cheshire County Council, the World Bank and the British Academy, amongst others. Unfortunately it is easier to describe the forms of teaching and learning that Palestinian colleagues are trying to shake off, or move on from, than it is to describe the 'new' forms of practice and knowledge being sought. In this respect parallels can be drawn with countries around the world, such as the UK, that are grappling with beliefs about knowledge ownership and control, with the inevitable tensions that arise from attempts to impose change on socially and culturally embedded practices.

Through experience in these projects and programmes we have come to interpret the concept of 'new' in the Palestinian educational context as a move away from 'traditional' learning and teaching methods. In this context 'traditional' means 'the teacher is the main maestro in the process' (Al Yamani, 2004, p. 67), and where learning is concerned with the reproduction and imposition of previously established knowledge, akin to Dewey's (1938/1969), 'boxed knowledge', with students being dependent on the teacher to validate their understanding. The move away from tradition, and the experiment with constructivist methods, aligns in part with Rancière's (1991) thesis on equality and traditional power relations in education, where his argument is for the teacher to be equal to the learner in ignorance and where both teacher and learner refer – and defer – to the object of study as the source of knowledge. The most relevant point being that the 'teacher as maestro' model potentially disables the learner, creating a dependency which Rancière argues is the real purpose of the learning that is taking place: learning to be compliant and dependent upon the authority of teacher. 'New' learning as we have come to understand it from our work in Palestine is instead concerned with learner autonomy, ensuring that access to knowledge is not governed and mediated exclusively by the external authority of the teacher.

Work with our long-term partners has allowed us to develop a more nuanced understanding of the tensions in contemporary thinking about education in Palestine than we had in the early days. Like many of the educators we have worked alongside, Al Yamani points to the special emphasis placed on the value of education since 1948 and the first dislocation of Arabs from the former Palestine Mandate. Education is seen as 'tough in its demands and methods, an indispensable asset that can be used in whatever circumstances in which a person eventually finds herself' (Al Yamani, 2004, p. 76). But she moves beyond the neoliberal end goals of social status and economic well-being to envisage education as

> a powerful means of changing the direction of society, for example, towards greater democracy or towards tyranny. It can shape citizens to be responsible, active, confident and creative, or dependent, timid and weak.
> (Al Yamani, 2004, p. 77)

Drawing on the work of Barakat (1993, 1995, 2000) Al Yamani does not shy away from the difficulties facing Arab societies around issues of freedom and justice and civil society. She contends that whilst Palestinian political parties have focused on the political aim of liberating Palestine, they have not considered seriously enough the socio-cultural aspects of liberation from occupation, which must include cultural attributes such as free expression in relation to the political discourses of equality and democracy. From this stance the freedom to question the cultural assumptions that shape personal life, and to freely reshape these in the way daily life is lived 'is the first step on the road to political freedom' (Al Yamani, 2004, p.75) She argues that authorities in Palestine have used educational policies more to control than enlighten; she points out that in the long history of education in Palestine, especially with the founding of Islam in the seventh century, the mosque became a place teaching about Islam and Jerusalem developed as an active centre for education and learning, mainly in the form of rote learning and calligraphy. Alongside this Al Yamani highlights the patriarchal Bedouin nomadic roots of the Palestinian peoples and argues that the legacy of both of these traditions continues to inform the Palestinian education system (2003, pp. 47–48).

Current education strategy and policymakers are looking outwards to establish stronger ties with the international community in their hope to guarantee educational rights for Palestinians, whilst simultaneously focusing inwards on the long term aspiration to reduce the learners dependency on the teacher and to realise forms of autonomous learning that include valuing the critical thinking, innovation and creativity (MoEHE, 2014). Educators in school, college and university classrooms are grappling with the challenges of developing and embedding such 'new' forms of pedagogy in a system that can be characterised as highly centralised with regard to its curriculum, textbooks, regulations and daily practices.

Dangerous and domesticated practices: creativity and democracy

The dichotomies of creativity and its relationship to daily practices and global politics have surfaced repeatedly in our collaborative practice and research in Gaza and the West Bank. Conceptions of creativity in Palestine are conditioned by the wider global context, as well as the immediate political situation and the requirements and realities of the formal education system. In our current work on creative pedagogies in the West Bank defining and agreeing what is meant by 'creativity', especially through linguistic and cultural mediation, has proved to be an enduring feature of our discussions. In this work we do not attempt to neutralise translation problems but to highlight instead the impossibility of separating linguistic issues from cultural ones, as we explore the possibilities for shared interpretation. For example, in terms of the ideals and virtues of creativity, we found that these were broadly shared with UK perceptions, but whereas creativity is often used in England as a euphemism for the enthusiastic delivery of a prescribed content, even where the teacher has had no agency whatsoever in its constitution, we have found that in the Palestinian context the term الخلاق *khāliq*, 'creativity', is also inextricably integrated into the current political situation, associated with a resistance to forcibly imposed orthodoxies, and has consequently acquired a special resonance. This led to a reconsideration of the idea of creativity as a liberating, emancipatory political strategy where the construction of space is conducive to creative and imaginative acting and thinking (Read, 1948).

Having said this a key challenge has been to find ways of working that do not become a means of primarily reinforcing ideological and political positions, for example using drama to didactically consolidate existing dogma or to be used as ingredients to spice up an otherwise dreary, formulaic core academic recipe. In the course of our work in both Palestine and England the state curriculum has become increasingly more didactic, and authoritarian, with frequent testing and the scrutiny of teachers' performance; assessment points have proliferated in both places, as have regulations.

In the West Bank C areas and East Jerusalem (Palestinian areas not administered by Palestinian authorities), teachers have the additional problem of a textbook-based curriculum policed by the occupying forces. It is not surprising that textbooks in societies in conflict present unilateral national narratives, which reinforce corresponding national narratives, and this is also the case in Palestinian textbooks in the rest of West Bank and Gaza where '[t]hey present the self almost uniformly in positive terms, motivated only by self-defence and the pursuit of peace. They fail to describe information about the other(s)' (Wexler in Sherwood, 2013, p. 42). Creativity as such plays little part in these curricula, other than, for example in drama, for the elaborate invention and interpretation of stories to known ends.

The uses of the term *creativity* in Palestinian education context also reveals its contradictory meanings in relation to teacher professionalism, and parallels can be drawn with the situation in the UK where '[a]n impossible tension is said to exist . . . in which teachers . . . are encouraged, on the one hand, to innovate, take risks and foster creativity, and on the other, are subject to heavy duty accountability' (Craft and Jeffrey, 2008, p. 579). Parallels can also be drawn with the increasing emphasis being placed on education as a means to secure personal advantage and economic well-being, for example the current Palestinian education strategy and policy (MoEHE, 2014) calls for the enhancement of entrepreneurship in student and teachers programmes. Whilst 'entrepreneurship' is being conceptualised in some national education systems such as Sweden as a democratic project, in others such as Palestine and the UK, it is very much the playing out of the neoliberal meritocratic vision in which success is dependent on individual effort and talents, rather than cooperatively or collaboratively (Verhaeghe, 2014).

In applying and securing funding with our Palestinian colleagues for our collaborative work we have been acutely aware of the agendas of some large international funding agencies, where individualism, marketisation and self-management are the preeminent neoliberal political messages, especially in the way individual freedom is associated with economic independence rather than social, cultural and political determinations. As Smith (2011, p. 142) argues, 'the steady incremental involvement of the international financial institutions in Palestine, particularly the World Bank . . . have left their traces in the policy-making elites' way of thinking'. We have also become increasingly aware since the 'Arab Spring' that whilst democracy with its inherent demands for equality can be considered as a dangerous threat to existing hierarchies, it can also be a means by which inequalities and injustices are legitimated with the appearance of consent. In the light of this context we have been forced to continually critically reconsider the democratic principles that we wish to uphold in our work and what our collaborative work might represent. We wondered how possible it is for teachers and educators operating under a closely monitored system to collectively establish any kind of authority over the content of their teaching and pedagogical methods, or over the conditions under which they work. In this context we have found that teaching is very much constructed through specific practices and governed by the proclivities and politics of the given social situation, resulting in an often singular, inflexible, educational micro-culture, which can provoke sharp and deep contradictory reactions and responses when challenged.

Insistence and resistance: dramaturgy in non-formal and formal education

In one of the most recent analyses of Palestinian theatre practice Jawad Rania argues that whilst the field is understudied there is much evidence of theatre being used:

> as a pedagogical tool, as a way to make visible the performance in the everyday . . . as a strategic means to confront the colonial power . . . by critically reflecting on questions of culture, nation, resistance, and violence
> (Rania, 2013, p. 2)

One of the most well-known centres is the Freedom Theatre in the north West Bank which explicitly aims to use theatre to empower young people and women and to use the potential of the arts to effect social change. The roots of the theatre are in the concepts of 'Freedom and Learning', which is also the name of the initial project set up during the first intifada, which used theatre and art with children in the Jenin refugee camp. The perceived relationships among freedom, knowledge and peace implicit in all the work of the Freedom Theatre runs deep in the education system and in the arts organisations with whom we have worked. We first encountered this grouping of concepts as graffiti on a wall in Gaza in 1996, part of a school running three shifts of pupils and staff each day to ensure the right to education, and these concepts were closely woven in to many other programmes. For example, the Alrowwad Cultural and Theatre Society based in Aida refugee camp, Bethlehem, recently offered alternative education to the children of the camp following the indefinite strike of the Palestinian employees of UNRWA in order to force the UN agency to meet their demands (PNN, 2014). Alrowwadd stepped in with the support of the strikers because there had been no schools in the 19 refugee camps in Palestine for two months and the children risked losing a whole academic year of studying, as well as facing danger on the streets.

These two theatre and arts organisations are offered as examples drawn from the 30 or more operating in Palestine, many of whose aims go well beyond raising the quality of performing and visual arts; they offer much more

> space in which children and youth can act, create and express themselves freely and equally, imagine new realities and challenge existing social and cultural barriers.
> (Freedom Theatre, 2015)

This includes using the arts to promote positive change in their community using an approach that is often international, seeking to reduce the cultural isolation separating local communities from the wider Palestinian and global communities.

Utilising theatre and drama as educational methodologies has a history in the Middle East region dating back to 1989 when the first Theatre in Education group was formed in Jordan at what was the Queen Noor Centre, Amman, Jordan – known now as the National Centre for Culture and Arts (NCCA, 2015). Theatre and drama have been used to teach other subjects, to inform the curriculum and to encourage critical thinking. The influence of the centre in the region has been significant in providing training opportunities for members of theatre companies to develop skills, knowledge and understanding of the use of interactive theatre in the educational process and the promotion of social change. Courses have also been run in Palestine for school teachers to use the arts as a medium for learning, but the level of activity is relatively low by comparison with Jordan (Jackson and Vine, 2013).

The point we are making here is that there is ample evidence that theatre groups, and the cultural centres from which they often operate, are concerned with young people's welfare and education and the contribution that the arts can make to the development and maintenance of a civil society constituted by human rights, democracy and freedom of expression, prominent examples being Al Hara Theatre Bethlehem, Al Rowwad Cultural and Theatre Society Bethlehem, Ashtar Theatre Jerusalem, Yes Theatre Hebron, Safar Theatre Ramallah, Freedom Theatre Jenin, Theatre for Everybody Gaza, and Az Theatre Gaza. The presence of these active theatres manifests itself in two complimentary ways: one being 'resistance' to political occupation through the overt, direct and collective representational possibilities of theatre and drama and the other being the 'insistence' of identity, the right of self-determination and expression, and the right to critically question within the 'safe' space of the drama studio; in the words of Juliano Mer-Khemis, the activist and theatre director killed as he walked out of the Freedom Theatre, 'who we are, why we are, where are we going, who we want to be' (Mer-Khemis quoted in Khalidi and Marlowe, 2011).

There is, however, much less evidence of formal mainstream education being concerned with the contribution that theatre and the arts can make to these democratic elements of civil society, but our work has brought us into contact with many of those who are working to change this. For example our ongoing collaboration with Al Yamani led us to work with academics from University Faculties across the West Bank and Gaza on the 'Creative Pedagogies – Revitalizing Palestinian Education' programme (2011–2012). It was on this project that we worked with Alafandi at Al Quds University, Jerusalem, who articulated the importance of the concepts of 'insistence' and 'resistance' in serving educational process that, in his words, 'can make a difference' (personal correspondence, January 2013). Our first collaboration in Gaza, on which the following case study is based, was backed by the Ministry of Education, head teachers and teachers, and even though 20 years later many of the same challenges persist, as pressing as ever, there are continuing and newly emerging examples of democratic practices that are still being realised.

Dramaturgical form in the case study

The forms of drama we employed in the project drew directly on the drama in education tradition pioneered by Heathcote (Drain, 1995) and developed by O'Neill, (1995), Bolton, (1998) and Neelands (2002; 2004). At the heart of the practice in this study is the opportunity for 'self-other imagining' (Neelands 2002, p. 6) through a dramaturgical approach intended to allow for 'attempts to reconnect our own reality with the realities of others' and to 'explore, question and comment on the social world' (Neelands 2004, p. 50). Whilst being strongly associated with schools' drama education, these methods have also been applied under various guises and in various forms in a much wider range of social settings, where they are often located closely to those of Boal (1979; 1995), and in particular his concept of the 'spectactor', the participant who alternates between watching, listening and doing. Fleming's term 'percipient' (Bolton 1998, p. 199) is not as transparent as Boal's but has been adopted by some practitioners as more accurately reflecting the nature of engagement, in which participants immerse themselves in the reality of the drama whilst simultaneously distancing themselves from it, where they make things happen and realise that things are happening to them, where they are able to consider their own contradictory biographical narratives in relation to others, to 'negotiate and renegotiate a sense of who they are and who they might become, in narrative and through conversation' (Nicholson 2005, p. 149).

One other key feature that has developed in our approach to the use of all the drama forms we use is that the emphasis is on the self in relation to Other. This has been an on-going conversation in our collaborative practice as we asked, 'How do each of us "look"? How do each of us deal with the other?' We use this concept in the well-established social sense to suggest self requires Other to define itself (hooks, 1994) and the term *Othering* as shorthand for the process whereby certain people are de-humanised as they are exploited by those who say they are 'civilising' those they believe to be inferior.

Said argued that very little of what he calls 'the detail, the human density, the passion of Arab-Muslim life has entered the awareness of even those people whose profession it is to report the Arab world' (1978, p. 12). Said's term 'Orientalism', used to denote the skewed understandings he believed many in the West had of Arab culture, has been critiqued by many scholars, but regardless of increased coverage of Middle Eastern affairs in the popular press, or perhaps because of it, we believe these distortions still hold true and that what he called 'crude essentialised caricatures' are perhaps stronger than ever (Owens and Al Yamani, 2010, p. 21). Said's call to 'speak truth to power' acknowledges the critiques of this idea, whereby power already knows the truth and is not challenged by the speaking of it. We accept this impasse, arguing that creative acts, to have any effect, need to be dynamic, perpetually adaptable, and critical; we align these with the insistence on identity proposed in Bhabha's concept of 'the right to narrate':

> By the right to narrate I mean to suggest all those forms of creative behaviours that allow us to represent the lives we lead, question the conventions and customs that we inherit, dispute and propagate the ideas and ideals that come to us most naturally, and dare to entertain the most audacious hopes, and fears for the future. This might inhabit a hesitant brush stroke, glimpsed in a dance gesture, a camera angle that stops your heart . . . suddenly in painting, dance or cinema you rediscover your senses, and in that process you understand something profound about yourself, your historical moment and what gives value to a life lived in a particular town, at a particular time, in particular social and political conditions.
>
> (2003, p. 180)

In Bhabha's conceptualisation this is a democratic imperative whereby an individual with others creates spaces based on dialogue and conversation, where the emphasis is not on consensus but dissensus, the right to be heard and disagree with what is being said, to take part without taking over.

The bird in the cage: a drama pretext

Our case study considers the context that gave rise to a particular drama pretext and the detailed and highly context specific thinking that shaped the activities within it. Our presentation and analysis of the creative event presents a form that is a manifestation of a particular practice, which, although it is transferable and replicable in terms of recognizable structure, exists only in the moment of the event during which it unfolds. Data were collected in the form of field notes written up after each participative performance of the pretext, 10 in total. The research questions are embedded in, and arise from, the context outlined in the previous sections and concretely, from practice. We frame this as an example of practice as research and where interpretations are determined collaboratively through dialogue as the drama itself unfolds. Rather than trying to pass interpretation off as fact, we try to present the case as a 'specific, complex, functioning thing' (Stake, 1995, p. 2) in some detail, messy though it might be.

The pretext was originally created in our first project 'Integration in Grades 1 to 4' and was used as a means of developing the ministry's capacity to support school-focused development, which it was hoped would inform district and national policy and planning. We were to work directly on the ground in schools with head teachers and school district supervisors and at a policy level directly with the ministry. This was being driven by an improvement agenda in a mainstream educational system that was thought at the time to be fragmented and distorted (Owens, 1997).

The initial step of our first project was to run two study visits to the UK for Palestinian ministry of education supervisors and head teachers. The visits were arranged to allow Palestinian colleagues to choose the content, form and focus of two pilot projects. The approach would be based on a classic pilot project model in which the learning environment of the young people would be improved through first-hand experience and testing of new teaching ideas in practice. Members of the curriculum focus groups would then begin to support other teaching colleagues to adopt new ways of working. One of the two pilot projects chosen was drama, because it was thought to provide a concrete form of active learning, with minimal resource implications.

The only resource apart from space that we used to capture the interest of participants at the beginning of a drama session was an old carved wooden spoon, half a meter in length, onto which were tied small objects; these carried significance for us of our lives and travels around the world and included feathers, old and new keys, woven strips of worn wool, blue beads, tied silk handkerchiefs, rings, a metal golden fish, a faded cloth flower, bracelets, a silver heart, a little glass jar full of tiny shells, a deep purple ribbon and a metal golden fish and small bells. Together these formed a colourful visual and acoustic curtain of objects hanging from the 'story spoon' (see Figure 3.1). Each one of the objects symbolised a participatory drama and it is from the physical handling and referencing to these that the move into dramatic action was made.

These objects were to serve as a physical embodiment of the texts we were to work with, a living curriculum which gave primacy to the spoken word and action rather than privileging the written word. The spoon itself was inspired by a metaphor used by Heathcote of drama as a kitchen. Metaphors for drama and theatre practice abound, for example as a weapon, a barter, a vehicle or a laboratory; the 'spoon in a kitchen' was intended to convey the image of stirring things around together to make sense of them, to understand them better. The way in which we used the spoon and story is recognisable in many cultural traditions and practices. For example the 'talking stick' in some first-generation American Indian peoples is used as a means for a just and impartial hearing. In Japan when Buddhist monks travelled they would draw people towards them as they unrolled parchment scrolls illustrated with pictures to enhance their stories and lectures. We also used this unrolling technique with the story spoon which, when first introduced, was wrapped in a piece of cloth inside another, and the observation was made that drama may appear to be about one thing but is often about another; in other words, the use of metaphor in dramatic form is like the unfolding learning process itself.

Each member of the Gaza curriculum focus group used resources available, including sticks, plastic bags and coloured stones, and selected their own objects to symbolise the stories they told to their pupils. This was the point at which we first encountered the original Palestinian story of 'The Bird in the Cage'.

Figure 3.3 The story spoon: the living curriculum

It was told by one member, an elementary school teacher in Gaza City, who then invited us to watch it as an example of the drama work she thought could often be found in Gazan schools. It told of a child who was keeping a bird in a cage, how the caged bird loved to sing and longed to be free, how the bird spoke to the child and demanded freedom and how the child then set the bird free.

She explained that two children at a time were invited to come to the front of the class and act out the scene between the child and the bird as accurately as it had been read to them. The teacher would then make the teaching point that it is wrong to take away freedom, just as it was wrong to take away the freedom of the people of Gaza, to keep them in a cage. In our discussion with the rest of the Gaza drama focus group it was clear that the use of analogy in story form to reinforce the narrative of resistance to the occupation of Palestine a given. Together we started to explore the implications of this to consider how the story might be re-created in drama pretext form, to allow for deeper levels of engagement and for criticality.

This started with a search for other connected sources, and three in particular informed the next stage of the development of the pretext. The first was a photograph that a colleague shared with us of a woman from Jabalia (in Gaza) looking directly at the camera with her words denoted in a caption beneath: 'We feel as if we are in a cage. The noose around our necks is tightening more and more and the world looks on while our people are slowly being strangled'. This provided the driving urgency of the dramatic through-line and has remained highly salient in terms of the relentless, deteriorating situation in Gaza:

> On the ground the machine of destruction does not stop for one day. We therefore don't have the luxury to wait any longer. Time is not on our side. We know that while we wait, many terrible things are happening.
>
> (Pappe, 2014)

The second was a reproduction of a child's drawing of what we thought was a concentration camp in the Second World War but which turned out to be a drawing by a Palestinian child of the camp where in 1948 she was forced to live as a refugee in her own country. This raised one of the first key questions of the pretext: 'If we were subjected to such forms of de-humanization could we then subject others to the same experience?' The final source was the poem 'Sympathy' by Dunbar (from which Mayou Angelou took the title of her book *I Know Why the Caged Bird Sings* in 1969):

> I know why the caged bird sings, ah me,
> When his wing is bruised and his bosom sore,
> When he beats his bars and would be free;
> It is not a carol of joy or glee,
> But a prayer that he sends from his heart's deep core,
> But a plea, that upward to Heaven he flings –
> I know why the caged bird sings.
>
> (Paul Laurence Dunbar, 1899)

The poem provided a train of thought that, when woven into the pretext generated further dramatic tension through the questioning of the bird by participants, trying to understand why the caged bird sings when the wrapping is first taken off the cage; why, in other words, do those under occupation still remain defiant and what are the consequences when they fall silent? It was the weaving of these sources with the basic folk story outline that allowed us to create the pretext framework for participation, not as a means to deliver a message but to ask questions and allow participants to engage in a dissensual process where the good friction between ideas and positions could lead to a questioning of perceptions and, perhaps, the identification of unquestioned assumptions. The main questions that surfaced in the process of re-creating this story was, What stories do we tell our children, young people, educators in times of occupation? How do we tell these stories in ways that allow the participants voices to be heard? and Who is it that needs to hear these voices? (Owens and Al Yamani, 2010).

The story through-line was shaped elliptically, by which we mean gaps were accentuated or opened in the narrative structure that begged questions and allowed for individual and collective imagining. The use of ellipsis opens up the narrative to participants for interaction through drama education conventions. Drama conventions are ways of organising space, time and people to create reconfigured learning situations in which the outcomes and pathways taken cannot be predicted. Imaginative play is central to this dramaturgical approach to create the 'as if', whereby we engage 'in the risky activity of make believe' (Schechner 2002, p. 81).

The discussion about the opening frame of the drama was concerned with establishing an initial connection between the carefully observed reality of the imagined world that was to be created and the often casually observed reality of everyday life. One of the group suggested we could use birthdays as a common connection point where participants would be asked to arrange themselves in a line of months of the year. This quick activity necessitated conversation and movement, focused on the self in relation to others and ensured that each person's voice was heard by the whole group as participants give the date and month of their birthday in order down the line. The link between the two worlds, story and actual, was that this story started with a birthday, a young boy's, and participants were asked to choose his name and age. The first narrative sequences that formed the pretext storyline was then narrated:

> There was once a boy called (boys name) who loved his father very much and his father loved him. He had no brothers or sisters and sadly, his mother died when he was younger. Son and father lived alone together in their big house, but he never felt lonely. The reason was quite simple: (boys name) had many, many relatives and though they all lived far away in different countries, they always kept in touch. He was part of one big extended family.

In groups of four or five the participants created a composite character, as one of the boys' relatives, deciding where in the world they live, whether they were rich or poor or somewhere in between. They were encouraged to use their imagination and have fun with their choices, before the next narrative sequence was told:

> (Boys name) was very excited. Tomorrow was his birthday and there, on his bedroom floor, were all of the presents from his relatives. They had been arriving through the post every day for the past week. Every time one arrived he would look at the postmark to see where it was from, hold it up to the light and feel it to see if he could guess what was inside. (Boys name) remembered what each relative had bought him last year.

The composite character groups decided what present the character bought him last year, and what this year. These were each noted on a piece of paper and placed on the floor, as if on the floor of the boy's bedroom. The last present was that given by the father and a chair was placed near the other presents to represent this. Where the presents were based on stereotypes this was raised humorously; the humour allowed the group to acknowledge and move beyond these tropes. Emphasis was placed on the irony of age or culturally inappropriate presents sent from distant relatives, and this playful imagining had the function of generating laughter and easy conversation about oneself and inappropriate presents received in the past. The drama form used here drew on the conception of 'serious play' and on what Brecht often referred to in his writings as 'spass' (fun) (Brecht in Willet, 2001, p. 7).

The drama conventions of 'composite character creation' and 'defining space' used in this way established the context for the subsequent dramatic action and introduced the boy as seen by others. The next story sequence was then narrated:

> Of course he was looking forward to opening all of the presents but the present he looked forward to the most was the one from his father. That evening, just before (boys name) was about to switch off his light, his father carried a huge beautifully wrapped present in to the room (a chair is placed near the other presents to represent this). He set it down carefully and said: 'Son, I am really sorry but I have just had a phone call and I have to go on a business trip tonight. I will be away for several weeks. Something unexpected has come up. I am so sorry that I will not be here tomorrow morning for your birthday. But you know that I love you and have never missed your birthday before. I will try and phone you tomorrow. This present is very special. It took me a long time and a lot of money to get it. Don't let anything happen to it. I have arranged with the usual agency for someone to come and cook your meals and take care of you while I am away'. (Boys name) felt very sad that his father would not be there in the morning, but he knew that he loved him and that business was business. Finally he drifted off to sleep wondering what on earth was inside that big box his father had carried in to the room.

In the morning he jumped up and pulled back the curtains. He rushed over to the first present and tore it open, then the second and the third until only the present from his father remained. He ripped off the paper and then sank down to his knees in silence at what he saw. There in cage, right in front of him, was the most beautiful bird he had ever seen. It was the same sort of bird that he remembered seeing at the zoo that day, years ago when he and his mother and father had such a wonderful day. He remembered saying how much he would like a bird like that and how his Dad had said that it would be impossible to get one. And now here he was with his own bird, in its own cage in his bedroom.

(Boys name) did not bother with any of his other presents. He just knelt in silence and listened to the beautiful song of the bird. When the man from the agency knocked on his bedroom door and bought in his breakfast he waved it away and just carried on looking and listening. Mealtimes came and passed as he waved the food away. As night fell he carefully covered the cage, climbed into bed and, feeling happier than he had felt for as long as he could remember, he fell fast asleep. In the morning he was up with the sun, pulled off the cage cover and sank down again to listen to the bird sing. When his breakfast came he ate some but did not once take his eyes off the bird. It was then that the bird stopped singing.

The teacher-in-role 'phones' one of the relatives and asks for advice as to how to get the bird to start singing again. 'Teacher-in-role' is a key drama education convention that allows for behaviours, attitudes and emotions much wider than those usually exhibited by a teacher in the classroom. Whilst still being the figure of authority in the room the learning that is taking place is not clear. There is no request for transmitted knowledge to be reproduced, nor is it clear what knowledge is to be validated or how this is to happen. As percipients, the participants know that this story is about something, but that something is not necessarily what the drama is about (Alen-Ohern in Ostern, 2001) and that a playful game is unfolding. The following is an example of the improvised dialogue and the decisions made about dramatic action that have been generated by the drama conventions of teacher-in-role spontaneously interacting with small groups of participants as composite characters:

(Teacher in role) 'What's wrong bird? Why have you stopped singing?' (Narration) The bird seemed to hang its head and look the other way. The boy moved around the cage. 'Come on bird, sing for me. I like you singing'. The bird looked the other way. 'What's wrong bird? Come on?' No matter how much he talked the bird would not sing. (Boys name) phoned his father on his mobile but the number did not work. He began to get angry. He took the (a present chosen from a family member), and ran it along the bars of the cage (surprisingly violent action). Then he took (another present) and poked it through the bars so the bird had to duck its head (again very violently).

The teacher momentarily switched roles to become the bird so that a look between the self and the other can be established. The drama generated laughter, but then became uncomfortable, as a result of the indignity of the boys actions, the latent violence of which was embodied in the performance.

> 'Hi, it's me. Thanks for the present. Look, I've got this other present off Dad, it's a bird and it's been singing but it's stopped and I want it to start again so what can I do?'

The person chosen by the group to speak 'on the end of the phone' said, 'Give it some water', followed by the other 'relatives' who suggested 'food/company/sing to it/let it out of the cage to fly around a bit'. The participants seem to know or sense that the 'freedom' suggested is the action the teacher is manipulating the group dramatically towards but still seemed to enjoy working through all of these suggestions. The boys' infringement of the birds' personal space and dignity was made very clear. For example, when food was suggested, the teacher presented this though the narrative:

> There was the food behind the cage. He ripped open the packet and tipped the whole lot in, spilling all over the floor. Go on then, eat, I've given you all you need – and more!' (The teacher-in-role tipped food grossly all over the floor of the birds cage); (Narration) He got angrier and angrier.

Finally one of the groups suggested giving the bird some freedom by letting it out of the cage to fly around the room.

> (Narration) After the (boy's name) had checked that the window and door were shut he bent down to open the cage door. 'Right bird, I'm going to open the door so you can fly out. If you try to escape I'll break your wings'. The bird looked straight into the boy's eyes as the door opened.

This was the turning point in this pretext session, when the teacher, having modelled the role of the boy sufficiently for participants to adopt it themselves later, let go of it for a while to model that of the bird, by asking them to use the drama convention of 'hot seating' – to question her/him in role as the bird. The major purpose was to appropriate the emotional content and empathy that are core to relational pedagogy and to drama education. The teacher became 'relationships manager', still retaining, as Aitken, Fraser and Price (2007) argue, the 'ultimate say of how aesthetic, social, political and power dynamics will be organized within the drama', remaining in role with a license to provoke, confront through non-verbal signs, use of symbol, metaphor and examples or other experiences in order to engage the participants in a dissensual process. From this point onwards the participants decided on the form themselves, with support.

The task of the teacher-in-role is a very different form from those usually undertaken by educators in classrooms: it is to portray or embody human-ness, just as it had been with the boy. In the case of the bird it denotes the position of someone who is trying to maintain their last vestiges of human dignity, someone who has been wronged and knows that the situation is not right. The bird may have food, water, shelter and the chance to live, but this is on someone else's terms and conditions. In this case freedom is conditional on the whims and moods of a young boy. 'Human' rights have been taken away. The bird is in a cage, it feels as though a noose is tightening around its neck and no one cares or is doing anything, and so from the source material parallels are drawn, through the dramatic structure, with actually lived life.

By this point the participants were beginning to suggest solutions, and as the dramatic frame was now so clearly established, they could step into the drama and improvise. The form they choose depended on negotiation, and included: work in pairs (one person as the boy, the other as the bird); forum theatre, in which the teacher played the role of the boy and the participants replayed the scene when the bird was deciding whether to fly out or not; small groups making wall drawings of the roles the boy and the bird, trying to find the words that opened up the motivations, concerns and needs of each. Whatever form was chosen, the last frame of drama was always the point of return.

At this point in the unfolding dramatic action the participants worked together to choose the dramatic conventions, that is the forms that would best enable them to progress the action and address the questions arising from it. They were, in other words, choosing 'how' they would talk about what they are talking about. As Giroux (2014b) argues, it is not only participation in education that is important but also the way in which the education provides the means towards governance. The conventions opened up spaces where opinions could rub against each other or collide, where there was no 'right' answer to the situation, and the teacher was not the only person able to validate the knowledge and experience: peers in the group, and 'others', were another possible source of validation. For example, at the point where the participants spoke to the bird, a wide range of opinions was expressed, opinions clearly rooted in both the reality of the drama and the reality of life under occupation:

> You can carry on living life, by doing exactly what the boy wants, when he wants, but this is no sort of life with dignity. True he would give you food and water, but only so you will sing for him. This is slavery.
>
> You can carry on singing and try and reason with the boy. But belief that a boy of this age can 'be changed' is nonsense. I bet his father has even stronger opinions!
>
> Remember Schiller. By the time a boy is five, you have the man.'
>
> When you try and reason with these people they keep you talking for years and years, your life slips away and they laugh behind your back knowing that all of the time they are getting what you want. Some of your family have died while others keep on talking. This is naïve.
>
> You can keep on talking, making the boy think all is okay but really you are looking for a way of escaping. But this will not solve the problem for all

of your family. You might find a way back home but they will still take others away and imprison them. You are not just thinking of yourself but of others and those who come after you, future generations.

You can stop singing and refuse to eat anything. You might die. It might seem pointless but it will be a decision on your own terms. Maybe if enough birds just die in cages then people will see that they cannot and should not be kept in captivity. No one will buy such birds, the shops will stop taking them and so you will have sacrificed yourself for the good of others.

You can fly out of the cage and peck the boys' eyes out. This is something you cannot imagine ever of having thought before and cannot believe you are saying, but it might bring peace for others if you sacrifice yourself.

Imagination, agency and political action are woven here into the metaphor of the bird in the cage. As we argued earlier, we are interested in such moments of critical creativity that stem from models of democracy akin to Mouffe's (2005), where the process can accommodate, but never settle, opposing views; the accommodation in the form of ongoing dialogue and exchange is the end, not merely the means. Imagination at play, expression of subjectivity, the political dynamic at work is the goal, and in so doing the participants of the drama also become the de facto 'citizens' of a democratic polity, even where no sovereign nation yet exists.

Between the present and the future

At the start we set out to find the pedagogical approaches and conditions most conducive to critical learning in the Palestinian context. We initially chose these creative arts-based approaches represented in the case study for our work in Palestine because the PNAME viewed creative education as basic as numeracy – in one instance – at that time. The formal education system no longer privileges creativity in this way, but our ongoing programmes are still acknowledged as offering more than merely something to spice up a dreary curriculum and are recognised as having the potential to increase awareness and criticality. Democracy and social justice continue to be a very real struggle in Palestine, but not without hope. Creative practices can help to realise these democratic goals by fostering the collective imagination, to envisage better ways of being together through creative behaviours that allow us in Bhabha's words to

> question the conventions and customs that we inherit, dispute and propagate the ideas and ideals that come to us most naturally, and dare to entertain the most audacious hopes, and fears for the future.
>
> (2003, p. 180)

Chapter 4

Independent and democratic learning

This chapter explores autonomous and democratic creative learning practices with young children. The main case study is Room 13, which is an international organisation that has incorporated independent learning methods as an influential adjunct to mainstream state primary education using contemporary arts practices (Adams, 2011). Through this discussion we utilise examples of young children's creativity from our experience professionally and domestically and explore features such as pupil autonomy, independent learning, artists in residence and the forms of collaborative creative learning adopted by children. The chapter is based on Dewey's theories of democratic education and citizenship and explores a range of relevant institutional and pedagogical theories. This chapter asks questions about teacher authority and the place of creative and cultural learning through contemporary art practices in state education.

Forms of democratic education

Dewey and experience

Dewey was perhaps the most well known of academics to align democratic with educational principles. Although his work is arguably specific to the period in which he was writing – early-20th-century American philosophy – he nonetheless remains one of the most important thinkers on democratic education and the concept of progressive education. This is relevant to our contemporary situation because reactionary political forces, through their media outlets in the US and UK in particular, have successfully managed to equate the notion of 'progressive' with many of the ills of education, and even of society in general (i.e. Johnson, 2014). This acquires significance for the degradation of democracy and, with it, creative education in particular, given the parallels between democratic and creative education outlined in this book. It is therefore worth revisiting the concept of democratic and progressive education as it was originally outlined by Dewey, to explore and possibly salvage those aspects that retain salience for contemporary notions of creative and arts education in the contemporary cultures within which we work.

For Dewey learning is an infinite, lifelong capacity, which should never be exhausted, since it is a prerequisite for a fulfilled life, in the ideal sense, and for the permanent engagement of the citizen with a continually developing society, in the democratic, political sense: 'the most important attitude that can be formed is that of desire to go on learning' (1938/1969, p. 48). For Dewey, however, this orientation to learning that he considers to be so essential should not be mistaken for an abstract conception; it is rooted in a situated conception of education based on the learner's experience. This is developed in his work *Experience and Education* (1938/1969), where he presents a detailed argument in favour of the experiential situation as a condition for learning. This is a precursor for the more contemporary notions of 'habitus' and 'situated learning', developed by Bourdieu (1986) and Lave and Wenger (1991), respectively, and popular with contemporary analyses of arts education (Grenfell and Hardy, 2007).

The experiential and the practice of the arts are deeply entwined, hence the enduring prominence of these ideas and theories of arts education. It is arguable that to practise any art is to pay attention to one's agency and being in the world, an experience that goes beyond the task in hand to encompass one's feelings and reflections on the social, cultural and physical conditions that were precursors and prerequisites to the moment of the creative event:

> [T]he first intimations of wide and large redirections of desire and purpose are of necessity imaginative. Art is a mode of prediction not found in charts and statistics, and it insinuates possibilities of human relations not to be found in rule and precept, admonition and administration.
> (Dewey, 1934, p. 349)

Persuasion and consultation, as opposed to coercion and authoritarianism, should be fundamental features of a mass, state education for Dewey (1938/1969). This is because he sees education as modelling democracy, an active and dynamic preparation for the democratic process to come when the child assumes citizenship status as an adult in a functioning democracy. Therefore, the model of progressive education that he advocates must necessarily incorporate, and indeed highlight, the responsibilities and rights of the learner, just as democracy demands the same of the participant citizen (Adams, 2013). In keeping with this democratic vision of education, Dewey demands that education should be voluntary: learners must voluntarily subject themselves to a learning process, and moreover, that this process should endure beyond institutionally organised education, to the extent where the learning is literally lifelong (1938/1969, p. 4)

It is this long-term view of education as an internalised process based on ethical principles that lays the basis for Dewey's association of education with democracy – that progressive methods of education 'resemble' democratic methods (1938/1969, p. 34; Adams, 2013). Dewey pursues the notion of representation through his metaphor of semblance: the correspondence of democratic ideals to the same qualities in progressive education; this correspondence is recognised by the democratic subject and an affiliation is made: the political system of democracy and the educational system of progressive education can share the same features and characteristics; they can be signified by identical representations of experience, articulated by Dewey through ideal virtues such as 'freedom, decency, kindliness':

> Can we find any reason that does not ultimately come down to the belief that democratic social arrangements promote a better quality of human experience, one which is more widely accessible and enjoyed, than do non-democratic and anti-democratic forms of social life? Does not the principle of regard for individual freedom and for decency and kindliness of human relations come back in the end to the conviction that these things are tributary to a higher quality of experience on the part of a greater number than are methods of repression and coercion or force? Is not the reason for our preference that we believe that mutual consultation and convictions reached through persuasion, make possible a better quality of experience that can otherwise be provide[d] on any wide scale?
> (1938/1969, p. 34)

Dewey's concern with an education system governed by consultation and, interestingly 'conviction', through persuasion rather than coercion, is a theme that runs throughout his work. This microcosm of democracy in the classroom with which he is preoccupied, has at its heart the concept of a high-quality experience for the learner. This can only be achieved, as far as Dewey is concerned, by satisfying key conditions: the first he calls the 'agreeable' or 'disagreeable character' of experience, and the second is its longevity, which he refers to as the influence upon future experience (1938/1969, p. 27). What this means in practice is that the relational aspects of the classroom or studio environment is conducive to learning: the learner is respected and takes responsibility for learning within a shared and agreed framework, so that lifelong habits of learning are produced in these positive circumstances. One can immediately see the centrality of this idea to educating for democratic citizenship; if the ultimate goal of education is the production of participating citizen in an active and dynamic democratic policy, then it is as necessary for education to instil this capability and desire for democratic agency as it is for the acquisition and mastery of knowledge. For Dewey this means the involvement of learners as participants in the conceptualisation and reasoning that underpins their education: 'the formation of purposes' which govern their learning', as he puts it (1938/1969, p. 67); this should be a hallmark of a progressive, democratic education, and he berates traditional models of education for their 'failure to secure the active cooperation of the pupil in the construction of the purposes involved in his studying' (1938/1969, p. 67).

Dewey insists on an epistemological hierarchy, whereby knowledge gleaned from, or generated through experience is superior to knowledge that is imposed by authority (1938/1969, p. 49). The latter he describes as 'boxed' knowledge, and his objection to this form of knowledge is that its meaning or relevance to the learner is proscribed by the demands of the immediate situation; once this moment has passed, because it was not sought nor desired by the learner, it can be quickly forgotten. The artificial nature of imposition therefore brings about its own doom, according to Dewey; the authority of forced knowledge is flimsy in comparison to the substantial grounding of knowledge driven by curiosity, desire or relevance. This grounding is experiential, because a great deal of knowledge in the arts is necessarily both procedural and conceptual, meaning that it is produced through doing, expressing or making – which might be in the realm of the visual, haptic or performance.

Habits of democratic experience

If learning through experience is one of the prerequisites of education, and the arts are well disposed to provide this form of education, then establishing the conditions for creative practices within educational frameworks is of paramount importance. By these means habitual learning experiences are established which emulate democratic participation. In anticipation of Bourdieu's (1986) notion of 'habitus', Dewey lists features of habit that, in a broad sense, constitute the 'attitudes' required for participation in a democratic society: '. . . the formation of attitudes, attitudes that are emotional and intellectual; it covers our basic sensitivities and ways of meeting and responding to all the conditions which we meet in living' (1938/1969, p. 35). Such ways of working and thinking, whereby the democratic is synonymous with the educational, do occasionally occur in institutionalised educational settings, and these instances, such as our example of Room 13, provide evidence of democratic practices simultaneously at work with creative practices in education.

Habitual practices arise through social and physical interaction with the learning environment (Dewey, 1938/1969, p. 39). Pedagogically this presents a great challenge for the teacher, for, as Dewey explains, managing the environment is difficult, because the interactions must fit with the proclivities of the individual, rather than the individual conforming to the conditions set by the environment, as in traditional forms of education (1938/1969, p. 40). The repeated adherence to these experiential and interactive modes of learning provide continuity, another of Dewey's requirements for democratic education (1938/1969, p. 51). Thus, the habitual models of learning are derived through participative practices, which have implications for the whole concept of 'the teacher' and where authority resides in the learning environment.

Dewey explains that the role of the teacher is not to impose authority: the teacher should not have to openly exercise authority because the learners will have sufficient understanding of the rules to know that they are for the good of the whole group and not for personal power (1938/1969, pp. 53–55). Teachers should not enforce control through fear of chaos, because the same arguments are used against democracy itself – so why should education be different to democracy? (1938/1969, pp. 187–188). Dewey develops this argument, using the example of slaves (where their 'purpose' in actions is determined by someone else). This is a fundamental issue of ethics for Dewey, arising from his focus on the 'moral principles of education' where he argues for a shift from the selfish to the social (1938/1969, pp. 195–197). He gives the examples of games that children play where the authority of the rules of the game are adhered to and are not questioned – it is only infringements of the rules that cause dispute. He argues that order has to be kept and imposed by the teacher in traditional education and forced on the learners because of the absence of pedagogies that generate shared responsibilities.

The institutional conditions for creative learning

Creative and relational education require conditions that are conducive for them to function productively. Nowhere is this more important than in the institutions that must accommodate them, such as the school or the college. Simons and Masschelein (2012) have explored the idea of the school and provide us with a three-part structural analysis of the *form* of this institution. They argue that the school, using the Greek origins of the term, is primarily a place of 'free time'; by this they mean that the school, above all else, should not be a place of social reproduction, that is the replication of the wider world, either in terms of social class relations or even the 'real' activities of work but, rather, a space that is deliberately divorced from all of these worldly considerations, providing instead a space for new and free thought. This is achieved in three parts: by 'suspension', by 'profanation' and by 'making attentive' (Simons and Masschelein, 2012, pp. 72–73). Suspension is a term that Simons and Masschelein use to indicate being 'freed from' the world and 'free to' explore knowledge and ideas; profanation refers to freedom from the common orthodoxies of society, and being able to transgress them; 'make attentive' refers to the freedom to be interested in, and to study, objects or events freed from partisanship or other indicators of social interest.

The problem with this, and other idealised structural forms that institutions might take, is they assume that it is possible for people to 'leave behind', like hanging your outdoor coat at the door, their preconceptions, values, interests, ideological conditioning and so on. The concept of the 'innocent child' relies on this understanding (or rather belief), and exposes the idea of child-centred education to attack. Nonetheless, this ideal outlined by Simons and Masschelein does provide us with a reconceptualisation of the idea, and the ideal, of the school as a condition for learning and understanding the world, and provides a starting point from which it might construct a democratic space for learning.

Smyth's (2004) research into the institutionalised attitudes and the pedagogical approaches of teachers towards their pupils reveals that these can be inadvertently exclusionary:

> One of the most significant 'exclusionary structures' militating against the accumulation of social capital is the 'institutionalization of distrust and detachment' (Stanton-Salazar, 1997, p. 17) – the subtle, and not so subtle, ways schools convey to students that their backgrounds and cultures are not valued.
> (p. 27)

He argues for inclusive pedagogies, consistency and, perhaps most significantly, 'an affirmation that the school attaches importance to the attributes students bring with them' (Smyth, 2004, p. 27). This last point reinforces the idea that the students' culture, dispositions and proclivities are elements that the institution should accommodate if learning is to take place. Once these conditions are established, Smyth argues, then 'mutual respect' can be established, a prerequisite for an engaging educational experience. It may well be the case that if the institution does not acknowledge the cultural life of the students then it will emerge in other more negative ways, as hostile sub-cultures, for instance. Willis's (1977) research into working-class children gives ample evidence of just how entrenched such cultures can be, even when the institution adopts an apparently progressive outlook.

Democratic learning through art practice: Room 13

Room 13's creative practices provide us with evidence of many of Dewey's conceptions of democratic education in action. Room 13 originated in Scotland in the 1990s through an artist in residence scheme in Caol Primary School (Fort William; Room 13, 2015) and since then has developed into an international network of young people engaged in creative activities, either as an adjunct to their traditional school studies, or through independent workgroups. Through media exposure and substantial grants from both the private sector and the state, Room 13 has established itself as a collaborative entity synonymous with contemporary creative practices (Adams, 2011). At its most democratic, Room 13 is a dynamic model of participative education adhering closely to Dewey's principles. Each Room 13 has developed its own character according to the nature of the institution or the organisations to which it is attached. This is true even in Scotland, where the original Room 13s in two schools barely a mile apart are quite distinct and have their own procedures and regulations, although as far as their working ethos is concerned they have more in common than they have differences.

Internationally the creative practices of Room 13s tend to reflect the dominant cultural trends in their location; it is no surprise then to discover that the UK Room 13s are those most interested in contemporary art practices as might be found in, say, the Turner Prize. By now there are a number of iconic artworks produced by Room 13; a television programme, exhibitions at major art galleries and substantial grant funding have over the years given the group's work significant media exposure, in which their artworks often feature. 'Solar Girl' is one such (see Figure 0.1); it was the UK winner of the Unilever International Schools art prize, and was exhibited at Tate Modern in 2009.

A striking feature of Room 13 practices are its independent learning strategies, whereby children are allowed to organise their participation in the group during school time according to their own independent timetabling; this means that children are able to leave their timetabled lessons in order to engage in Room 13 activities. The children understand that they must not fall behind with their normal timetabled curriculum work, and so the responsibility for maintaining their work schedule rests with the child, rather than the teacher. This idea derives from the democratic models provided by Summerhill (Neill, 1962/1976) and William Johnstone's (1941) pedagogical practices, both of which established that children can be given a responsibility and authority over their education, and can practice experiential, democratic learning. Similarly, the Folk High Schools for young adults in Denmark, which model their learning on democratic principles, provide a precedent for Room 13. What is remarkable about Room 13's practices is the underpinning principle that a child may organise their curriculum around the desires and needs of their creative practice, should they wish to do so. In doing this they not only emulate the progressive educational strategies advocated by the likes of Neill, they also establish the primacy of creativity at the heart of education.

Most Room 13s have management groups drawn from the pupil participants, and in the case of the Scottish groups, these have been established for many years and their working methods and practices have developed traditions of their own. Often children who participate in Room 13 have older siblings who were former managers of the group. The range of activities for which the management groups take responsibility varies greatly but has encompassed such responsibilities as accounting, scheduling of exhibitions, organisation of accommodation, and application for funding grants as well as the day-to-day administration of the group. Occasionally the management may involve themselves in entrepreneurial activities such as commissioned artwork or photography for local businesses or services, as were well documented in their TV programme (Room13/ZCZ Films for Channel 4, 2004).

> Being and artist in residence at Room 13 is a very strange creature, because you're not in charge, your managing director is in charge. Most of the time that's the way it goes, but it only requires the alarm to go and immediately they cede responsibility to you, everything's done as required; as soon as the fire alarm has finished you come back in again and you're again one of the team; I find that very interesting.
> (Rob Fairley, artist in residence and one of the founders of Room 13, interview with the author, February 2011)

Room 13s normally operate continually throughout the school day, and often before and after as well. The pre- and post-school activities resemble many other 'normal' after-school clubs, but the continual operation of the groups during the day means that the extended times offer continuity and opportunities for creative work that may not be possible otherwise:

> anybody who comes in can just pick what they do: someone would walk in and start doing a picture, maybe someone else might paint a folder; we do lots of different things; some stuff's modern, some stuff's traditional, some stuff's just random.
> (Room 13 members, Caol, interview with the author, February 2011)

In its early stages Room 13's existence as an integral part of the school was challenged on the basis of its contribution to the curriculum; if pupils were to leave lessons to attend Room 13, then Room 13 should be expected to provide experiences that covered all areas of the curriculum. Fairley collaborated intensively with teachers at the school to research into ways that this might be accomplished. The idea of children being able independently to decide to leave lessons in order to attend Room 13 has been a contentious issue right from the outset, however, and the tensions that arise are indicative of the broader educational debate about institutional authority and governance versus the rights and responsibilities of children to determine their own learning. In the case of the oldest and most well established Room 13s, such as those in Scotland, much experience has been gained over many years, and now there are strategies and models to accommodate this singular creative learning phenomenon. For instance, some children have effectively negotiated their own timetable by regularly attending Room 13 activities at given times. At other times, as Claire Gibb, International Coordinator and a former member of Room 13 explains, this is circumstantial; considerable amounts of continuous time may be given over to Room 13 activities prior, say, to an exhibition. The management group may be given privileged, timetabled meeting times. Significantly, however, there are the impromptu moments when children may decide that they would like to carry out creative work irrespective of other timetable and curriculum requirements. Inevitably, these are the most taxing for a formally timetabled institution to accommodate, but nonetheless they do occur in Room 13. Sometimes, as Gibb puts it, children simply 'find themselves at a loose end and turn up', although she is at pains to point out that this is not in the least anarchic, as it may sound, for all movements of the children in and out of lessons and Room 13 are regulated between the pupil and the class teacher.

Practices within Room 13 encompass far more than a typical project-led art class might; Gibb describes the group as an intellectual entity: 'Room 13 is a way of thinking' (correspondence with the author, 2009). As she explains, the studio is not simply there as a place to produce art; artists have to do more, they have to challenge taken-for-granted thinking, and interrogate contemporary moral and philosophical problems: 'to raise their level of thinking about what they're doing, why they're doing it and what it is to be an artist' (Gibb, 2012). Is it noticeable that for many participants in Room 13 the dilemmas of how to be an artist, and ways of artistic being, can dominate the discourse, most famously in the title of their home-made television programme *What Age Can You Start Being an Artist* (Room 13/ZCZ Films for Channel 4, 2004). *Artist* is used to mean a social and interactive way of being, as well as a creative one. As Gibb explains,

> [o]ne of the values of room 13 is that we're just here as people, and all we've got to draw on is our morality and integrity as artists, so you don't approach a child or any other person with a procedure in mind, which immediately distances you from them. It's a sort of alienating thing; you approach them purely as a person; just as you do with every person that you meet you make decisions about how you're going to interact with them on a day-to-day basis.
>
> (interview with the author, February 2011)

Both Fairley and Gibb are emphatic about their status within Room 13 as artists rather than teachers; this is consistent with the belief, widespread in Room 13, that art, not education, is the primary impetus and raison d'être for the group: 'We don't get taught; they don't tell us how to do art, we just do it' (Room 13 members, Caol, interview with the author, February 2011). Gibb rejects the proposition that Room 13 is itself an educational institution, instead privileging art and creative practices above those of education:

> [F]or my part, I would say that Room 13 remains at heart a contemporary art movement. You [the author] used the word 'fundamentally' which I think is the correct word. Given the nature of the work we do and the fact that the majority of our studios are located in schools and places of education, there is a tendency for Room 13 to be considered mainly from an educationalist point of view. In fact, I would say that the educative elements of Room 13 are a by-product of the fundamental arts practice which underpins our work. Our 'educators' are artists, and as such the making of, and discussion about, art is their first and foremost motivation.
> (Gibb, correspondence with the author, 6 October 2009)

The demarcation between educator and artist may be exaggerated by the context in which she and many Room 13 collaborators have to work, which is alongside – and in concert with – a school: an institution that by definition is 'educational'. Gibb's ambivalence about Room 13 as an educational project and her rejection of the epithet 'teacher', when applied to Room 13 artists in residence, are reinforced by her corresponding averseness to being pigeonholed as a 'progressive' educator, a term derived from Dewey which has become pejorative in neoliberal discourse (e.g. Johnson, 2014); she is wary of the concept, preferring instead to liken their practices to a cultural model:

> Room 13 is frequently hailed as a 'ground-breaking' and 'innovative' initiative. Yet the children themselves are entirely unremarkable; their achievements are a consequence of the timely application of principles that are ancient, and align more fully with the Renaissance model of apprenticeships than any modern-day ideas of progressive or liberal education.
> (Gibb, 2012, p. 240)

Gibb's favouring of the idea of an apprenticeship owes much to the traditions and culture of arts education, which, as she points out, originates in much earlier times when artists were more commonly thought of as artisans. The apprenticeship concept is credible when applied to the working practices of Room 13, because the youngsters do emulate and acquire the techniques and ideas of the senior members of the group in situ, eventually filling their position as expert practitioners. This is reminiscent of Lave and Wenger's (1991) situated learning, and when spending time in the studio with Room 13 at work, it would be hard not to equate the relationships and practices that one is observing with a community of practice, as elucidated by Wenger (2005). In particular, Wenger's framework of 'belonging', comprising engagement, imagination and alignment, seems to fit well. Our observations of the studio at work would indicate intense practical engagement with the projects by the group; our interviews with the artists and the participants demonstrate their ability to imagine the scope and potential of the concept of Room 13 as a creative community and their place in it, and they orient and negotiate their practices in order to bring them into alignment with their understanding of what Room 13 means. This is confirmed by Roberts, who points out, based on her observations of Room 13 at work, 'teaching and learning occur primarily dialogically, with questioning being the main stimulus for growth' (2008, p. 23). In many ways the participants of Room 13 constitute a textbook example of a community of practice as Wenger would describe it.

The apprenticeship model proves rather inadequate as a means of describing the diverse nuanced range of practices evident in the Room 13 studios, however, and contradicts the group's proselytising of reciprocity: the medieval and Renaissance apprentice could not presume to critique the master's work nor dictate its intellectual direction, both of which youngsters readily do on a daily basis in Room 13. Indeed, Fairley describes his own arts practice as stimulated by the realisation that working with young people in the studio provided him with a critical feedback that he was unable to obtain elsewhere. He attributed this to their uninhibited willingness to provide a commentary on his work, a feature he found was lacking in the more typical studio because of the adult politeness of his colleagues there. When asked about working procedures Fairley frequently refers to the influence of the young Room 13 artists on the adult artist in residence and emphasises that all practices that occur in the group have reciprocal effects. He contrasts this with the traditional classroom arrangement where the children expect to be directed by the instructor or teacher; for Fairley this reciprocity is a fundamental feature of Room 13 (Fairley, interview with the author, February 2011). This view of pedagogy aligns with Rancière's (2010a) notion of education emerging primarily from an equality generated by a shared investigation of the object of study; then it is possible to view the creative art experiences of Room 13 as simultaneously creative educational experiences, the main difference being the pedagogical methods employed.

Many Room 13 practices are characterised by a propensity to collaborate, although this can take diverse forms, occur at any stage in the life of a work from conception to presentation, and vary in degree from group to group, as Fairley points out:

> Room 13 Lochyside ... across the corridor from our office ... is a strangely open area where the young artists seem to work in a hugely collaborative manner with it being rare for ANY piece to be completed by a single hand ... in Room 13 Caol (20 mins up the road) this way of working would be sacrilegious and if anyone dared make a mark on a piece of work that was not theirs' trouble would ensue!
> (Fairley, correspondence with the author, 2009)

Problems with collaboration may occur when social interests such as friendship groups dominate over the creative activity, but these are overcome by studio-to-studio collaborations, where objects are sent back and forth and to which each group contributes graphically to the ideas of the others. One of the most distinctive features of Room 13 collaborative activity is the direct collaboration between the artists in residence and the children participants, which can occur spontaneously and with great enthusiasm, enhanced by proximity and the shared working studio space. The conditions for collaborations to occur, irrespective of the form they take, are greatly enhanced by the absence of any formal assessment regime: there is no requirement to distinguish one participant's contribution from another in order to allocate marks or impose any other form of calibration. Nonetheless, the children were well aware of the nature of each other's contribution when restarting work that had been left dormant in the studio for some time – a common occurrence in Room 13 – and where a work is considered completed the children are quick to recognise and attribute each other's inputs.

Common methods of assessment used elsewhere in the school were emphatically rejected by Room 13 children at Caol, on the grounds that they could not accommodate the practical, intellectual or relational complexities of their work: 'If people mark it, and say they don't like it, you might get a bit upset, because it's your best drawing you could do' (Room 13 member, Caol, interview with the author, February 2011).

The willingness of many Room 13 participants to engage in collaborative art production and its conspicuous absence from mainstream education is one of the positive effects of the liberation of children from externally imposed and highly competitive assessment regimes. Assessment in Room 13 is internal and self-generated, and has many forms, most often a constructive, formative dialogue, and is practical, with specificity demanded by the medium in hand:

> Instead of marks we give compliments, and, say, somebody is painting a picture of a tree, then you could say something like 'you could put a bird' there'; like try to help by giving more detail
>
> (Room 13 member, Caol, interview with the author, February 2011)

Room 13 pedagogy

Fairley describes Room 13 pedagogy in terms of its creative working procedures and argues that there are shared principles that bind the different groups despite their international diversity. These commonalities are to be found less in the physical attributes of space, number or type of institution with which they are associated, and more in their working ethos:

> The basic ideas of Room 13 have not changed . . . There are now many subtly different models but the basic tenets remain the same. Nearly all the ideas come from the youngsters themselves . . . sometimes drawing on discussions with the older artists . . . and these now are just as likely to be older kids dropping in after High School.
>
> (Fairley, correspondence with the author, 2009)

Fairley's reference to the interactions between the older and younger participants, and the wide age range of the youngsters that occupy Room 13s, is important because, unlike the standard practice in many Western educational systems whereby children are grouped with assiduous attention to their calendar age, Room 13s more often resemble family age groupings. As Fairley points out, this has an important pedagogical function, with ideas emerging and disseminated across the age range. It is also another correspondence between Room 13 and the artistic communities on which they are modelled. As Gibb (2012) argues, this cross-generational approach supports a mutual respect, which is characteristic of Room 13s. The artists in residence take all work seriously and instigate a studio culture in which 'intense discussion and critical discourse' thrive, and avoid direct instruction, preferring instead to cultivate a momentum for serious artistic practice predicated on intellectual rigour, irrespective of the age of the participants (Gibb, 2012, p. 239). Underpinning Gibb's understanding of artistic practice is a belief in criticality, the idea that a work of art should be subject to an ongoing critical review throughout its production: 'A work should be moving or exciting or disturbing – somehow emotive – or it fails as a piece of art. In our studios, the work of all artists is subjected to this basic test of integrity' (Gibb, 2012, p. 240).

That Room 13 is an intellectual as well as a practical phenomenon frequently crops up in accounts of the group's activities. One former member of Room 13 Lochyside, when asked to recount the most memorable aspects of his experience as part of the group, mentioned that philosophy was as important to him as the art work – at that time he liked to think of himself as a philosopher, 'an eight year old Socrates' (Mark, former Room 13 participant, interview with the author, February 2011). He recalled that much of the Room 13 work derived from current events, and this was something that interested him and made the work of the group distinctive. The customary role of the teacher itself comes under critical scrutiny in Room 13, presenting problems for the functioning of group as part of mainstream education in Mark's view:

> I think the adults would definitely need to be trained to think that way because it's a traditional thing for the teacher to be the one who's got to think ... teacher and pupil need to be on a level as long as they respect each other
> (Mark, former Room 13 participant, interview with the author, February 2011)

He also turned the traditional concept of age-related development towards independent thinking on its head, arguing that his primary school experience of Room 13 encouraged an independence and autonomy that was to diminish instead of increase in his secondary mainstream education:

> Even more than today I was responsible for my own learning; I think younger children have this enthusiasm for learning and discovering and I think as you grow older you kind of fall into a routine that other people devise for you.
> (Mark, interview with the author, February 2011)

These practices are not without their dilemmas. Critically questioning an idea or an image that children are making, even with constructive intentions, may have effects that are wholly negative, as in one example that Gibb provided of just such an incident in a life drawing class: 'the kid who had been drawing confidently was suddenly faltering and wanted to rub it out; the kid was suddenly presented with a dilemma and decided that she had done something wrong' (interview with the author, February 2011). Similarly, adults working in the Room 13 environment encounter the perennial problem of children's loss of confidence and disillusionment with their drawing ability, a culturally dominant trend in the UK, frequently accompanied by the proclamation: 'I can't draw'. In Room 13 this has become known as 'going blind', and workarounds have to be found, a scenario familiar to many mainstream art educators. There are also times when the artist in residence is presented with dichotomies over the need or requirement to intervene in the Room 13 children's creative practices according to the requirements of a current project, commission or impending exhibition. The tensions that arise vary according to the urgency of the project at hand or institutional constraints.

Room 13's marginal existence in relation to the host institution – the school – is important, for this arguably situates it in a 'third place' (Oldenburg, 1989), which is to say that it simultaneously belongs to the school but is not *of* the school. As one Room 13 participant put it, 'It's kind of part of the school and not part of the school'. Working in Room 13, like playing a game, can be thought of as occupying a distinct and important arena; as Huizinga puts it, 'temporary worlds within the ordinary world, dedicated to the performance of an act apart' (1944/1949, p. 10). It is important to bear this in mind when considering the relational possibilities of creativity within the group. This bracketing off of a distinct temporal space has implications for their artwork, where the room itself and its social history of artistic practices, and the performance of those practices within the confines of that space is of great significance to the current participants and their ad hoc collaborations. This is because the collaboration is often determined by an understanding or memory of a previous collaboration that occurred in the same space. These artistic traditions make it possible for the group to operate democratically, with a conspicuous absence of adult or teacher authority, and yet still retain a fairly high degree of regulated and organised practice. It is neither an autonomous artistic community nor a school art class, and yet in a way it is both. This ambiguous third place is fully exploited by the artists and the participants of Room 13 in their artistic production. One of their most memorable characteristics, particularly striking on visiting their studio at work, is the sheer pleasure evident when artists of greatly different ages and experiences work together in an environment relatively free of arbitrarily imposed social hierarchies, and in which the discourse is entirely focused on the subject in hand: the artwork.

If the purpose of education, where not an end in itself, is to reproduce democracy and the flourishing of a culture, then childhood may be considered as a period when one can be supported to be creative, sociable and collaborative, in preparation for a lifetime of critical enquiry. Room 13 is an instance where this seems to occur as a matter of course.

Pedagogical methods

The teacher's role in the democratic learning environment is intensively organisational rather than instructional, facilitating and managing an experience that is mutually beneficial (Dewey 1938/1969, pp. 30–31). The structure and form of arts pedagogies are arguably more conducive to this ideal of experience that Dewey outlines; the teacher in the creative classroom has the potential to create learning experiences that are centred on mutual interests in materials and issues that constitute the production of an artwork. Although directly instructional demonstration activity may well be required, and even demanded, where techniques are instrumental to a project, more democratic and collaborative activities are readily introduced. This is because the concept of the 'artist in residence' is deeply entrenched in the history and traditions of Western art education, and as a consequence many teachers see themselves in this dual role (Adams, 2011). In this configuration the teacher and learner are engaged in mutual exploration of creativity. The teacher-as-artist explores the problem to hand alongside the learner, and in some progressive situations, Room 13 being a case in point, the influences are reciprocal. Although the teacher may occupy a privileged position by virtue of experience and technical expertise, creative imaginings will just as easily be produced by the learner as by the teacher. If the teacher is confident enough to be receptive and amenable to artistic prompts, then a creative engagement can emerge.

Matthews, concerned with democratic ways to create learning situations with children, developed a pedagogical model of working which he describes as 'conversational' (2003). This is a respectful way of working with young people and forges a middle course between direct instruction and passive encouragement, both of which Matthews condemns as being well meaning but counterproductive. Like many educators and parents sympathetic to progressive and expressive education, he sees instruction as reductive and proscriptive, the imposition of adult values that efface those of the child. Unusually though, for educators of this persuasion, he is also wary of hands-off, non-interference methods that uncritically privilege children's expression. Like Vygotsky (1933), Matthews recognises and acknowledges the significance of adult interaction and the unavoidable cultural exchanges that occur, even if the adult assumes the position of passive respectfulness. However, he sees Vygotsky's imposition of adult understandings and values as patronising, something that children both desire and to which they must inevitably acquiesce; he argues instead for a more circumspect and respectful dialogue.

Matthews's work arises from painstaking studies of his own children, filmed and photographed at every stage of their creative development, from the earliest childhood scribblings to sophisticated teenage projects. Over the decades of studying his children he amassed a huge database composed of drawings, films, photographs, notes and recordings, from which he has constructed his analyses. Although Matthews's focus is primarily on visual representation, he is keen to incorporate all other forms of expression that pertain to children's meaning making and, indeed, argues that it is necessary to have a broad review of how children make creative responses to their world, and confining oneself two one domain of analysis, such as the visual, reduces and limits our understanding. For example it may well be the case that a young child's drawing may be little more than a few apparent scribbles, but when the child is seen in the act of actually creating the drawing it may be readily apparent that the performance of creating the work, the gestures, sounds and narration, are as important as the drawing itself. Added to this we should consider the others in proximity to the creation of the work – adults and other children, and their influence and how this impinges and determines the child's response. All of these relational features of the creative act have, in the final analysis, to be considered within the greater cultural context within which the event occurred.

An instance of this relational, conversational and multimodal creativity occurred when Luca (at four years old, the grandson of Adams) created a painting in a domestic setting, the kitchen. The topic of the painting underwent transformation in the process of its making, and despite the size and scale of the image – which was quite large for a small young child, being a rectangle equivalent in its largest dimension to his own height – he appeared to be in full and confident control. Luca was willing to narrate the 'story' of the painting throughout its creation; for 40 minutes he spoke as he worked, assembling his narrative from a variety of sources, mostly drawn from his recent experience of watching television and listening to stories that had been read to him. Moreover, these stories were tempered and adapted by the feedback that he received during the making of the painting. Consequently what appears to be a painting of a volcano (see Figure 4.1) spewing fire may also, and probably more accurately, be interpreted as a bricolage of marks corresponding to a verbal recounting of recent freshly remembered stories, from TV programmes, books and family tales, and reinforced by the adults in the room that prompted, encouraged and reinforced the ideas that he was venturing.

The performance of creating the painting was a rehearsal for Luca of recent events, in which he was situating himself in the landscape of his social world in relation to the dominant features of that landscape – the people who were listening, watching and commenting as he worked – all of which was tempered by the media to which he had recently been exposed. This creative event is relational in a conversational sense, in that it is the product of repeated rehearsals by the child, which are presented as a performance through gesture and verbal expression, as well as through the painting, and reinforced continually by the others who were present. The reinforcement takes the form of a performance itself, as others in the room prompt, question and encourage; the subtleties of facial expressions or even silences, the very absence of encouragement, affected Luca's production. Taken as a whole from a relational perspective, the event is a reciprocal engagement, an exchange of ideas, thoughts and feelings, which are very difficult to separate out, as they occurred rapidly and simultaneously; they do seem to conform to

Figure 4.1 Luca's volcano painting

Dewey's idea of habits formed through experience, as Luca manifestly incorporated world views into his painting and his thinking as he worked.

Contributions, both verbal and gestural and were made throughout the painting period from all of the three adults present, each eliciting a new response from Luca, although the reaction took different forms, sometimes overt, sometimes less obvious. For example, Luca created the large horizontal red outline shape at the base of the picture in two confident delineations with his brush, the loaded paintbrush running out at the end of each manoeuvre. It caught the adults' attention: '[W]hat's that?' 'It's a mole contraption' he responded, after some thought. There was a moment's silence, with an exchange of perplexed expressions. Luca clearly enjoyed the enigma of the moment and started to chuckle, repeating this title several times, louder with each iteration. Arising from the side of the mole contraption, filling in the narrow gap between the triangle of the volcano and the picture edge, Luca painted what was to become his 'poppy tree', on either side of which he drew in figures representing his grandparents (as he explained when questioned). A key moment in the production of the painting was his extensive use of black in the central large triangle representing a volcano. There been some discussion in the room as the paint was being prepared, which involved squeezing tubes of acrylic paint into the wells of a mixing pallet, which emphasised the importance of economy of paint, that is only putting out what was needed, which developed tangentially into a discussion of the potentially deadening effect of black paint (a discourse well rehearsed in the colour experiments of 19th-century European Impressionist painting). This was not intended as any kind of guidance or advice to Luca, merely an aside between the organising adults in the room, yet this was picked up by him even though he had not been a contributor to the conversation at the time. As the painting commenced he loaded his brush with as much black paint as was practically possible and began the enormous large black triangle that dominates the pictorial space of the image. A few suggestions were made to him about the possibilities of other colours, but his clear desire was to offer a challenge to this conventional adult wisdom and for humorous mischief.

Throughout these exchanges the picture was growing dynamically, overlaid with a narrative peppered with jokes; thinking of the picture relationally, it can be seen as the product of the intersubjective relationships in the room, rather than the produce of an individual child. Influences were at once everywhere and yet hard to discern as discrete entities, difficult at any one time to ascribe a particular utterance as the cause of any specific aspect of the work. Nonetheless, it would seem undeniable that the presence of responsive people had a profound effect on Luca's work on this occasion. The picture event was arguably a collaborative production, with Luca as director, more akin to film production than to the more conventional notion of an artist's individual expression.

It is an interesting coda to the painting episode that at its conclusion Luca showed little interest in discussing or explaining the image or even looking at it again. The following day his interpretations of the various elements of the painting were not consistent with those given during the event itself; new stories were spun, but now, without the simultaneous process of painting, were invented without enthusiasm, it seemed that the painting as a finished object only existed at the margins of his experience and could only be conceptualised during the event itself, when he had considerable agency as a creative practitioner and was accompanied by his makeshift audience. It was not the colour black that had the deadening effect on the painting; it was its objectification, from the relational ground of performance into an aesthetic object, which appeared to kill his interest.

Luca's painting could also be understood, when presented as the finished object, in conventional European art historical terms; for example it could be described as a picture bearing the features of composition, form, colour, texture, pictorial space and perspective. It can also be interpreted as both portrait (the pair of figures that can be discerned either side of the red 'tree' shape to the left of the canvas) and landscape (the central black volcano spouting fire); the handling of the paint could be analysed as painterly with an economy of the broad calligraphic marks, but all of these are examples of post-event interpretation, at some distance from the performance of the painting itself.

Atkinson, observing a video of Luca creating another painting at an earlier age, theorised on the ways we interpret his performance and his painting. Using Rancière he argued:

> Such enquiries further our understanding along established lines of thought and bodies of knowledge. That is to say, such enquiry presupposes or is predicated by establishing epistemological frameworks through which Luca's painting practice can be understood. . . . Such enquiries are predicated upon particular distributions of the sensible, upon distributions of the visible and the speakable in which the child and his practices can be comprehended
> (Atkinson, 2011, p. 4)

Atkinson goes on to argue that these epistemological frameworks should not be taken as benign, simply as a means of analysing creative events in order to make them comprehensible; instead, they structure the acts and events themselves, reconfiguring them in relation to pre-existing orders of knowledge. In other words, the process of understanding the creative event should itself be seen as actively intervening rather than passively absorbing; the square peg of the creative event is transformed as it is forced into the round hole of our predetermined comprehension. Atkinson pursues this idea in order to explain the ways in which arts education, whilst providing the ground for creative learning to occur, simultaneously represents this learning within the orthodoxies and conventions of the institutional culture within which it has been produced. This is important, not only because of its transforming or distorting effects but also because of its potential for discrimination and the reinforcement of inequalities. It may be that the act of making a creative work or event comprehensible necessarily requires these reconfiguring process, and immersed in our culture as we are, we may find our awareness of this process opaque or at least elusive; nonetheless, its effects are apparent and available to us for scrutiny.

This is particularly the case, as Atkinson points out, when artworks are subjected to assessment and evaluation, where cultural and ideological positioning often masquerade as the taxonomies of objectivity. This, as educational reproduction theorists like Bernstein (1966/2000) and Bourdieu and Passeron (1990) explain, is an important instrument in the ascription of individuals to categories of social class. What may appear to be an objective and transparent process, the assignment of the characteristics of an artwork to specific attributes of competence is imbued with cultural value. This, Bernstein argues in his discussions of the symbolic codification of language (1966/2000), becomes a device for the segregation of children into cultural groups that are as likely to be determined by class (to which one might add race or gender) than by ability. He points out that the relational attributes of language use, to which working class children have ample access, are trumped by conceptual attributes, to which middle class children are more likely to have access; thus the assessment of a facility with language is covertly the site of the conferment of privileges by means of class.

Contrasting with this Matthews (2003) argues that all aspects of a child's life have the potential to be represented in the event of a creative production such as a drawing. This is not limited to the drawn image on the page, but includes the performance of drawing: gestures, utterances and all the sounds and motions that occur during its production. Consequently, Matthews urges us to pay attention to all of these modes of expression and not limit our reading of a work to the drawing itself. All marks a young child makes are significant, never pointless, even if we have difficulty making sense of them or understanding their source; these problems, Matthews argues, are our limitations as adults, not those of the child. The role of chance and improvisation are fundamental to the drawing process, just as they are to the cognitive and affective development of children generally. For Matthews the adult's role in this creative moment is crucial (2003, pp. 20–21), neither as an instructor nor as a bystander but, rather, as a partner in conversation, which is his model for the creative relationship between adult and child.

This model of working with children in this conversational manner is arguably critical for the development of creative independence and for collaborative interdependence. Just as Rancière argues in the 'Ignorant Schoolmaster' (2010a), the relationship between adult and child or teacher and pupil is determined by the practice, not by authority bestowed externally. Each responds primarily to the work in hand; the practice is the learning vehicle, and equality is established at the outset. Through making and performing a creative dialogue is established. This dialogic process is context specific, and learning is contingent on the creative process as much as it is on the democratic principle of equality within which it is established. Just as two artists are able to learn equally from each other by engaging with their painting practice, irrespective of their prior knowledge or understanding, however great or uneven, so too with children and the adult or teacher, when their relationship is constructed through a dialogic relationship such as this.

Chapter 5

Contemporary creative pedagogies: Japan

This chapter discusses an example of contemporary creative and relational pedagogical practice in relationship to the institutions that hosted it. Designed to offer an alternative dramaturgical approach for students in higher education in Japan, the project focus was placed on the use of participative drama to create spaces for dialogue and understanding. The resultant exchange of creative practices challenged pedagogical and cultural assumptions such as those derived from reductive imaginaries of 'Western' individualism contrasted with the 'Far Eastern' collective.

From bystander to actor: applied drama in Japan

Creativity/souzouryoku 創造力

This example of creative pedagogy is drawn from our experience in an Anglo-Japanese long-term intercultural applied drama project (since 2000). For the purposes of discussion about relational creative learning and pedagogical practices we focus on one Japanese stage of the project, as it was particularly significant for the development of our thinking about creativity and democracy. The locus of creativity in this case study is a higher education institution in Japan that forms part of a wider network of practice we have established, which includes a theatre company, a National Children's Theatre Association, and a range of schools associated with the network. Our focus in this chapter is on second-year diploma drama students at the higher education institution. Before turning in detail to the social relations and forms of practice developed in this project, we set out the cultural and political context of the project in Japan and its indicative relationship to democracy.

The changes resulting from new technology and the process of globalisation that characterises post-industrial societies such as Japan and the UK have been profound. Bauman explores some of the unsettling nature of these (Bauman, 2001, 2002, 2004, 2011). He uses the phrase 'liquid modernity' (2001, p. 79) to describe the feelings of uncertainty and sense of insecurity that characterise such societies with what he refers to as 'the illusion of ever extending choice'.

Bauman points to the form of neoliberal fatalism that endless choice has bought with it, and considers alternative routes by which the move 'from bystander to actor' (Bauman, 2002, p. 205) might be made possible. He argues that security is a necessary condition and a key aim of the applied drama project is to create spaces where participants feel safe enough to discuss the relationship between the individual and the collective. Security in this sense is not taken to mean warm togetherness but an equal opportunity to put forward personal opinions within a process characterised by dissensus, like Mouffe's (2009) model of agonism in recognising that this permits struggle and conflict to persist within the democratic process, in this case within the applied drama space.

Post-industrial nations such as Japan and the UK are not the same, nor are they 'whole cultures', composed as they are by quilts of cultural confluences and influences. Our understanding of the culture and politics of Japan continually shifts as we reposition ourselves as a result of our engagement in the projects; this is part of the process of uncovering our assumptions in order to gauge how these inform the drama and research process. For example, we started this project with a strong sense of working within a culture of conformism. However, the more widely we read, worked, listened and talked, the more we began to realise that this highlighted rather than concealed issues of individual and national identity.

Giddens suggests that our quest for self-identity is a problem originating in Western individualism (2000), but our reading suggests this is not necessarily the case; whilst there may be much truth in the advice to 'always seek the social to understand the Japanese phenomenon' (Gluck and Sharpe, 1998, p. 4), a consideration of 'identity' would also yield much understanding. Gluck and Sharpe argue, having made the point that democracy is differently constructed in different contexts,

> If as some say the great theme of Chinese History is unity, that of Indian history, continuity, then the corresponding theme of Japanese history would be identity . . . in Japan democracy tends to be defined socially as co-equal individual access to material and social goods. The social sharing of benefits among the people is considered fundamental perhaps more than political criteria like voting in elections.
>
> (Gluck and Sharpe, 1998, p. 4)

Whilst in the early stages of the project we questioned this form of social closeness in which those who 'creatively disrupt' are resisted rather than encouraged, we slowly began to see the strengths of a social and cultural web that has offered coherence and cohesiveness in the face of the uncertainty which neoliberalism generates and thrives on. The use of applied drama as a means of organising reflection on the construction of individual and societal identity in this context constitutes the second key aim of this project.

Giddens's concept of the self as a reflexive project has been criticised by those seeking to re-couple the politics of identity with the politics of equality (Fraser in Bauman, 2002), but this concept does offer a useful take on our project as extrapolating self-identity from the daily constructions of ordinary life to provide Gidden's 'altered self' (1991, p. 33), which can be explored and constructed through a drama process intended to promote a sense of agency through vibrant 'agonistic' contestation, exploring personal changes within the wider context of social change.

In summary the key aims of the applied drama project were to create spaces where participants felt secure enough to discuss the key philosophical question, 'How shall we live?' when considering the relationship between the individual and the collective. These were achieved within an applied drama process in which the aim was not to settle conflicting voices in order to achieve resolution but to engage in the model of creativity itself, allowing participants take the step from bystander to actor by voicing their own imaginative conjectures. If politics is commonly thought of as what Badiou calls 'an action with place' then our project may be seen as part of his search 'to find a new way in politics – in a very complex distribution of truth, politics, democracy, philosophy – we probably have to find something like an action without place' (Badiou, 2006). We see the potential in the rich paradox here between the notion of the search for 'action without place' and Casey's argument that 'there is no creation without place' (in Olsson, 2007, p. 2).

The Japanese context: the relationship between education and creativity

This case study primarily comprises the experience of students studying in the drama department of a university in Tokyo. Students are recruited from all parts of Japan and the socio-economic backgrounds from which they are drawn vary considerably. It is impossible of generalise about the particular educational experiences that the students have before arriving at the university, so we tried instead to get a sense of the structure and scope of the Japanese education system and some of the current debates in order to understand more about the expectations that the students might bring with them to our collaborative work.

Japan has the second largest higher education system in the world with 3 million students enrolled in more than 700 universities comprising national government and local municipal public and private institutions. The latter serves the majority of students and has expanded extensively to meet the post-war popular demand for higher education. Only nine universities have performing arts programs and our case study university is one of these, having strong connections to professional acting agencies. It was a former junior college prior to becoming part of a much larger university, and in common with other specialist institutions, it has its roots in post-war US occupation policies, which were conceived to broaden opportunities and participation in education, in conjunction with their New Deal influenced fostering of democracy.

Japanese educational levels rank highly in international statistical tables. At the time of the project the OECD figures confirmed Japan's place as one of the top three countries in almost every international educational standards statistical table.

The education system is very centralised with examinations and testing at its core requiring extensive memorisation, teachers as a source of knowledge, an emphasis on student effort and self-discipline, with a low tolerance for deviating from conventional patterns of thinking; the characteristics of anti-dialogical pedagogical methods. University entrance examinations are based on a transmission-reproduction form of pedagogy, which consequently dominates the education system; at the time the Japanese Ministry of Education, Culture, Sports, Science and Technology (known as Monbukagakusho, 2005) was one of the most powerful and influential ministries.

However, as we became familiar with the system and gathered further data we quickly began to realise that the situation was more complex than this set of generalisations allowed for. Young people in Japan are often presented as either obedient learners under strict parental control or antisocial rebels. Yet we also have evidence to suggest that there are also highly motivated young people finding their way creatively through an education system that does not privilege flexibility or creativity. Factors that restrict creativity were present, however, including bullying, low self-esteem and self-respect, school nonattendance, self-harm and even serious criminal acts. On the other hand, there were clearly factors usually associated with encouraging the development of creativity such as free play, open space early child settings, very good basic skills, a reputation for persistence in practice to master skills, and pedagogies, particularly in the primary school, that instilled motivation.

As we probed further with staff in state and private, primary and high schools, we saw and discussed examples of creative practice. On the other hand, teachers also told us that it was hard to be creative when struggling to manage classes, and official figures confirmed that this was the case in a significant number of classrooms throughout the country. Reading, working and thinking further into the practice, history and philosophy of formal state education in Japan led us to understand that the system 'is like' that of the UK in its continual review and revision of provision, and its search for a new direction in order to keep pace with rapid globalised social and economic developments; it was also attempting to address many of the issues outlined earlier, especially non-attendance, difficult behavior, low self-esteem, and the alarming rates of self-harm. Consequently government programmes have been launched to promote: 'Kosei-ka': internationalisation; 'kokusai-ka': the zest to live; 'Ikiru chikara': freedom for leisure; 'Yutori': creative activities (Ministry of Education Culture, Sport, Science and Technology, 2005). The education system is unlike like that of the UK in that there is an openness about socialising children as Japanese citizens, and issues of educational reform most often revolve around ideological and moral notions of what it means to be Japanese and what social behaviours this entails (MacDonald, 2015). The emphasis in education has traditionally been placed on the valuing of the collective; for example, the Ministry of Education publicly states that 'unharnessed individual freedom' represents 'a direct threat to the collective' (Ministry of Education Culture, Sport, Science and Technology, 2005).

Saito and Imai argue that against a background of a traditional culture of conformism the search has been underway for some time for a new relationship between the public and the private in post-war Japan; in particular a search for a 'transformative language and vision of what it means to be and become a human being and of what it means to be free' (2004, p. 591). Our work corresponded with Saito and Imai's argument for the need to employ pedagogies in Japan that work towards re-conceptualisations of the relationship between the individual and the collective, and working through applied drama practices that privilege neither the Western imaginary of the individual nor the Japanese imaginary of the collective.

The relationship between art and politics

The form of dramaturgy in the project ran counterculturally to that usually engaged in by students, lecturers and visiting artists in the drama department. Full-time staff had pastoral care of students and coordinated timetabled sessions taught by specialist visiting artists who employed a predominantly transmission–reproduction form of pedagogy, whereby the expertise and knowledge of the artist was transferred through demonstration and repetition. Departmental staff had started the larger project collaboratively with us three years earlier to deliberately offer an alternative form of pedagogy to that currently offered. They were interested in the imaginative organisation of pedagogy offered by a particular form of dramaturgy which they thought might provide an alternative dynamic of participation that would be relevant to the changing interests of their students.

Rancière claimed that he wrote *The Ignorant Schoolmaster* 'to inject some life in to debates on the purpose of public education by throwing in the issue of intellectual equality' (1991, p. 3). In *The Emancipated Spectator* (2010) he develops these ideas further, particularly those of intellectual emancipation in relation to the subject of the spectator, and this is particularly relevant in this case study context to the relation between art and politics. Rancière takes issue with assumptions made about the spectator traceable back to Plato, namely that the spectator is *de facto* a passive being engaged in watching not 'doing', and calls for a theatre where all those present learn from being 'present'. He is not, however, talking primarily about changing theatre form in either the direction of 'distanced investigation' or of the direction of 'vital participation.' His point is that the spectator, like the pupil in school, is never passive in the sense of simply sitting and receiving the knowledge transmitted to her by the director or teacher; they use their expertise to make a bridge between what they know and what the pupil or spectator do not know. The transmission model, like Freire's (2001) 'boxed knowledge', is based on the unquestioned assumption, often by visiting artists, that teaching and learning are unproblematic: the teacher transmits and the learner receives, just as the actor acts and the audience spectate. The department staff wanted to offer an alternative to, but not to totally replace, the transmission model to one that acknowledged and encouraged the active reception and co-creation of knowledge. Rancière calls for a form of theatre, like Freire's calls for a form of education, which enables rather than actively disables the ability of the spectator to construct: 'the path from what she already knows to what she does not yet know, but which she can learn as she has learnt the rest' (Rancière, 2009, p. 14). He argues that that the learner does not learn in order to become the teacher, but rather

> to practice the art of translating, of putting her experience in to words and her words to the test; of translating her intellectual adventures for others and counter-translating the translations of their own adventures which they present to her.
>
> (2009, p. 15)

To create the space safe enough for participants to do this was, and continues to be, an important aim of the project. Another challenge has been, and continues to be, for us as dramaturgs and pedagogues, is to resist the conventional pedagogical stance of a bridging expert, between our knowledge and the students' deficit of understanding. Our aspiration, in Rancière's words, has been to 'uncouple' our 'mastery' from our 'knowledge' (2009); the ignorant schoolmaster and dramaturg's art lies, he suggests, in the ways in which they allow their learners or spectators 'to venture in to the forest of things and signs, to say what they have seen and what they think of what they have seen, to verify it and have it verified' (2009, p. 14). The ignorant director or the teacher does not know what the learner or the spectator should do or know:

> Each will take something different, something unanticipated and unplanned for away for the encounter. This is the meaning of the ignorant schoolmaster: from the school master the pupil learns something that the schoolmaster does not know himself. She learns it as an effect of the mastery that forces her to search and verifies this research. But she does not learn the schoolmaster's knowledge.
>
> (Rancière, 2009, p. 14)

Emancipation and the dramaturgical form: applied drama

The project forms part of the history of theatrical exchanges, appropriations and 'slanted–readings' (Drain 1995, p. 291) between Japanese and European theatre, which is long and complex and can be traced back at least to the beginning of the 20th century. The intention in our project has never been to import wholesale the slippery genre of applied drama but, rather, to translate it into forms of work that can shift between cultural contexts and still connect with participants in a wide variety of cultural settings. Applied drama is a generic term that can be given to a range of practices such as that of process drama used in this project. 'Applied' in Thompson and Schechner's sense of a word means 'in translation' (2004, p. 11), and we use this term because it has currency with our collaborators who have stuck tenaciously with the shorthand term *appliedo* to describe the social applications of the work we engage in together. The Japanese word for *applied* is *oyo* (n), *oyo suru* (v) and the translation carries with it the suggestion of many ways of doing something, of flexibility (Owens and Green, 2010).

The participative form of drama we collaboratively create is intended to act as self-referential and an experiential metaphor for the social construction of reality. It is a reflexive form of practice in which everyone is encouraged to consider the realities that shape them to which they contribute. This concern with agency and structure is one of the defining features of the approach: participants are given the opportunity to become 'other' than they are in everyday life and yet paradoxically more like 'themselves'. The 'transformational' aspirations of applied drama practice are an ongoing concern of those in the field.

We use the term *applied drama* to mean an inclusive of process and performance-based work, and the term *participants* to refer to those taking part (Nicholson, 2005, p. 5). Whilst we also use the term *practitioner*, our understanding of it has been enriched by the Japanese term *shinkouyaku* – the word that the Japanese students and staff feel most closely approximates to this role. This is like the word *navigator* in English in suggesting someone who determines a position but is unlike it because it also implies working with others to determine a set of positions. The notion of individuals working together to determine directions in which they might move has resonances with the collective, and dialogic, dissensual processes on which much practice in this book is based.

The particular applied drama form used is process drama which is located within the range of participative, communal performance genres in the oral and communal aesthetic tradition. Emphasis is placed on 'the construction of possible selves and alternative realities' (O'Neill, 1995, p. 142) as participants engage in drama to make sense through the 'imagined experience' of a particular phenomenon or a dimension of their lives (Neelands, 1992). The mainstay of this approach is 'the collective negotiation of meaning', and its particular strength is 'to invite tension and contradiction, and help students work within the ambiguities in a collective, but not necessarily consensual process' (Gallagher, 2000, p. 61).

Case study: the dreamer

This long-term project moves between Japan and the UK for 7 to 10 days in each country, and for the purposes of this discussion we focus on one of the Japanese stages. The Tokyo-based part of the project involved thirty-two Japanese second-year diploma drama students, studying at a higher education institution, some of whom had been involved in previous projects. They participated together for two days in a drama pretext, then worked for three more towards an open public session that they themselves ran in their own institution for a theatre group in Tokyo which incorporates young people with special educational needs. This study focuses primarily on the students first two days of participation but does refer to the open public session.

The focus was on the idiom that had surfaced on a number of occasions when we were working in the first three years of the project: 'Derukui wa utareru'/'Standing Nail Must Be Knocked Down'. Initially we understood this to mean that individualism should not flourish at the expense of the group, that being different will ultimately be a difficult experience, as the individual nail standing too tall has to be hammered down to the same height as the other nails for the good of all; that great things can be achieved by always placing the social before the personal, the collective before the individual. The students' opinions of the idiom's relevance in their lives and Japanese society varied greatly and brought the interrelationship between the personal and the social, the tension between structure and agency as dimensions of the relationship between creativity and democracy, sharply into focus. We began to reflect further on the different values and emphasis placed on this balance by individual students, ourselves, the translator, our collaborating colleagues and between the Western performance traditions fascinated with dramatising the tensions between individuality and conformity, and the performance traditions of Japan.

The question that we formulated at this point informed the direction of the project: 'To what extent are we shaped by the structures that envelop us and form our horizons, and to what extent do we in turn shape these structures through our own actions?' Answering this question in practical applied drama terms led us to notions of working and dreaming, and the creation of a process drama based on an individual who goes against accepted practices.

The dreamer pretext: planning for the possibilities of dissensus

On a two-year higher education course priding itself on its vocationality and the students' dreams about what work they might do were never far away, nor were the thoughts of our fellow collaborators responsible for giving their students the best possible chances to use drama as a means to find employment. We sensed the learning possibilities about 'dreaming differently': new understandings about the individual and the collective in ways that would be relevant to students' and our lives, and we recalled conversations in past projects about 'freeters', young people who choose not to spend intensive working lives working for material gain, and who take casual jobs and enjoy the freedom this allows to pursue their own agendas. Unsurprisingly the government viewed this as a threat rather than the opportunity perceived by the young people, and we began to think of the ways in which the pretext could resonate with this situation. The central metaphor was eventually developed from four sources: the rich histories of Japanese and British seafaring traditions, the biblical story of Joseph, Geraldine McCaughrean's novel

The Kite Rider (2001) and insights into the relationship between knowledge and power from Foucault's *Madness and Civilisation* (1967/2002).

The pretext was shaped to 'energise the democratic confrontation' (Mouffe, 2005, p. 6) whereby discussion arising from the drama would not be limited to establishing compromises. This involved creating a space, through dramatic analogy, of mutual interference where the students could engage in a process of dissensus in which existential questions were 'actively recovered and brought forward into public debate' (Giddens, 2000, p. 244). It was structured to provoke reflection about the relationship between the personal and the social, the public and the private, in ways which might allow us 'to conceive of these in new and richer terms' (Saito and Imai, 2004, p. 590).

The dreamer: synopsis

> The drama is set in the days after Japanese isolationism/sokoku, when the great trading ships sailed the seas. It is based around the character of H, a young member of a ship's crew who dreams, with an almost spiritual fervor, that one day he will be able to fly. Meanwhile, with the Captain's protection, he contents himself with making kites and flying them from the deck.
>
> When the ship docks to load cargo, H's sister knows that she must, for his own safety, make him see the fury that is building up in the rest of the crew as they work while he plays. Just before the ship sails two friends persuade him to stop talking about his dreams, stop making kites and do some work. The ship sails, but the plan fails.
>
> Without permission, H takes some of the rationed food, to nourish his dreams and share with the crew in an attempt to 'help them slow down and enjoy life a little more'. One thing leads to another and before they realise what they are doing the crew's anger erupts, they strap H to a canvas hold cover, tie a rope to it and haul him high into the air above the sea until he is just a dot in the sky. The rope snaps and H is swallowed-up by the sea.
>
> The Captain appears on deck and asks the crew why they are standing so silently in a line, holding a rope and staring into the distance.

In *Madness and Civilization* Foucault identifies the three salient themes that are at the heart of this applied drama pretext: 'Disobedience by religious fanaticism, resistance to work, and theft' (1967/2002, p. 255). H commits all three of these major offences against bourgeoisie society's essential values, offences that Foucault argues are not even excusable by madness. H's inability to work and follow the rhythms of collective life lead to a tragic rupture in the life of the community on board the ship and provide the arc of potential drama action.

The structure of the pretext requires a constant shuttling between life onboard the ship and life in Japanese society, the individual and the collective, which is intended to keep dialogue open and resist entrenchment of opinion through the use of irony.

In the drama, H represents the archetypal standing nail, and the careful construction of the pretext was intended to allow for as wide a range of opinions as possible to surface in response to his behaviours, attitudes and values. The moment the captain appears on deck to find the crew with a broken rope in their hands is intended to be a point of departure, or rupture, in the development of the emerging narrative where the 'intentional arcs' of the participants engage. There are at least three levels, or takes, of the structure/agency dialectic built into the pretext, each of which might illuminate the other, and inform the nature of the unfolding dramatic activity.

First, the students' behaviour as participants in the reality of the drama has been 'structured' by the practitioner through the pretext so that they find themselves responsible for the possible death of their 'brother'. In other words, the participants' experience in the drama has been shaped by its structure, but they also now have the opportunity to shape the structure of what follows through their own agency and acting.

Second, within the reality of the drama-world, the way in which the crew unquestioningly accept an exhausting seven-day working week as a given, a world where individual choice is subsumed in collective action suggests a 'fatalism' in which there is no possibility or hope of shaping the structures that determine the crew's experience of work.

Third, the moment of rupture causes those ideologies about work, leisure, personal and social responsibilities which might otherwise be presented as folkloric 'common sense' (Freire, 1998, p. 36) in Japanese society, to become the intense focus of necessary analysis and critical 'theorising'. This moment of rupture within the art form is shaped to open, 'a moment of silence, a question without answer' (Foucault, 2001, p. 274). The rupture in this metaphor is structured to allow us to 'emerge from daily living' (Freire, 1998, p. 93) and by distancing ourselves from the object of consideration, in this case 'work', to paradoxically come closer to understandings of it.

The correspondence between the 'common sense' need to 'pull together' onboard a sailing ship, and the need to work collectively against a background of a 'traditional culture of conformism' (Saito and Imai, 2004, p. 591) in Japan, are deliberately fantastical if somewhat obvious. The choice of the ship as a symbol of 'freedom on the high seas' and paradoxically as an instrument of colonial oppression is less obvious. The intention was that the pretext would provide the means to break the surface agreement about the value of 'pulling together', of 'teamwork as common sense' in a way that allowed for 'spontaneity, improvisation and interpretive risk' as we 'reflected upon taken for granted ways of knowing' (Britzman, 2003, p. 43).

Emergent issues

Four patterns emerged from our research. These were kaleidoscopic in the sense that they were not fixed, coherent or constant but, rather, patterns of possible meaning that shifted and could only be recognised through repeated rotation of the data collected from a drama process that was itself created to allow differences of opinion and ideology to surface. We used these to facilitate the discussion under four headings: first, 'inherited opinions', which Mill classifies as those passed down from previous generations (1859, p. 68), and, second, 'adopted opinions', defined as those newly acquired but which can quickly form a new, but equally rigid, orthodoxy (1859, p. 68). The third pattern is presented under the heading 'resisting fixity', the notion of 'fixity' being taken from Bhabha (1994, p. 37) and suggestive of a more complex hybrid understanding. Finally 'negative case opinions', which was included to acknowledge the pattern of voices that represented students who did not view the drama or research process positively at various stages.

We are not suggesting that any of the student biographical-narratives were completely coherent or unproblematic and we were aware of the difficulties in organising rather than normalising the stories told. Certain voices have been privileged here, and in presenting patterns of voices in this brief way we run the risk of writing a narrative in which the students' voices are 'affixed . . . to the unified subjects' positions of humanistic discourse despite the fact that they were continually becoming undone by the slippage of this very discourse' (Britzman, 2003, p. 41). In fact, the movement between reflection on individual identity and consideration of social structure within these patterns has proved to be one of the most telling aspects of the case-study data.

Inherited opinions

The first pattern of voices represents those students whose opinions reproduced and reinforced the dominant ideology, in this case the understanding that the standing nail must be knocked down immediately for the good of society as a whole. Within this selection of voices we identified three motifs. First, the unquestioning reinforcement dominant ideology characterised by the reactionary: 'H makes me angry, these kind of people should die and that's all.' Second, an awareness of the ideological imposition, but a belief that this is in everyone's best interest, characterised by certainty: 'Japanese society is still vertical and conformist, it is a price worth paying, this is how we live in Japan. People equate it with common sense', what Clifford Geertz describes as 'common sense as a cultural system' (2000, p. 73). Third, an awareness of the ideologies and structures shaping lives, a desire for change coupled with a sense of powerlessness: 'If H stands too high he will die. He has courage to continue as standing nail. I want to be a standing nail but I am Japanese; I can't.' Responsibility was also seen as a challenge and best to be avoided:

> The Japanese nationality loves working together, co-operation. Individualism destroys the group. We have to protect ourselves from abuse, this is exactly how I live in Japan. This is what we all can do, be the same and survive.
>
> I think that if you want to stand up you must have lots of responsibility. In a group society you don't need responsibility. It is a much easier life if

you are the same as the neighbours. Lots of students see this as an easier life. Responsibility is a bit scarier for them.

Many students talked readily and often about having ideas and emotions, but finding it very difficult to express them. The sense of frustration in not being able to communicate ideas and opinions, particularly between generations was strong and they pointed to what one students called they called 'the vertical systems' that 'keep us in place.' These included parental authority and strict control through education that stresses the importance of placing collective harmony before individual needs:

I must kill my feelings to live in Japanese society.

There was recognition by some individuals, that performing arts students were not necessarily representative of students studying other subjects, let alone the rest of Japanese society:

I still think an equal society is best, but we are different to normal Japanese students in education, we don't want to be the same as everybody else – yet still see what we do!

Some students felt keenly that Japanese society was changing, and this was characterised by uncertainty, 'In the past you had to be self-effacing, you had to melt into the group. Modern Japan is more individualistic'. Others were in agreement with the student who wrote, '[A]lthough the surface changes underneath things do not.' Many students felt that it was 'safer,' and 'wiser' in everyday life to remain 'surfaces to each other', rather than 'soaking beneath the surface' (Beck in Bauman, 2001, p. 147).

Adopted opinions

The second pattern consisted of voices that appeared to passionately 'adopt' new opinions that challenged the dominant ideology whilst often having no interest in looking at things from other people's points of view. They were heard most strongly in relation to issues of pedagogy. For example a visiting artist was invited in to help work towards the open public session and chose to work on restaging the moment when H was hauled in to the sky. In journal entries and evaluations following this pedagogic approach was rejected outright by many students and with outrage by some students who felt that this was an oppressively transmission–reproduction teaching approach:

The teacher decided everything that should be – everything! I can't agree with it. But why am I thinking this? Maybe because I have experienced applied drama.
This was not right, it was not applied. He told us what he wants us to do. What about . . . ? [the group we are going to work with] He had not met

them. We have, we know what they can do and the drama is for them. What were we to do?

When everyone saw sensei's direction they were very impressed, how he is a professional director, all students never doubted this. They thought this is what we want. Nori and Tabu (pseudonyms) said, 'It is wrong. This is not applied drama.' These key words completely changed everyone's mind. We don't need a professional director – we must do everything ourselves. Has the Sensei seen the group we are going to work with? If the director decides what happens flexibility is lost- this is a disadvantage as we can't find out other peoples' ideas.

When trying to make sense of the data, we began to consider if these students had, in their own ways, rejected the idea of pedagogy that they had 'inherited' only to 'adopt' with fervour a rigid version of a new pedagogy. The artist teacher skills in restaging these were impressive and the result very effective in terms of staging. In one sense this pattern of student voices showed how challenging it is to develop the ability to 'be critical' rather than simply exchange one conformity, one doxa, for another.

Resisting fixity

The third pattern of voices represented those student understandings of the tensions between the individual and the collective that were more complex than those in the first two patterns. They resisted the fixity of inherited opinions as they crossed borders (Giroux, 1997, p. 147) by engaging in a seemingly wider range of discourses as they explored and constructed the 'altered self' (Giddens, 2000, p. 33):

When I listened to what others said, I looked back on myself, reaffirmed or revised Myself.

At various points in this student's narrative of resistance, issues were used that had arisen through the project to revisit past incidents in her life in order to feel her way into the future:

To be honest I firmly believed I would become a medical doctor, everyone pushed me. I nearly died. I was so ill, I experienced a different world, my anorexia was so heavy. Even my doctor said, 'I can not believe that you are alive. You are lucky that you got your life back, now you can do anything you want to.' At that time I first realised, right, so I only have one life, of course I can do anything I like, so I don't want to go backwards. I started drama. Now I can become so strong because I am doing things my way. I can survive. Maybe the majority of people think that a secure feeling is the most important in the future. But what is secure? I am feeling especially now days in Japan that we don't need to think about that.

In replacing the dreams her parents and teachers had for her with those of her own Aiko (pseudonym) appears to use the drama space to rethink and retell the story of how she has reached back to reposition herself and continues to revise her biographical narrative 'as part of a reflexive process of connecting personal and social change' (Giddens, 2000, p. 33). Perhaps this is what Aiko has in her mind when she envisages applied drama as 'a thinking plaza':

> Respect. I learnt this word from the project. Nobody said this, but I learnt it. Even if people have the opposite idea to my opinion I respect it because these people gave me the opportunity for thinking. Applied drama is like a 'thinking plaza'.

As a social agent, Aiko is not a passive bearer of ideology. She appears to be trying to 'tell the truth' about herself by showing that 'in part she is constituted across a number of power relations that are exerted over [her] and that [she] exerts over others (Foucault, 1967/2002, p. 454).

Negative case opinions

A pattern of negative voices in the data related to dramaturgy and pedagogy. One student was cynical about the project because her father lost his job prior to the project:

> I feel very cynical. Now I have to think dream and work. My family has always lived together, father never left home, now he has to live separately from us. I can't think of the project. Financially this is very difficult. My dream is to carry on working here but this is expensive. I feel guilty and maybe will stop college. But work in the college is my dream. I can't concentrate. I am cynical.

When we read this report we seriously questioned the way we had moved so quickly from exploring the pretext at the students' own level into a rehearsal process that allowed little time for continued explicit exploration of issues arising from the work. Another student pointed to the potential tyranny of democracy:

> You said, 'You can do what you want', but this didn't work, for example when we discussed in a group. There were some scenes I didn't want but the group decided to have them and this made me angry. A minority opinion is wiped out by a democracy.

The power of peer pressure was also stressed by the same student who said that it was one thing for us to say that if people preferred to make sense by watching instead of doing that was OK, but it was quite another to not be seen to be doing by others who would judge you as being lazy. Katherine Paterson, the young peoples' novelist who has lived in and written extensively on Japan, states that '[i]f we teach young people to think they will grow up to question us' (1989, p. 82). It was of little comfort to these students to know that their questioning itself was welcomed precisely because they felt able to question and criticise the practitioners they were working with. In this sense the wider vision that some students realised was at the cost of frustration and confusion for others.

Summary of interpretations, connections and claims

We have tried to resist explaining issues away by identifying causes and effects, arguing that these are intricately wired to political, social, historical and personal contexts. We point instead to the ways in which the creative applied drama process resonated with these contexts in ways that allowed temporary and distinctive understandings to be made of them.

In concrete terms 'The Dreamer' provided a central metaphor that enabled us to ask why H and the ship's crew behaved and thought in the way they did, what differences and similarities there were between these and the way people behave and think in our own societies. It was structured to allow for a process of dissensus where conflicting voices about working and dreaming, individuality, the individual and the collective could sound out between 'adversaries' not 'enemies' in a relationship Mouffe envisages as 'agonistic' (Mouffe, 2005, p. 20). The cost of this for the individual can be high in a situation where power between the two parties is not equal such as between teachers and students. On the other hand, the risk can generate a sense of agency and so can open many possibilities, and we offer one example of this.

After the students had participated in 'The Dreamer' they spent three days planning and rehearsing how they could run the pretext for a group of young people with special educational needs who were part of a theatre group that met nearby. After the two-hour session when the young people had departed the students met in a public forum with the teachers and actors, who had come to observe the drama and a microphone was passed around the room. Many of the teachers present felt that the session had been too much about play with far too little structured learning and no outcomes to show. One student Yasuo (pseudonym) kept rising to his feet throughout this discussion until he finally got the microphone. When he did the atmosphere in the room was already charged, and he was shaking with the cost of what he was about to say:

> I have to say something. I absolutely learnt this in school. I hated my infant school because the teacher was so strict, pushing me to work, to study hard, to do my homework . . . if you don't do this you won't go to university, if you don't go to university you won't get a job, work hard, study hard, study hard, this is my life! I really wanted to play, to decide myself, this is what I want to say, why must we always work hard? I . . . [silence]

Afterwards, he said that it was one of the bravest things he had said in his life, but at that precise moment he ground to a halt. It appeared that the creative, collaborative, dissensual process had created a space for Yasuo's words. There was a strong sense for us that he had stopped speaking but had started communicating: 'everyone has known such a situation in which the rift between the saying and the said opens up' (Lingis, 1995, p. 108). In creating a space for the students to act and speak on their own behalf the project had perhaps momentarily 'energised the democratic confrontation' (Mouffe, 2005, p. 6).

This was not 'democracy . . . viewed as a basic question about people becoming "nicer" to each other' (Mouffe,, 2005, p. 54). It was rather an aspiration for a democracy generated by 'a type of education that fosters . . . the development of individuals with the capacity to be self-reflective, passionate about the collective good', and bringing ideas into the public realm (Giroux, 2014). Participants heard conflicting voices arising from dramatic action in process, sounding out between adversaries rather than enemies, an agonistic relationship. They engaged in a process characterised by the notion of good friction, challenging and disagreeing with each other as they reached back to their life experiences, making connections between abstract systems and themselves in a reflexive mobilising of self-identity.

If, as Bauman suggests, we are all bystanders now, then there is evidence here that some, but certainly not all, students who wanted the responsibility to temporarily take a step into action appeared able to find routes to do so through a drama and research process structured to allow for the move between bystander and actor. We draw parallels with Rancière's argument that the collective power of the drama/theatre art form comes not from the fact that participants are all members of one collective body but, rather, from their ability to make distinctive connections, to create unique stories from their own understandings in the company of other storytellers as equals. Although the telling in action and critical reflection the space that was opened, exposed for some the illusions of official dogmas where these could be at least partially penetrated and contested, a space created for struggle and potential change where the task of drama is like that of philosophy which, as Foucault suggests is to

> describe the nature of today, and of 'ourselves today.' . . . It is a time like any other, or rather, a time that is never quite like any other . . . [not] a simple characterization of what we are, but instead – by following the lines of fragility in the present – in managing to grasp why and how that which is might no longer be that which is. In this sense any description must always be made in accordance with these kinds of virtual fracture, which open up the space of freedom understood as a space of concrete freedom, that is . . . of possible transformation.
>
> (quoted in Nealon, 2004, p. 42)

Chapter 6

Creative interventions

In this chapter we look at the ways in which entrenched world views and hegemonic prejudices might be opened up by particular types of creative practice rooted in notions of justice and egalitarianism discussed earlier. We analyse the kinds of contingent learning and understandings generated by such interventions as participative pedagogical events. The case study is based on a research project with Gypsy Roma Travellers focused on the use of imagined experience to create a space in which existing understandings could be opened up, acknowledged, shared and challenged by creating anti-racist social and educational spaces in schools and local authority institutions in north-west England. The practice employed is that of research-based applied drama and theatre, and the pretext 'Michael's Story' is presented as part of our ongoing research into everyday racism.

This project did not exist in a vacuum. Particular climates, political and otherwise, together with specific circumstances and policies gave rise to them. These are considered in relation to the creative initiatives, artistic and pedagogical practices that were shaped in response to them. In doing this we also reflect on the wider international context, such as that occurring in Europe, where at the policy level, integrating Roma and itinerant communities within their localities continues to fail in practice, and in the Middle East, where the vulnerable indigenous Bedouin communities face an ongoing policy of home demolitions and forced displacement. We ask in whose interest is it to brand Travellers as scapegoat figures for collective public revulsion and anger, and wonder if this is this another means by which, as Tyler (2013) argues consensus is achieved for the continued neoliberalisation of the state and society.

Michael's story: developing understandings about Gypsy Roma Traveller culture

This case study is based on a three-year project (2011–2013) funded by Race Hate Crime UK in which we collaborated with our Local Authority Department of Education and Department of Planning to investigate the potential of pretext-based process drama to develop understandings about the Gypsy Roma

Traveller culture of young people in school, the professionals who work with them and the managers and leaders who run the system and devise the policy that shapes this. The key participant groups were young people, teachers and the wider workforce, including governors and local politicians. The locus for creativity was in primary schools and local government meeting facilities. The approach taken was the use of imagined experience, through a pretext-based drama and research process, to create a space in which existing understandings could be acknowledged or challenged. The three initial objectives of the project were to raise awareness of Traveller cultures with the non-Traveller population, to build understanding about Traveller cultures amongst children in the 7–11 age range and the adults who work with them and to introduce educators to a critical creative form of pedagogy that they could use with the young people with whom they were working.

The wider context

The challenges faced by itinerant cultures such as Gypsy Roma Travellers in Europe and the Bedouin in Palestine are usually ignored in a rush to condemn. A key challenge common to many cultures are a set of unquestioned assumptions by the non-itinerant population about itinerant cultures. These are often biased, inherited and based on superficial media reports and limited personal contact, all of which leads to widespread mistrust, unchallenged everyday racism and, in some cases, violent conflict. The European Union has produced recommendations relating to Gypsy Roma Travellers and 'itinerant cultures' (Council of Europe, 2011) as has the most recent five-year study in the UK by the Department for Education (DFE; 2010) in relation to education. Current research in the UK strongly suggests that more respectful attention needs to be given to the heritage and lived experience of Gypsy Roma Traveller children if the serious risks associated with cultural isolation and sleepwalking into segregation are to be mitigated (Allen, 2014).

As discussed earlier a touchstone for the well-being of a democratic society in Western nations has been free access to high-quality education and the notion of education for all (Carr and Hartnett, 2010), but what of the rights of those who want to access it but are driven away, or the right not to access state provision at all? Gypsy, Roma and Travellers have a long record of resisting demands to be accountable to teachers, schools and government in the UK and across the world. There is also evidence of Travellers facing emotional and physical violence when attending schools, with consequent non-attendance, and this is particularly true at secondary or high school level. Such non-participation implicitly questions the assumption that mainstream capitalist models of education offer inclusive, culturally neutral, high standard benchmark provision. Our research-based practice takes place in a context where structures in schools are not accommodating or even acknowledging the unequal social relations that occur in the wider society between the Traveller and non-Traveller population but, rather, as Rancière

(2011) argues, appear to be replicating and perpetuating these through the education system itself.

Gypsy Roma Traveller culture in the UK

In the context In the UK it is not easy to say exactly 'who' Gypsies, Roma and Travellers are, because in reality they are a disparate and culturally entangled group that are 'just like other social groups, whether they are fully nomadic, static, or only periodically settled' (Garratt and Piper, 2008, p. 116). In Gypsy Roma Traveller studies, as in all other study fields, terms are contested, but the following groups are identified by Richardson and Ryder (2012): Gypsies or Romani who were first recorded in British history in 1514; Irish Travellers who have travelled in the UK at least since the 19th century; New Age Travellers, who became identifiable first in the 1970s and through the 1980s; and Roma from Central and Eastern Europe. The Gypsy Roma Traveller groups that live in one local authority in Cheshire belong to the first two groups, and they are the oldest recorded ethnic minority group in the UK, with records stretching back some 500 years (Richardson and Ryder, 2012). In the UK the population is reported as approximately 300,000, with 200,000 in settled housing. In Cheshire West and Cheshire Council (CWAC) there are 14 known private sites of various sizes; the largest has 25 pitches, the smallest two pitches.

Richardson and Ryder (2012) cite the survey by Mori (a UK polling company) commissioned by Stonewall (Valentine and McDonald, 2003) which found Gypsies and Travellers to be one of the most reviled groups in society. In a recent UK government plan to 'Tackle Hate Crime' (H.M. Government, 2012), the under reporting of hate crime against Gypsy, Roma and Travellers is cited as a significant issue. In Cheshire, a young Traveller was kicked to death in a playing field in a racist attack in 2003, and prejudice is evident in local and national press reporting. The Gypsy Roma Traveller education adviser for the local council asked if we could create a pretext to tell a story in a non-threatening but engaging way, one that could provide a safe environment in which to discuss Gypsy Roma Traveller lifestyles and cultures. We took the opportunity to try and understand our own responses as well as those of others, and to try challenge these through a drama-based research process with a wider audience.

As Garrat and Piper (2008) argue, accounts of Gypsy Roma Traveller culture tend to follow one of two stereotypes: the criminalised and dangerous or the romanticised and nomadic. This project attempted to use a polyphonic pretext-based drama and research process that allowed participants to encounter, listen to and hear voices other than their own and the dominant media narratives. The aim was to create a space for dissensus to generate data that would allow us to validate and disseminate understandings in ways that did not 'reinforce inappropriate and stereotypical responses that would perpetuate the status quo' (Garrat and Piper, 2008, p.121).

Drama education, identity and democracy

For Rancière equality is a starting position and a key point in what he terms the distribution of the sensible (2004, p. 85). This is an implicit law governing what are perceived to be, unquestionable, self-evident facts that are based on that which is visible and audible, on what is said and done in a society. He suggests that those who have a share in this are those who have time and space to consider what should be common to the community. In this project, drama was used to create time and space for such consideration. Our drama practice is intended as a way of doing and making to intervene in the construction of perceptions and understandings about Traveller culture. The 'stage', in this case an open space for participative drama, was constructed as a 'locus for public activity, and the exhibition space for fantasies [which] disturbs the clear partition of identities, activities and spaces' (Rancière, 2004, p. 13). In the dramaturgical approach employed, we did not begin with a view of ourselves and others as defenceless in the face of the oppressive structures we confronted, nor as unitary, unproblematic sets of attitudes and behaviours such as victim and perpetrator. We saw ourselves rather, in Bhabha's terms, as 'quilts of confluences and influences . . . very carefully put together' (Bhabha, quoted in Eakin, 2001, p. 21). In part this position acknowledges self-identity as a reflexive project where we have to acknowledge the many, often contradictory, culturally specific influences and prejudices that inform, affect and determine our approach. We also sense the importance of forms of 'conflictual consensus' or good friction through which this can be challenged. We sense a resonance between the agonistic consensual conflict of democratic debate and the tension that drama needs to function. As Rancière states,

> [i]t is not a matter of claiming that 'history' is only made up of stories that we tell ourselves, but simply that the 'logic of stories' and the ability to act as historical agents go together. Politics and art, like forms of knowledge, construct 'fictions', that is to say material rearrangements of signs and images, relationships between what is seen and what is said, between what is done and what can be done.
>
> (2004, p. 39)

Pretext-based process drama

In this specific form of drama education participants engage actively in a practical drama task that starts a learning process. The term *pretext* refers to the source of the drama activity, which begins simply but which can rapidly develop towards more complex problems (Fleming, 2001). Instead of talking about a given dilemma chosen as an entry point in the consideration of a given subject or phenomena, participants step in and out of it, not to lose themselves in an illusion, but in order to see familiar things in a different way; in our case the given subject was Gypsy Roma Traveller culture in the UK.

The pretext method was 'enactive', which can be used on two senses from a social-constructivist point of view: first, to mean that learning is relational (Gergen, 2009) and begins with an action (Bruner, 1996), which in drama often involves bodies as well as mouths moving as an important part of thinking, coming to know, make sense of things and understand (Powell, in Bresler, 2007). Individuals grow into, arise, shape and are shaped by their relational role with the world and process drama aims to create opportunities for interaction and reflection on this. In the second sense enactive refers to the ability to take on a role and let go of it, to continually step in and out of the carefully observed reality of a collectively imagined world in order to make connections with the largely unobserved realities of our own everyday lives. The idea that we learn through direct experience and vicarious experience through observing others has long been established in the field of sociology (Bandura, 1986). In the field of arts, in process drama, learning takes place through direct collective imagined experience, observing others and reflecting on the implications and consequences of this through the connections made with our own lives and those of others.

At the heart of the practice is the opportunity for 'self–Other imagining' through a drama approach intended to allow for connecting our own reality with the realities of others (Neelands, 2004). The pretexts were constituted as events; we use the word *event* in three ways: Goffman's (1974), as an occurrence that replaces a familiar frame of reference and meaning with another one; Sauter's (2000), as a questioning of dominant narratives; and Rancière's (2004) as a means, within the forms created, for those present to reflect upon how to look, talk and think about the world.

Multiple perspectives and dissensus: the metaphor of the kaleidoscope

Metaphor can articulate something of the density, complexity and multi-dimensionality of this form of drama practice and research that values both the intuitive and imaginary as well as the analytical and rational. Metaphor as a literary device is the backbone of social science writing, and readily applies to the arts, since it is at its essence making a representation of one in the terms, or likeness, of another. Ricoeur argues that metaphors are valuable because they force the reader to translate them; translation in this sense is an intrinsic part of the metaphoric process where what is needed to comprehend the representation is imagination and intuition, and where metaphorical truth is produced by certain tensions, the most important being the way in which metaphor preserves the 'is not' within the 'is like' (2003, p. 302). For example Hamlet's situation 'is not' like that experienced by the average citizen today in terms of revenging murder but 'is like' the Third Space situations in which 21st-century citizens often find themselves – neither being able to carry on as things once were nor knowing how to go forward.

The metaphor of the 'kaleidoscope' provides an organising construct for this practice. The 'turning' motion creates an endless variety of attractive visual images to enjoy and interpret, created as thirty or so shards of glass of different shapes and colours settle into place before being turned again. Like pretext-based drama, the images are fleeting, their value lies in the space created to enjoy, look, imagine, interpret, discuss and change. The pretext mobilises a metaphoric circling around the given phenomena or subject, in likeness of the kaleidoscope shards turning in their round tube within a triangle of mirrored sides; 30 or so human beings in process drama move and settle in the space. The parallel with the notion of 'turning' in definitions of translation is drawn here. If the translator is 'the one who turns', to 'look at from many angles', this co-constructed process is about the practitioner working alongside the participants, creating images, imagining, interpreting, expounding the significance, expressing one thing in terms of another and trying to articulate understandings.

Scholars who have explored the metaphoric promise of the kaleidoscope (Gray 1991; Gonnami, 1998), allow for a consideration of the 'is like' and 'is not' of drama as the kaleidoscope, a plaything, which also acts as a tool for social understanding, for rethinking the social world and our place in it. Whilst the roots of the kaleidoscope can be found in ancient Egypt, the instrument as it is known today was invented in 1816 in Scotland by Sir David Brewster. The clue to the nature of such understanding lies in Brewster's coining of the word *kaleidoscope* from the Greek *kalos*, meaning beautiful; *eidos*, meaning form; and *skopeo*, meaning to look at (*Oxford English Dictionary*, 1998, p. 342). The idea of the kaleidoscope not being of any 'practical' use in itself, but allowing interpretations and perceptions to be clarified, shaped and shared through the aesthetic in a series of successive phases that hold for a while before the next shift, resonates with how understandings are constructed in pretext-based process drama. The turns are planned and occur on many levels, from the reality of the drama to the reality of everyday life, actual worlds to possible worlds, imaginary to rational, analytical to intuitive, conscious to subconscious. The kaleidoscope turning generates unfamiliar conjunctions of knowledge that Gray argues 'excess meaning' or knowledge creation originates from

> [a] perceptual chaos framed by order; a rearrangement that disassembles the familiar images of nature by multiplying it through a series of reflections into an unfamiliar pattern . . . a generative force for visual unfamiliarity . . . the persistent presence of this nursery plaything . . . its interest in lawful messiness, its interest in change.
>
> (Gray, 1991)

The simplest pieces of coloured glass appear at the far end of the tube in surprising, strange formations, no longer bits of coloured glass but intricate, complex original shapes, the everyday made strange and beautiful. A connection can be made here between Gray's notion of 'a generative force for unfamiliarity' and Brecht's (1936/1964) *verfremdungseffekt*: the familiar unexamined realities of everyday life rendered strange through powerfully beautiful dramatic form.

In this sense the turns in pretexts can be envisaged as turns of dramatic form, turns of the kaleidoscope, where one part of the story is carefully set off against another to acquire a disconcerting look as 'something general' becomes 'a principle'. The process is driven forward by interpretation and questioning allows for 'adaptive understanding' where

> [t]he understanding you have had before may turn out to be restricted, false, and your learning horizon breaks down into pieces, and you construct a quite new understanding of some existential horizon in your life, of other people's thoughts and of society.
>
> (Ostern, 2001, p. 16)

Moving from metaphor towards a rational diagrammatic model, the sequence of process drama may be summarised thus: a contract to clarify levels of participation; if appropriate a physical metaphor in exercise form to introduce the given subject or phenomena, followed by a sequence of four turns: first turn – narration, the step in to a possible world through story; second turn – imagining and doing: participants are invited to solve a dramatic task through 'doing/drao; third turn – watching, listening, feeling, thinking, where participants collectively and individually interpret and make connections; and fourth turn – discussing and interpreting, participants collectively share and discuss interpretations and connections. The four turns are repeated with different tasks in order to spiral around the given subject or phenomena to allow for the articulation of multiple perspectives and dissensus.

Pretext and process drama research methodologies

The field of 'performed research' includes a wide range of methodological practices and discourses and pretext-based process drama is another (Owens and Al Yamani, 2010). As Pässilä (2012) points out, '[f]ormal ties between theatre and research, particularly in terms of the analysis and interpretation of research results have developed only recently, over the past three decades' (see also Bresler, 2013; Gallagher and Ntelioglou, 2013). Pretext-based process drama form as referred to in this case study is an aesthetically centred form of participatory action research in which the drama form is used both as a learning process and to generate, collect, analyse, validate and disseminate data whilst always being open to further scrutiny and interpretation. It is simultaneously concerned with expression and understanding.

There are many aesthetic, methodological and political challenges in such practice located at 'the intersections of art and academic inquiry' (Bresler, 2013), and this is particularly critical given the research territory of the intercultural where one key purpose is to allow for understandings of 'other.' Mindful of the ethical troubling dimensions of drama work with, for and about marginalised cultures and communities (Nicholson, 2005), the decision about who would be the focus for our project was inevitably problematic and had to be carefully considered. Non-Travellers rarely have the opportunity to hear views about Travellers other than those they have often unquestioningly inherited. On the other hand, Travellers are often mistrustful of non-Travellers. Bringing peoples from both sides together to share experience in real work time is thus extremely challenging. Taking this reality into consideration we decided to focus on young people just about to make the transition from primary school to high school and to do this through methodologies centring on imagined experience using creative interactive participatory approaches. There was consultation and ongoing checks from the outset with members of the Traveller communities about the pretext. We were concerned throughout his work about the position we speak from and in the name of what or whom (Rancière, 2004). In this project there was never any deliberate attempt speak on behalf of Travellers, and a conscious effort was made to acknowledge our own position as research-based drama practitioners interested in understanding the perceptions of non-Travellers.

Two pretexts were created in a three-year period, both designed to open a space in which existing understandings could be acknowledged, shared and challenged. The first, 'Michael's Story', involved teachers and the young people they worked with (aimed deliberately at 10- to 11-year-olds) and was used to generate and capture data. The second, 'Working with Diversity', opened Michael's Story, disseminating interpretations of the data and the research literature to the wider education workforce including governors, local politicians and local authority workers. It was also used to generate further data in response to these interpretations, and to an imaginative engagement through a scene added to the pretext specifically for this purpose. Both pretexts not only had to be able to play in one hour in order to get commitment from busy professionals but also had to be flexible enough to extend to two to three hours for further exploration by young people.

In terms of scale and scope the project took place over three years (2010–2013), involved 240 young people (aged 9–11), 159 teachers, lecturers and support staff, 115 trainee teachers, 89 head teachers, governors, local authority officers and elected local politicians. The nine primary schools involved self-selected participation following a blanket mailing. The two pretexts were run a total of 26 times ranging from one to two-and-a-half hours. All sessions were audio recorded, and participants wrote and drew in response to a series of pre-formulated questions at the close of each session. The ongoing, long-term relationships among the local authority, the schools and the university were important in terms of trust throughout the project.

For the purposes of this chapter the focus is only on the drama practice in sessions run for the teachers, head teachers and support staff in the pretext 'Michael's Story' (Owens and Pickford, 2014). This was always run for the entire staff of a school, took place in the hall or a large classroom after the young people had left, and lasted between one and one-and-a-half hours. As the pretext requires an imaginative commitment through active participation, we asked participants to take part at their own cognitive and affective level, but kept on asking how they thought their young pupils might respond. The intention was to ensure professional appropriateness, in other words they were imaginatively engaging in order to gain insight into how the young people they were working with might engage, and what understandings might be allowed for through this process.

The pretext introduces the participants to Michael, a popular pupil in the class. They are given the opportunity to show, interpret and discuss the characteristics of his popularity before being taken on a journey to visit Michael's home created through narrative and projected visual images. Michael introduces them to his life on a Traveller site, invites them into his trailer for tea with his mam and shares his granddad's passion: the restoration of an old Gypsy wagon. The students are given the opportunity to ask questions of Michael, his mam and his granddad (members of the research team in role) which may have arisen during their visit before returning home to share their experiences. Within the safe and familiar environment of the school, students are given the opportunity to consider, explore, discuss and share their understandings in the light of those of others. The first part of the pretext builds identification and the positive context. The second part of the pretext opens possibilities to problematise the positive context and opens possibilities for dissensus.

Translating and understanding in action

Rancière (2004) explains that understanding is constructed by the way knowledge is packaged and presented to learners, which normally ignores the way the personal interpretations that participants might naturally bring with them or that may be generated in the course of an event. In contrast to this we were interested in using drama to allow learners to test their perceptions against those of other participants present, to test for themselves if they were valid or not, and in doing so go beyond their received opinions. As in 'The Dreamer' case study, we were trying in Rancière's terms to uncouple our mastery from our knowledge. In the highly charged context in which we were working we were aware that the creative practice, if effective, could well challenge the host institution itself, in terms of whose knowledge and perceptions about ways of living and learning should count and be of value. The applied drama process in this sense had risky and potentially disruptive qualities in its aim to develop understanding.

In addition to Rancière's problematisation of understanding we also draw on Gadamer's 'understanding of understanding' in which he argues that 'what one understands makes a difference to what one does' and so from this stance 'all understanding is practical' (in Dostal, 2002, p. 3). We used the four classifications of understanding identified in Gadamer's work: 'understanding as intellectual grasp' in the sense of 'I get it'; 'understanding as practical know-how', which is about an ability to 'do' something; 'understanding as agreement' in the sense of we understand each other even if we do not agree with each other; 'understanding as application and translation' which is concerned with the temporary nature of understanding which when applied does not necessarily hold true forever and, like translation, is always provisional (Dostal, 2002, pp. 36–51).

Translation is the entry point to the practice and we write deliberately from our perspectives as practitioners. This involves talking through our intentions and interpretations of the process to give the feel of how we see translation in action in pretext-based process drama as being kaleidoscopic. In this sense the writing leans to the auto-enthnographic rather than a reported case study, using Steiner's four-beat hermeneutic motion of translation (Steiner, 1998).

Michael's story

First of all the participants are asked to rehearse a scene which shows why 'everyone just feels better' when Michael is around. As each is scene shown the rest of the participants interpret these by offering words that are written around an outline drawing of Michael, the most common being that he is 'kind', friendly', 'caring', 'generous' and 'funny'. Having established the positive nature of Michael's character there is a turn in the dramatic kaleidoscope as participants are suddenly presented with the image of a Gypsy Roma Traveller site. They are asked if they were surprised to find that Michael lived there. Responses from the teachers predicted that the response from their students would vary, from 'Yes, I thought he would live in a big house' to 'No, I knew he would live there.' When asked 'Do you know anyone who lives in a caravan/trailer?' the turn is from the reality of the drama to the reality of everyday life as connections start to be made between the world of the drama and personal and professional worlds: 'My sister lives in a caravan'; 'I have been to visit some of our pupils who are travellers.'

The next turn takes participants further in to the dramatic context, to play with animals and have lunch with Michael's mam in a caravan/trailer that is spotlessly clean and tidy (shown in projection). The visual turn offers a different interior than that which was usually imagined: a familiar thing – the caravan – yet so unfamiliar inside, full of cut glass and expensive china. The next turn allows for the rational and intuitive through the question: 'Michael has been at the school a year but has not invited anyone home until now, why do you think this is so?' The answers in the context of the pretext launch the process of dissensus. Often very different opinions started to reveal understandings through implicit and explicitly stated attitudes, beliefs and values. 'He might be worried they would not be his friends if they knew where he lived'; 'His parents probably would not want him to bring any one who was not a traveller home.' The task of exploring how this unfolding drama 'is like' and 'is not like' (Ricoeur, 2003, p. 5) the realities of the participants' lives and the understandings they have, has begun.

The initial trust of the participants suggests there is something in the metaphor of this young boy of difference that requires understanding (Steiner 1998, p. 313). Suggestions from the group often led participants to the conclusion that this could be any boy anywhere and almost anything is interpreted as representing difference, but having recognised there was often an attempt to interpret and understand. As Steiner argues, 'understanding, recognition, interpretation [are] compacted' (1998, p. 313). Slowly we circle this figure through various turns until the initial two-dimensional representation can be viewed through the lens of the drama, as a hologram that we can view from different angles. Having looked at Michael through his friends' eyes, we meet his dogs and horses, and then his mam and his granddad. Participants are invited to put themselves into Michael and his family's position to try to understand perceptions not initially our own and, in so doing, dissipate otherness through familiarity. Steiner suggests that there is sadness if we have failed, but also sadness after success; we have the chance to become at home with what was once different or other, an act of incorporation, which may give energy or may destabilise and stop us in our tracks. He argues that we need the final 'piston-stroke' of the four-stage cycle, the act of reciprocity to restore balance and level any feelings of disequilibrium. In the pretext a step is taken towards that on the level of narrative closure devised in groups; the groups are prompted by the idea that we can now see that there is more to this young boy and this situation than we have observed hitherto. New forms and interpretations emerge in the drama, and the significance of each may be transformed as we reflect on how each situation is like or not like that of their own lives. In Steiner's words, '[t]here is more here than meets the eye . . . some translations edge us away from the canvas, others bring us close up' (1998, p. 317).

This case study is intended to illustrate how time is arrested to allow different perceptions of the event to be voiced, different understandings to be heard, to exploit what Boal refers to as

> the imprecisions, ambiguities, ambivalences and polysemies, which may be mingled with the perceptions of a scene or event . . . suppositions, double meanings, the nebulous, the fields of 'could be yes, could be no, maybe who knows?'
>
> (1995, p. 96)

In Ricoeur's (2003) terms this approach allows for different perceptions of 'is like' and 'is not' to be voiced or quietly considered. Boal argues that it is precisely here in what he calls 'the realm of supposition' that 'something is concealed, some piece of knowledge which can be aesthetically revealed, seen, sensed, felt' (1995, p. 96). In social constructivists terms knowledge is co-created rather than 'aesthetically revealed', but there is nonetheless an appropriate sense of the translational–transformational potential in his metaphor of 'the realm of supposition'.

Identifiable changes occurred within each of our four categories of understandings (Owens, 2014). In respect of the first category, the 'intellectual grasp/I get it' factor, insights were gained through participation in both pretexts, and a significant number of participants indicated that they learnt about Gypsy Roma Traveller culture and how it is changing. We asked from the outset about perceptions of what we were doing and, importantly, how we were doing it, and many participants with no previous understanding of pretext-based drama claimed to have 'got it' in terms of recognising some of the potential in enactive learning.

In terms of the second, 'understanding as practical know-how', which is critical in enabling us to improvise our way through life, one of the forms adopted was the use by some participants of the language of anti-racism during sessions, for example choosing between the words 'all, many, some, a few' when making statements about Gypsy Roma Travellers as a culturally entangled group. Sometimes the effort taken to choose between these words was visible on a participants face and in their body language, an example of Aristotelian phonesis or practical knowledge being applied, not in abstract terms but in action, a 'doing', a change. To keep these claims in perspective, whilst these instances were exceptions, neither were they widespread.

'Understanding as agreement', the third of Gadamar's categories, is the sense of 'we understand each other' even if we do not agree with each other. The degree of dissensus varied greatly in each context, but there were a significant number of examples of clashes of adverse opinions leading to explicitly stated changes in understanding. For example, in one session a school governor took an extremely strong 'all Travellers' position during the pretext in which the school caretaker articulated a much more nuanced stand. On the following day the school governor made contact to say that having reflected over the night, she was now questioning the position she took. When, in Gadamer's words, 'understanding fails', it is hard to quickly articulate new understandings: 'The unsayable is only the unsayable in the light of what one would like to say but cannot' (in Dostal, 2002, p. 42); if the perplexed situation of Gypsy Roma Travellers in the UK was an easily resolvable situation it would have been resolved by now.

The fourth conceptualisation, 'understanding as application and translation', suggests that understanding can only be provisional. Interpretation of the data drew on much evidence of participants attempting to come to grips with their and others' understandings with a sense that this can never be absolutely final, as expressed be their need to find out more. The curiosity engendered in many participants suggested a readiness to disagree, to leave things open enough that there is room for a plurality of possible interpretations, since none are exhaustive. Understanding according to the experientialist position of Lakoff and Johnson is 'not cut and dried; it is a matter of constructing coherence' (2003, p. 227). Inglis clarifies this further for us when he refers to the instances where time is taken to establish a temporary understanding not as a mental process, but in the sense of 'now I know how to go on' (2005, p. 12). 'Now I/we know how to go on' as a definition of understanding also implies a preceding moment or period of uncertainty where, 'I/we did not know how to go on' or in Bhabha's terms, a Third Space experience (1994, p. 37). We suggest that there is such an implication in Inglis's definition, in that 'I/we will not know how to go on forever', and that such experiences where I/we can go neither forward nor backward, are signs that my/our understanding is turning. This brings us back to the metaphoric promise of the kaleidoscope which, like Jones's (2012) view of democracy, is a fragile, contingent and momentary occurrence, which has to be constantly reinvigorated.

Chapter 7

Democratic trends in the politics of creativity and innovation

This chapter moves beyond formal educational institutions to look at the place of creativity in organisations and business in a wider community context. It is offered in keeping with Dewey's democratic vision of education that he envisaged enduring 'beyond institutionally organized education, to the extent where the learning is literally lifelong' (1938/1969, p. 4). We conceptualise the use of arts in organisations as forms of socially engaged practice that can have a pedagogical function, which is to say that our understanding of the social world may be realigned by our exposure to them. The case study on which our discussion in this chapter is centred is an Anglo-Finnish research-based and creative initiative, through a public participatory consultation and engagement process. The project focused on the public use of a town-centre building, and is one of a series of participatory innovation events we are piloting across Europe led by Pässilä from the Lappeenranta University of Technology, School of Business and Management (LUT Lahti), and RECAP, University of Chester, UK. All of this is considered in relation to the changing nature of liberal democracy in the UK and Finland, the ascendancy of neoliberalism, the stresses and tensions in local democracy under neoliberal austerity and Third Way politics, as well as presenting possibilities for wider participation.

Arts-based initiatives in organisations: Finland and the UK

The project on which the case study is based is part of an ongoing trajectory of work concerned with what we call the 'Turn to Learning' in arts used in business, public and third sector organisations. To illustrate what we mean by this we discuss the use of Arts-Based Initiatives (ABIs) as a means of organising reflection, defined as the collective and subjective reconsideration of practice, in one of our UK-based projects in 2014. The locus of creativity – *luovuus* in Finnish – for the case study is a social enterprise limited company, part of a wider network that we have established in Finland and the UK. Our specific focus is a public brokerage process concerned with the use of the 'Goods Shed', a deserted railway building in a town in north-west England. It involved participants across the age range, from young people to senior citizens, and across the socio-economic spectrum. Before looking in detail at the social relations and forms of practice developed in this project we discuss the relationship between creativity and innovation in organisational contexts, and in order to frame the practice culturally and politically we also consider the wider context of our work in Finland and the UK in terms of its relationship to democracy.

Innovation and creativity in organisations

From the field of innovation, creativity and education, Robinson (2011), offers a shorthand distinction between creativity and innovation which he conceptualises together with imagination in the following sequential way: imagination allows us to 'step out of the here and now' in order to anticipate many possible futures; creativity involves 'actively producing something' in a deliberate way, a form of 'applied imagination'; innovation is the process of putting that 'something', such as new ideas, into practice, a form of applied creativity (Robinson, 2011, pp. 141–142). Robinson also observes that just as the dominant assumption in creativity literature is that 'creativity is good', so the dominant assumption in innovation literature is that 'innovation is beneficial.' Unsurprisingly this has become wearing, and there have been calls for more critical approaches to both innovation and creativity (Gielen, 2013). We return to this critique later, but at this point simply want to highlight the conceptual link among imagination, creativity and innovation.

Robinson (2011) suggests that education and business face many common challenges; he argues that regardless of the many alternative schools of thought developed in the last 40 years about the principles and practices of organisational culture the prevalent current forms are still based on the mechanistic model originally designed in the interests of those who were driving the industrial revolution in the 19th and early 20th centuries. This is premised on the belief that any problems encountered in organisations can be dealt with by rational adjustments to the systems of operation in place. This emphasis on the technical overlooks what Robinson calls 'the human factor', referring to the 'values and feelings, perceptions, opinions, motivations biographies' of the people and the networks between them which 'are' the organisation (2011, pp. 222–223). Believing that contemporary challenges cannot be met by models from the past, Robinson champions the potential of imagination, creativity and innovation in generating new models of creativity for collaborative and community use.

Like Robinson, Pässilä (2014) argues that in contemporary, fluid, perplexing situations, organisations including education systems cannot afford to privilege technical dimensions of innovation over the sociocultural. Whilst Robinson articulates the root causes of the disjuncture between the way education and businesses are organised to meet the complexities of contemporary societal needs, Pässilä focuses on the messy business of innovation in the workplace and resists any definition which suggests that this is an unproblematic process of putting new ideas into practice, drawing on a decade of frontline practice based research in business, public and third sector organisations. According to Pässilä,

> innovation has been understood as a technical project that can be solved by scientists, research and design experts, innovation management; the dominant assumption is that innovations generate valuable things . . . [whereas] innovation seems to be a more complex phenomena than previously understood.
>
> (2012, p. 15)

Pässilä is developing forms of Research-Based Theatre (RBT) through collaboration that involve rethinking the dominant conceptualisations of innovation. She defines innovation activities as 'learning steps aiming at the creation of innovation wherein all organisational actors are understood as critical innovators' (Pässilä, 2012, p. 16). This emphasis on inclusivity and collectivity resonates with Robinson's argument that '[a] culture of creativity has to involve everybody not just a select few' (2011, p. 4). In Pässilä's conceptualisation day-to-day practices are central to the social and interpretive dimensions of innovation. The creation of a space for collective reflection in and on change using the imagination through RBT methods is key to this approach.

We particularly value the broad-based approach to community and regional development pioneered by Melkas and Harmaakorpi (2012) and the use of ABI's within it, in this case a brokerage process run by the town Foundation, a social enterprise limited company, and with initial backing from the Royal Society of Arts Venture Fund (RSA; north-west England). ABIs were used to attract, engage and mobilise members of the community to envision the use of the old railway goods shed standing in the town centre. There is much rhetoric in both public and private sectors about enabling people to take an active role in solving problems in their own communities, and yet public consultation still usually takes a top-down approach and is consultant-driven. Conventional models of consultation in such cases in the UK usually take the form of quick online questionnaires or street surveys, which provide a useful indication of interest but are minimal in terms of public engagement. In the participatory approach to consultation, inclusive arts based methods are used to generate ideas as part of a research process that values dialogue, the collective and 'slow knowledge work' (Holtham, Ward and Owens, 2010). Our intention was to use ABIs to meet the need for a different approach that puts local knowledge and knowing into practice.

In summary, our aim was to give momentum to a public brokerage process, the key objectives being to create spaces where participants could articulate and test their own point of view against those of others, to create a form of 'good friction' (Korhonen and Airaksen, 2014) and in so doing to allow the wider community to hear and engage with these. The process was characterised by dissensus (Mouffe, 2007) in which the aim was not to settle conflicting voices in order to achieve resolution, but to engage in the model of creativity itself, allowing participants take the step from bystander to actor through voicing their own imaginative conjectures, in this case about the use of a public building.

The Anglo-Finnish cultural and political context

The valuing of polyphony, criticality and the right to participate are at the heart of our long-term research with Pässilä and her colleagues in Finland (Pässilä, Oikarinen and Harmaakorpi, 2013). Having said this we are aware that the Finnish cultural and political context differs significantly from that of the UK and that these continue to shape the participatory practice–based approach we are developing and trying to understand together. For example the Finnish Ministry of Education and Culture (MEC) has a remit to develop conditions for education that explicitly focus on 'creativity, social participation and well-being'. Two of the four values underlying this 'vast sector' are given as 'democracy and creativity' (MEC, 2014), and these directly inform the current national 'Strategy 2020' (MEC, 2010). In a 2007 report commissioned by the Finnish Parliament on the subject of democracy, Mannermaa opened up a debate on the individual's relationship with decision-making authorities arguing that this is 'an eternal one in that each generation has to devise its own interpretation of democracy' (2007, p. 10), echoing Dewey's argument that '[d]emocracy has to be born anew every generation, and education is its midwife' (1899/2008, p. 15) and concluding, 'People should feel that they are living in a society which they can call their own' (Mannermaa, 2007, p. 151). The distinctively Finnish models of societal development and participative decision-making are embedded in such statements in which the concept of democracy is seen as far more than a matter of formal societal governance:

> In order for a society to be democratic, the ideals of democracy have to extend to all processes that have an influence on a person . . . key components are economic democracy, the individual's right to influence inter alia his working conditions (company democracy) and, on the other hand, to act as an active consumer (client democracy). The application of democratic ideals in other such important arenas as . . . organisations, universities, schools and even in families is part of the broad interpretation of democracy. The formal societal processes of democracy function well and credibly only when the principles of democracy have been instilled from childhood and are applied in all areas of life.
>
> (Mannermaa, 2007, p. 10)

From outside of the country, Finland is often grouped with Scandinavian, and more accurately Nordic countries, and the perception is that social democracy is ideologically well embedded, or, as Acemoglu, Robinson and Verdier (2012) describe it, based on the operation of a 'cuddly form of egalitarian capitalism'. There are, however, significant differences between Finland and its neighbours, including the degree to which neoliberal ideological discourse has been adopted (Kenworthy, 2014). Given the specificities of the context it makes little sense to try to import wholesale to the UK a Finnish context-specific innovation process. Critics of the Finnish egalitarian approach also suggest this can lead to a 'consensus culture' (Korhonen, 2012), where management and decision making are seen as being about seeking solutions through negotiation in the attempt to please as many people as possible, rather than clarifying underlying issues or conditions, or establishing alternatives to be voted on. In terms of seeking consensus rather than allowing for dissensus or the agonism of open debate there are parallels with the forms of management and decision-making developed during the period of the UK's New Labour Party's Third Way.

UK Third Way politics (Giddens, 2000) is concerned with attempts to reconcile laissez faire capitalism with socialism, hoping to achieve politically sustainable consensus and participation, retaining social inclusion and cohesion, but letting go of the ideals of socialist equality, social justice and emancipation, a form of politics heavily informed by neoliberalism but within the context of reforms of our welfare state. Third Way privatisation and break-up of the welfare state necessitates the acquiescence of citizens who would retain the rights to participate within the diminished state democracy and where the value of citizenship can often depend more on participation in the economic system (Hewitt, 2012). In contrast, our project's aim was to allow for open democratic discussion and the debate and disagreement generated from a dissensual rather than consensual process.

One of the ideas of Third Way politics and the 'public good' is a version of civic liberalism in which public spaces are places where societal renewal can take place. Improvement to urban environments were very much part of this picture in UK government initiatives of the early 21st century, and this included the use of arts projects in which 'culture-led regeneration connects ideas of democracy and citizenship supporting local culture [which] it is imagined, renews the public realm' (Gibson and Stevenson, 2004). In the Goods Shed project we were not attempting an egalitarian opening up of culture to a wider audience, and we were sceptical of the paternalism inherent in Charles Landy's (2015) 'creative city' approach. We were arts practitioners and pedagogues providing a service, but not 'contracted to work within institutional parameters regulated by policy directives' which, as Hewitt (2012) points out, is the classic way in which artists are conceived as making their contribution to Third Way politics. Our use of RBT and other forms of ABIs were used as ways of framing how members of a community could explore and reflect on questions, problems and emotions in new social learning situations (Pässilä, Oikarinen and Kallio, 2013). The roots of the ABIs employed are in the field of organisational learning, in which arts practitioners work within innovation with employees, managers customers and citizens. This genre is still developing, and its forms, styles, purposes and values are still taking shape (Berthoin Antal, 2009; Pässilä and Oikarinen, 2014).

The turn to learning

One of the longer-term concerns of our Anglo-Finnish project is with what we call the 'Turn to Learning' in the practice and theorising of arts as used in organisations and business. We are trying to move beyond what Schiuma (2011) classifies as the two prevalent models of arts use in organisations: first, 'Observer' in which businesses and organisations sponsor arts by acting as patrons and spectators, and, second, 'Adopter', in which short-term, toolbox solutions in the form of particular methods are applied to complex problems. Schiuma presents the case for a third model of arts use in contemporary organisations, that of 'Integrator'; in this model 'technical knowledge' is integrated with 'emotive knowledge' as the arts are used to engage with 'the emotive and energetic factors affecting the behaviours of employees and the characteristics of an organisations infrastructure.' (2011, p. 3). The ecosystem of the organisation is also viewed within a wider societal context in terms of, for example, issues of sustainability. Consequently we align our Turn to Learning approach with the Integrator model, which takes the form of a combination of action research and arts-based learning in the context of innovation management, based on studies and experiences of Finnish practice-based innovation. (Melkas and Harmaakorpi, 2012).

RBT in the context of this approach to innovation offers a possibility for exploring organisational behaviour, cultural codes, processes, structures and ways of practising, as well as the underlying professional values, attitudes and assumptions. We are interested in conceptualising an innovation process that leans as much to a critically creative form of education – the relational, social and political – as it does to the individual, or training and economics. In this respect our work also appears to align with the research orientation of Critical Management Studies (CMS; Alvesson and Willmott, 1992) with its theorised approach to management and organisation studies seeking to challenge existing orthodoxies in Business Schools by for example valuing reflexive critique (Antonacopoulou, 2010). We find found the concept of CMS interesting in the way it has developed in many theoretical directions from early roots in critical theory in the 1990s. The political situation that gave rise to it is attributed to a number of possible causes including the increase in state funding for the subject of business in the 1980s in the UK, which attracted academics from the social sciences where state funding was being cut. At the same time workers and managers from business and organisations were attracted to universities believing that they had something to offer when contrasted with their experience of what they perceived as the outmoded modernist teachings of managerialism. The main point for us here is that the form and content of knowledge taught in business schools and subsequently operating in the world of business and organisations was radically questioned from the 1990s onwards as these academics began to apply a wide range of critical theory to the parallels and links they saw between managerialism and neoliberalism. They were interested in developing alternatives to the dominant discourse of free-market forms of globalisation as an inevitable, 'natural' phenomenon. For the purposes of this discussion it is the shared concern with organisational and social transformation that we wish to highlight.

Arts in organisations and business

At the same time that interesting discourses were starting in the field of CMS, others were also starting in other parts of the academy such Organisational Studies, about use of theatre in the context of organisations. For example in a special issue of *Organisational Studies* called 'Theatre in Organisations' it was suggested that theatre had 'moved from a metaphor to describe organisations towards a technique to change them' (Scheyogg and Hopfl, 2004), which resonates with other publications in *Communication Studies* (Boje, Luhman and Cunliffe, 2003) and *Management Studies* (Meisiek, 2002, 2004; Clark and Mangham 2004a, 2004b). Whilst some of the earliest theatre in organisation companies started in the early 1990s have gone on to establish themselves comfortably in the neoliberal policy flow of the business and public organisations sectors, other individuals have continued to develop critical and research driven theoretical lenses and forms of practice such as Clark (2008), Barry (2006), Meisiek and Barry (2007) and Barry and Meisiek (2010).

Parallel developments at that time were also taking place in the use of other arts forms including music, art and dance, and have continued to do so (Schiuma, 2011). Managers and artists have explored the potential of operating as partners to develop new ways of working to realise organisational change and innovation (Taylor and Ladkin, 2009). Pässilä (2012) suggests that '[o]ne of the most distinctive new dimensions of development in management thinking and education since the year 2000 has been the growth of the "Art of Management" movement'. Research, academic inquiry and practice have taken place in the educational context of university business schools (Meisiek and Barry, 2014) and in to the ways in which practitioners from across the arts work in private, public and third-sector organisations locally, regionally and nationally through academic inquiry in University Arts Schools (Lehikoinen, 2013).

Schiuma (2011) documents and analyses the evolution of the field in arts and business in which he is concerned with the form of 'organisational value creation capacity' generated by integrating technical and emotive knowledge through the arts as a knowing process. His main focus is on what is going on inside organisations when the arts are employed as products and process by management, 'the deployment of artistic products and processes [are used] to activate and induce the static dynamics that affect the emotive knowledge characterising employees and organisational infrastructure' (Schiuma, 2011, p. 11). Schiuma flags the challenge of meeting the growing expectation that business should be socially responsible, sustainable, culturally cognisant and ethical and argues that 'the private sector plays a crucial role as a co-creator of society' as it builds the 'ecosystem in which it operates' an approach predicated on recognising 'the human-based nature of the organisation', a form of business with humanity (2011, p. 11). Other scholars in the field such as Taylor and Adler operate from a liberal arts tradition in the valuing of self and how one relates to the world whilst taking a critical stance in the sense of seeing business and organisations as arenas for social change: 'How can we use theatre within organisations to facilitate social change?' asks Taylor (in Darsø, Meisiek and Boje, 2007 p. 92). Reflection as part of craft practice is important in Adler's (2010) thinking about the ways we learn to support us in creating the type of global community in which people can flourish rather than just survive.

In our collaborative RBT work critical reflection is used to make sense of practising in the workplace, using drama as a means of renewal and change in organisations. Our studies in the field of arts in organisations discuss how to organise or cultivate collective reflection and reflexive practices within organisational settings and innovation. We are looking at the process of organising collective reflection and reflexive practices, emphasising learning from experiences in workplace innovation as a mode of ABI (Pässilä, 2012).

Arts in organisations and democracy: claims and critique

Based on the discussion so far we suggest that the purpose, meaning and value of arts in organisations, business, the workplace and in universities are contested. We also note that there are a number of scholars and practitioners committed to using the arts in critically creative ways to question and challenge the assumptions of 'business as usual' in the working practices of organisations. The routine activity of global capitalism is resulting in unprecedented perplexity, and therefore in our interventions many difficult and occasionally unpalatable questions have to be raised, including a critique of the society of which the organisation is part and in which the individual lives and works.

To return to the field of Organisational Theatre, it was the pioneering practitioners themselves who were amongst the first to try to articulate the tensions between theatre and business – in other words using art in organisations as sites for social change whilst under no illusions that the bottom line was return on investment:

> We found ourselves with images of the duality of theatre and business, the virgin representing the purity of art and the actor prostituting that art and, the possibilities of the open space, the magic of theatre, being in the moment, the process of creativity competing with the need for outcomes.
> (Darsø and Meisiek in Darsø
> et al., 2007, p. 17)

As Darsø and Meisiek point out, 'when managers began ordering the plays, they also wanted to define the content, and participation was not always voluntary, but rather part of work' (Darsø *et al.*, 2007, p. 10); therefore, it was no surprise that tensions arose. These tensions have long been explored in the literature of the field of applied theatre (Kershaw 1992; Nicholson 2005). To keep the discussion framed in relation to the broader concepts of creativity and democracy in arts in organisations and business we explore the extent that socially engaged arts practices in organisations can be designed to produce forms of democracy through the Turn to Learning.

Prior to this we consider Gielen's (2011) critique of the phrase 'socially engaged art practices' through which he argues arts in organisations can be analysed. Drawing out a critical cartography of community art to talk about the political possibilities and limitations of socially engaged arts practices, Gielen opens the discussion around three critiques. First, he asks what happens when it becomes clear that in certain situations the perplexities being explored on the micro and meso level are being generated at the macro, and that systemic change is needed? Second, he raises the issue of 'repressive tolerance', whereby organisations tolerate a little bit of subversive art as a good thing whilst repressing it at the same time by keeping the door on discussion about systemic change firmly closed, or out of sight. His third critique is concerned with the methodology of the artists themselves who may be intending to help people with the skills of understanding one another through critical self-reflection but who, from another perspective, are merely interfering and inadvertently upholding the status quo.

Gielen (2011) does not, however, dismiss the whole project of socially engaged arts as much as ask for more reflexivity. He argues that there is 'a lot of nonsense' being talked about this by 'believers' and 'nonbelievers', and in his own words 'wants to take the subject seriously to find people who have written in order to broaden the concepts being used'. Gielen emphasises the need to create distance, particularly by those most involved where the challenge of self-reflexivity is to move beyond emotional response. He suggests that attempts for example to use the arts to achieve integration will not succeed because the issues are systemic but that the process itself has the potential to help people become aware of the values they hold and the rights that they have.

Creativity in the routine workday of global capitalism is often a euphemism for doing more with less. Gielen (2013) uses the example of project work to epitomise this. He coins the term *project-like-thinking* as shorthand for the ways in which the work of the individual educator, practitioner, researcher or whichever 'creative worker' is increasingly no longer embedded within the institution in terms of job security. She or he is now expected not only to generate creative ideas for projects but also to secure funding for them and, in many cases, to administer them. Employment is dependent on forever chasing the next possibility of work, which entails having to form and re-form sets of relationships in order to achieve short-term collective goals (Gielen, 2013, p. 48). There is little chance to reflect on long-term considerations as the worker assumes maximum personal responsibility in what is often framed as the pursuit of their own self-realisation, before moving on to the next project.

Gielen suggests that whilst the excitement of the collective energy of each new project may allow for creativity and productivity, it can easily shift in to a form of self-exploitation in the way it 'feeds on intellectual and physical stamina' which can in the long run lead to exhaustion (2013, p. 47). Project-like-thinking in this neoliberal conceptualisation, is also often concerned with short-term problem solving rather than the idea of problematizing issues in a critically creative approach. Being critically creative requires an environment of trust, established over time in which individuals can depend on and trust each other without feeling they have to agree.

Sennett (1998) points to the need to restore trust in others in order to allow for the disagreement that actually binds communities such as workplaces together. Citing Coser, he argues that 'people are bound together more by verbal conflict and by verbal agreement' stating that this is important in becoming a community in 'in the sense that people learn how to listen and respond to one another even as they more keenly feel their differences' (Sennett, 1998, p. 143). Sennett suggests a workplace team as characterised earlier offers only a weak form of communitarianism, uninterested, unwilling, unlikely and unable to create change at organisational level, let alone at individual and societal levels. How then to challenge this largely unquestioned logic epitomised by a shallow-communitarian project-like-thinking in which criticism is so often targeted at level of the individual or team and so rarely at the system within which they work. We use RBT and the concept of 'fictionalising the real' (Rancière, 2004) to frame examples of the practice and theory we are currently developing in this respect.

Fictionalising the real

Rancière argues that 'the real must be fictionalised in order to be thought' but urges an avoidance of the 'the notion of narrative that locks us in to oppositions between real and artifice', while pointing out that this is not about 'claiming that everything is fiction' nor 'a thesis on the reality or unreality of things', nor 'a matter of claiming that 'history' is only made up of stories that we tell ourselves' (2009, pp. 38–39). He draws instead a parallel between the 'logic of stories' and individual and collective agency:

> Politics and art, like forms of knowledge, construct 'fictions', that is to say material rearrangements of signs and images, relationships between what is seen and what is said, between what is done and what can be done.
> (Rancière, 2009, p. 39)

In the ABIs used in the Goods Shed project one of the key methods was 'aesthetic distancing' (Pässilä, 2012). The roots of this of this can be traced back to romanticist and modernist thinking about the potential of combinations of education and art, for example Russian formalists such as Shklovsky who saw their task as being 'to contribute to de-familiarisation of habitual perception through art' (Eriksson, 2014, p. 7). The shift from 'as is' to 'as if' is key to the form of aesthetic distancing we used in this project where drama conventions such as storytelling were used as de-familiarising devices to create fictions, as a protective device in a situation where there were very different strongly held views. Through this form of aesthetic distancing, reflection is realised by looking at the ordinary and commonplace with new eyes, making the familiar look strange, and the strange familiar, a form of productive alienation often associated with the critically reflective theatre practice of the German dramaturg Bertolt Brecht:

> The production took the subject matter and the incident shown and put them through a process of alienation: the alienation that is necessary to all understanding. When something seems' the most obvious thing in the world' it means that any attempt to understand the world has been given up.
> (1936/1964, p. 71)

In the Goods Shed project we worked with aesthetic distance to learn through play (Sproedt, 2012) in the form of a series of dramatic conventions including narrative in storytelling to

> re-configure the map of the sensible ... open up space for deviations, modify the speeds, the trajectories and the ways which groups of people adhere to a condition react to situations, recognise their image.
> (Rancière, 2004, p. 39)

Rancière calls these 'uncertain communities' where roles, territories and language can be called to question. He uses the term *la partage du sensible* (distribution of the sensible) to refer to 'the implicit law governing the sensible order that parcels out places and forms of participation in a common world' (Rancière, 2004, p. 85), arguing that this governs what is permissible to be thought or said or practised. Aesthetic distancing calls in to question the seemingly self-evident facts of our perception by allowing us to 'be spectators of ourselves in ways often denied in life, because we can distort time to give opportunity for reflection to be encountered' (Heatchcote and Hovda, 1980, in Eriksson, 2014, p. 8).

Case study: goods shed

The relationship between RECAP and the Frodsham Foundation was established through a series of meetings at events run by the RSA, who have an interest in public service and communities, learning and creativity, which are also the concerns of RECAP and the foundation (see Figure 7.1). The RSA's 'new world view' is that 'everyone has the ability to live creatively and take control of their own lives' (RSA, 2014; Taylor, 2014, p. 3), a central idea in neoliberalism. Taylor

Figure 7.1 The Goods Shed

proposes that the concept of 'the power to create' can contribute 'a more expansive political discourse' in the face of what he sees as continuing sterile debates between the major British political parties; he turns to aspiration, imagining a future where it becomes possible that others beside the existing social elite can live creative lives, defined as a life of fulfilment actively chosen. Social enterprise is an integral part of the RSA's landscape.

The Frodsham Foundation is a social enterprise limited company which has been set up to support and promote innovation and enterprise for citizens in Frodsham, Cheshire, which has approximately 25,000 residents, 1,200 businesses and 200 community groups. It is a company limited by guarantee, meaning that there are no shareholders so that profits made on any activity are invested in future activities and projects. The term *social enterprise* is contested (Teasdale, 2011) even though it is often associated with organisations that have existed in the UK since the mid-1800s, such as cooperatives that use return on investments to improve the economic situations of their members or disadvantaged groups. As Evans, Richmond and Shields (2005) point out they have developed hybrid organisational characteristics, for example multiple goals social, economic, government systems, in response to pressures from the market and the state and are seen as part of the New Public Management era.

In the UK in recent years it has been central government policy to adopt a social enterprise model to effect social change in the name of more efficient (or cheaper) delivery of services to the local community more. The shift to the increasing emphasis on earned income and participation in market activities can be referred to as social enterprise activity. The UK Department of Trade and Industry (DTI) defines social enterprise as a business trading for a social purpose whose surpluses are principally reinvested for that purpose or in the community, rather than established to maximise profits for shareholders and owners (DTI, 2002). Social enterprise can be seen as a social construct that can be viewed from varying perspectives ranging from philanthropic organisations with trading elements to commercially orientated businesses that still have core social aims (Teasdale, 2010).

A critique of both the RSA and social enterprise parallels the earlier discussion, where it was suggested that such forms of local activism and social regeneration, whilst ostensibly offering a third way between state provision of public services and privatisation, let the government off the hook through what is ultimately a market-based form of development. From this perspective social enterprise presents Third Way rhetoric in a discourse of power (Curtis, 2012). The risk here, as Curtis points out, is that the discussion becomes depoliticised by placing too much emphasis on efficient delivery of services rather than recognising the power and social structures operating. Curtis argues that social enterprises have a role to play in terms of grassroots democracy, but that this needs to be alongside 'long-term governance based transformation'. He calls for

> a novel ethos of research which simultaneously makes scholarly work more critical and reflective while rendering it significant for practising social entrepreneurs ... Littler narratives have to be heard and monuments and careful attention to the transgressive spaces of the workplace have to be called on, to inform the social and the internal mission of the social enterprise.
> (Curtis, 2012)

This case study presents one little narrative from one transgressive space.

The process of collaboration and research methods

An initial meeting with a member of the RSA on the local foundation together with its chief executive centred on possible concrete projects to work on together; these included strategy for developing local provision of care for the elderly and a consultation process for the development of the local town plan and a brokerage process for the use of the Goods Shed. Discussions allowed us to talk through in more detail the practice based innovation approach through arts-based initiatives that we were working on in Finland. We found common ground in the concept of bridging alternative world views as a means of generating potential for innovation. Following this the foundation considered its priorities and chose the brokerage process. Together with the local town council it had already conducted an online survey for use of the building; a large number of responses provided strong evidence that the public wanted the building to be used, but the remoteness of this digital form of consultation had not engaged enough of the community to provide the momentum to take things forward in a way that would convince the larger county council who owned the building to hand it over on a long term lease to the Foundation and local town. We agreed on four-month period for the process and division of responsibilities. In the first month the foundation would identify and contact the focus groups they wanted us to work with; in the second, the focus groups would be run; in the third, the evocative report would be created; and in the fourth, the evocative report would be presented at an open public meeting in which the next concrete steps to be taken would be identified.

RBT as used in this case constituted a form of participatory, action and collaborative research. The data sources which formed the empirical evidence base consisted primarily of narratives of involvement, and our reflexive narratives in response to this. The intention to research issues that surface within a community and then use the understandings that are generated from it for the benefit of those in that community has parallels with the function of applied drama and critical pedagogy. They are concerned with going beyond seeing the world as it is and creating spaces to think of it differently. A key question in this 'connected' approach to research is to ask how it is this possible and how are we to act in new and different ways (Schratz and Walker 1995, p. 125).

Nine focus group sessions took place over a one-week period, comprising a very wide range of participants: business and local entrepreneur groups, patient forums, community groups, school parent–teachers association members, community voluntary sector leaders, younger families and children, jobseekers and youngsters. The focus groups were run by our Anglo-Finnish team of four – two ABIs practitioners and two postgraduate students. Participants were aware from the outset that we were interested in not only the substantive topic of the focus group sessions, but also the ways in which we approach this, and were interested in what this allowed for. Each session began with an explanation of the research-based and arts nature of the brokerage process. The same aim informed each, which was to let as many voices as possible rub up against each other in the course of one and a half hours. The arts-based initiatives used in sessions varied according to context in order to realise this aim and the following three examples are presented to give a sense of the commonalities and differences in structure used across the nine focus groups.

The first focus group on one evening in a community church saw a large number of local entrepreneurs initially work individually, selecting visual 'work-story' theatrical images from which they were asked to select those that resonated with their view of the 'burning issue' that was most important for them in terms of the Goods Shed. Pässilä with the graphic designer Laura Mellanen created more than 500 theatrical image cards in order to create a process for sharing both experiences and embodied knowledge. These are used as a method of reflective inquiry during the research process, each being constructed according to image-theatre practice (Boal, 1995) and the five elements of drama; act, scene, agent, agency and purpose as proposed by Burke (1969, in Pässilä, 2012, pp. 56–104). This process led to work in pairs where the matters were shared, leading in to group work of five and six people constructing their narrative of issues about the Goods Shed. This was done visually on large white cloths using marker pens and the work-story images. Each group fed back and issues were recorded then coded visually on the wall in large written form to show the common concerns emerging and the individual points being made.

In contrast the approach used with the large focus group of young people aged 13 to 16 rested almost totally on map-making and had to accommodate individuals coming and going in the non-formal setting of an evening youth club. Map-making as a drama convention generates dialogue from local knowledge. Participants were asked to draw the town around central coordinates and recognisable features we had pre-drawn including the Goods Shed. We asked them to mark where they currently spent most of their time and where they most enjoyed spending time before then asking if they know where the Goods Shed was and what, if anything, they thought should happen with it.

With the group of senior citizens during an afternoon in a health clinic the first activity was to form a continuum with the person who had lived in the town the longest at one end, and the person newest to the town at the other. Continuum as a drama convention is used to physically regroup participants in order to allow for new dialogue partners. Participants were accordingly grouped according to the period in which they arrived in the town and talked about their first impressions and how that compared with their impressions today. We retold these as a storytelling narrative as a way of introducing the Goods Shed, asking the question of what, if anything, should be done with it. Storytelling narrative as a drama convention is used to create aesthetic distance between participants and the phenomena or subject in order to make the familiar strange, and so allow for possibly new insights in the usual landscape of the taken-for-granted. These participants were also invited to select theatrical images that connected their thoughts about past and present with the Goods Shed today, with smaller groups reporting their thoughts back to the whole group (see Figure 7.2).

The evocative report and textile artwork

The month between the last focus group session and the public meeting was used to analyse the data collected from the focus groups into a model to be used as a starting point for co-construction and action planning. The concept of evocative reporting was developed by Mellanen and Pässilä as an alternative to written reporting, which often only reaches a very limited audience and tends to quickly find itself on a shelf. It is designed to utilise multimedia approaches in allowing for collective voicing. We are developing the concept together with Chamberlain (2014) and in this project it took the form of a nine-minute film (Pässilä, Owens and Chamberlain, 2014) to disseminate and

Figure 7.2 Examples of theatrical image cards produced by Mellanen and Pässilä used as prompts in the focus group workshops

further engage the public in the questions rising from the data. Documentary techniques were used in the pursuit of inclusivity, for example the melody and music of the evocative report contained the combined conflated voices of all participate voices in the nine focus group sessions. This was made available via to the public via the Foundation website after the open public meeting together with photographs of a piece of textile art that was also created in the intervening month and finished during the public meeting. The large textile piece was made on a 2- by 1-metre wooden frame cross-woven with strips of bed sheet material purchased from one of the town's charity shops (see Figure 7.3). Each strip was coloured and overlaid with verbatim statements made by participants in the focus group sessions. These were written and woven in during the public meeting in the community church and the textile piece was displayed as a form of 'stained glass', recording very different opinions, dreams, hopes and

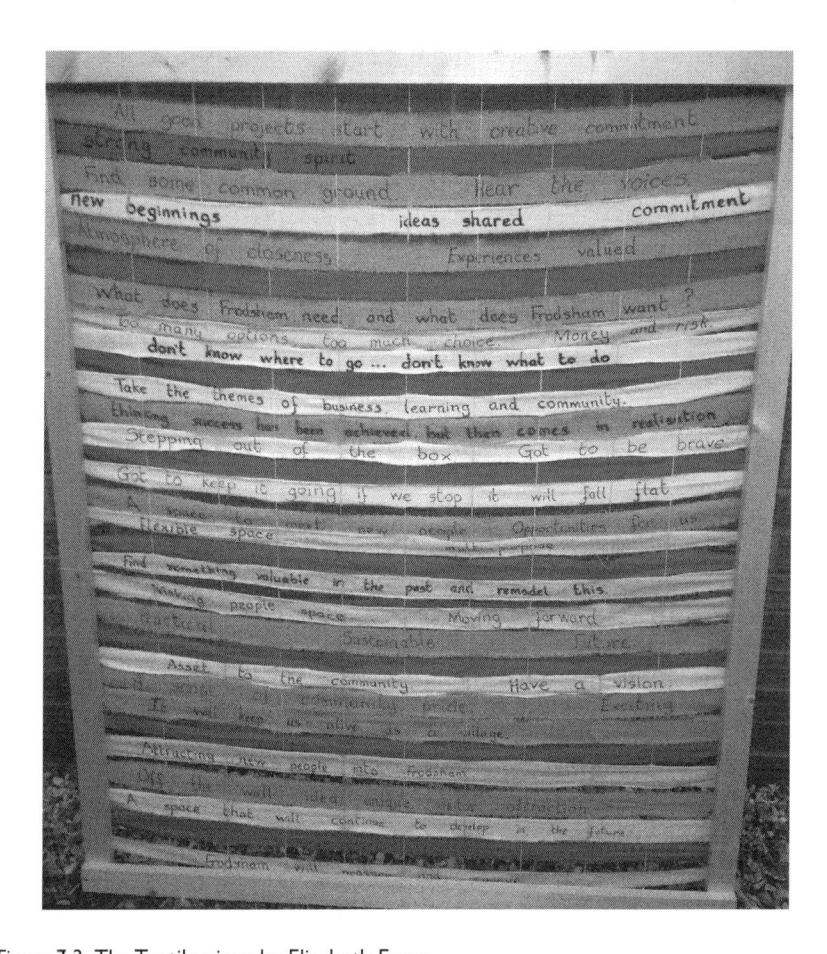

Figure 7.3 The Textile piece by Elizabeth Evans

concerns. We used both the evocative report and textile artwork to inform the subsequent discussions.

Outcomes and consequences

Given our close involvement in this continuing project, we attempt in this discussion to maintain a critical distance. We do this by looking at our practice through the theoretical lenses considered earlier in this chapter, turning to the questions that continue to trouble us. For example, a key claim in of the ABI process developed in this project is that it allowed for a reformulation of our practices and perceptions, whereby a blurring took place 'of the boundary between those who act and those who look; between individuals and members of a collective body' (Rancière, 2010b, p. 17), but did this happen? We suggest that on one level it did, in facilitating an incremental form of reformulation, allowing for an initial temporary suspension of inequality, at least in terms of who had the space and time to speak and be heard in the decisions that were being made about the way a public space was being shaped. We went to the participants face to face, and in places and times to suit them, fitting in with their ordinary meeting times, such as Friday night at the youth club, Wednesday afternoon at the health centre for the senior citizens, Tuesday morning for the mothers and babies, and Tuesday early evening for local business people. On another level we ask ourselves if the whole emphasis on 'being with' is more about creating our 'success story' as practitioners and researchers than reformulation and change.

Our intention was to use arts based methods that, in Rancière's words, might 'reconfigure the map of the sensible' through processes that 'open up space for deviations, modify the speeds, the trajectories and the ways which groups of people adhere to a condition react to situations' (2004, p. 39). For example in one of the focus groups organised for entrepreneurs and local business people, a prominent local business person came 10 minutes late in to the session to find the rest of the participants selecting theatrical images that they felt captured their thoughts, feelings, dreams or fears for the Goods Shed. She declined when asked to choose a couple of images, stating that her customers could not park when they came in to the town and that 'it should be knocked down, we need a multi-storey car park.' Another member of the group had already made it very clear from the outset that the use of the Goods Shed would only reproduce services already provided by existing publically run spaces such as the library and community arts space. We acknowledged both viewpoints and the fact that others would have their own opinions in the spirit of improvised theatre where there is no blocking and all ideas are accepted. Having said this, it was hard at points not to be attracted to those who appeared to flexible in their thinking and so get locked in our own rapidly forming opinions – something skilled improvisers readily recognise. The group was split and we asked each to share their chosen work story cards, talking through them and visualising ideas on a large roll of paper laid across several tables, to which we as researchers also contributed in the form of drawing what we were hearing. Once the drawings were completed each group then shared their thinking, referring to the cards, drawings and annotated questions. In the hour and a half the images allowed for summary and iteration, silence, dialogue, time and space to reflect in the light of others. The participant who was concerned about duplication of services continued to raise this until the end of the meeting, but began to allow that it might provide services that existing provision did not. The 'knock it down' participant said just before the close of the whole focus group session, 'We do need a multi-story car park, but maybe not there.'

This example is presented to give a glimpse of how a space for learning was created where participants could articulate and test their own point of view against those of others, to create a form of good friction (Korhonen and Airaksinen, 2014) and in so doing made time to think through their assumptions before voicing them again. The aesthetic distance created through the use of theatrical images and the conversation these generated deferred a return to the participants' default, 'self-evident' perceptions of the situation (Eriksson, 2014). This was also flagged in the opening scene of the evocative report, taking the form of a film shot looking down on the town from the hill as the light was fading. The narrator's voice was in the drama convention storytelling mode:

> It is the year 2019 and a lone walker is returning from a long walk on the sandstone trail. He stops and looks down at the town that was first recorded in the Doomsday book is he sees the lights of Morrison's Supermarket and just over the railway track there is a dark deserted building with large doors; he blinks and then the space is completely deserted and he blinks again and sees a multi-story car park; he blinks again and he sees a building that is lit with people coming and going from it; intrigued he makes his way down into the town and hears people talking about what they've been doing; he goes closer to the building and peers in . . . it's a hive of activity, warm, it seems to be a place for the community and business and learning; its incredible, and as he listens people seem to be saying how can we possibly have been managing when we did not have the Goods Shed.

Using a deliberately 'designed futures' perspective we were inviting those at the public meeting to step out of the here and now in order to anticipate the future by imagining they were looking back from it. The voices then heard over film footage of the main crossroads and streets in the town were reflecting on the town present, some being proud and positive, stressing a strong community spirit such as 'We believe that we are very welcoming community'; 'the good things about the town are our traditions'; 'a sense of connectivity' (see Figure 7.4). Older citizens regretted the loss of the town carnival many years ago, others pointed out, '[W]e've always been a town of small businesses, I think we really want to keep that dynamic', and '[P]eople meeting through buying and selling things.'

Figure 7.4 Still from the Goods Shed film

Another set of voices pointed in a different direction highlighting division and exclusion:

> 'I'm sure there are many towns just like us but it's almost two towns'; 'there are areas of exclusion and not everybody shares equally'; 'this is just not the place for young people'; 'we've got an ageing population'.

From these diverse voices presented in the evocative report, reflection through dramatic form in the collective sharing of individual experiences brought local knowing into practice. On another level a resource for building a sense of community was also being created.

The process in each participative focus group was characterised by dissensus, in which the aim was not to settle conflicting voices in order to achieve resolution, but to engage in the mode of creativity itself, allowing participants take the step from bystander to actor through voicing their own imaginative conjectures. The narrative story line of the evocative report played on these, shifting people 'back to the present' in a way used in each session to keep troubling the 'here and now' by stepping in and out of it:

> But of course people did manage before you, and if we go back just five years before the Walker stopped to look down to the year 2014 he would have seen groups of people meeting to talk about the possible uses of the

Goods Shed, he would have heard people talking about the culture of . . . [the town], invisible things like the atmosphere that there could be in such a building; he would have heard others talking about practical issues, whilst others were more concerned with the decisions that have to be made. Others were considered strategy and others could be heard talking fractions regional innovation and have a good shed could be a plan for the whole area's regeneration and the question is emerging about values and beliefs, about what should be and could be, about the shift from the 'as is' to the 'as if'.

This second narrative introduced the wide range of 'as if' thinking from across the focus groups. Some focused on inclusion, integration and signposting:

'I feel that there should be opportunities for jobseekers'; 'where younger people could talk about the ideas they like to try out'; 'a place to come and be part of the community'; 'where you can meet new friends'; 'various crafts areas for craft classes'; 'friendly'; 'it could be a place that signposts other places like the leisure centre and the library'.

Others focused on immediate needs – 'it could be a bus station' – or on workspace:

'You could start your business by borrowing or renting a table small size'; 'to have a table you could rent'; ' local produce stallholders have a local market'; 'should be high-speed broadband' and leisure, 'I think it should be skate park'; 'micro brewery'; 'can we have a shop?'

In each focus group the need for a café was strongly sounded out: '[I]t should be a cool retro Café old fashioned'; 'inexpensive Coffee, warmth, chat'. Another set of voices was concerned more with how the place would be organised and run:

'Constantly changing in someway or another'; 'it wouldn't be the same operate everyday it would be somebody knew was coming into try ideas'; 'available almost 24 seven'; 'it's got to be very cleverly constructed to allow for all different sorts of things to be brought in.'

Rather than simply making sure that those who would make change heard their personal viewpoint, participants were engaged in a learning process as their own viewpoints actively rubbed up against others.

The third narration introduced the themes interpreted from the data for further discussion:

And some people said the Good Shed is a gateway to communication, that's the place where you go to meet people in business or to do your work business, but also a learning lab for old figures in a community place, not just a draughty old community hall, and vibrant place like a Costa Coffee on wheels, and all managed in a user-centred way quite different from anything has ever happened before.

The themes were presented in one static visual over the top of the work-story images used in all of the focus groups: 'Gateway to Communication' was a key heading followed by three themes: 'Business HUB, Learning LAB, Community Corner', underscored by 'User-Centred Management System'.

Questions arising from statements made and the process itself were then floated on top of the film visuals, which by this stage had turned to the railway platform outside the Goods Shed where a young woman waits for a train:

> 'What does the practice-based approach mean?' . . . 'Who are the fundamental partners in this dance of cross-fertilisation?' . . . 'What kind of learning lab?' 'How would this experimental community space we created be run?'

Whilst underneath voices echoing the themes can be heard: 'The building could be a gateway into the town when coming off the train.'

The third narration acknowledged the threats:

> 'We shouldn't build something that we already have in . . . [the town]; 'it's maybe because no one is daring to do it'; 'car parking needed when people come in . . . yes knock it down'; 'I don't know what's worse to see: a derelict building or a multi-storey car park.'

The concluding narration was 'there is no beginning to small . . . what has to happen today for the first concrete steps to be taken?'

In terms of outcome, on a public level, change took place in the planned use and ownership of a building as a result of a process in which this ABI played a part. To return to Pässilä's definition of innovation activities as 'learning steps aiming at the creation of innovation wherein all organisational actors are understood as critical innovators' (2012, p.16), the organisational actors in each focus group were given space to be critical innovators, as were the general public in the open meeting. The 'learning steps' allowed the foundation to subsequently articulate the basic concept of the Goods Shed to the larger county council and the participative focus group meetings shared in the evocative report gave momentum to the request for a 25-year lease which was duly granted. From this momentum Project Make Space was launched as a design competition for RIBA (Royal Institute of British Architects) who were directed to the evocative report as a key research source. The designs were presented at a public exhibition and members of the community were then given the opportunity to vote for the designers of their choice. At the time of writing the next phase of practice-based research is being planned to allow for collaborative participation in the move towards the final use, organisation and design of the Goods Shed. This is important to us from a practice-based perspective in that the research actions we took have led to the next step of actions with the architects and to the next steps of collaboration with the members of the foundation.

Democratic loose ends

We have tried to illustrate how we invited people to themselves open and create spaces for social engagement and collective action and the forms these took in the brokerage process, but did our practices resist the conformism of market ideology? As a practice-based research team we reflected on our methodological approach and its consequences. We had a positive intention to work alongside people offering our skills using arts-based methods to assist with mutual understanding through critical self-reflection. But, to be provocative, our work could be viewed from another perspective as propping up a central government regime that has deliberately run down local government and with it local democracy and subject to manipulation by an unelected social enterprise company to smooth over social relations in order to liberate free-market economics. We would of course strongly contest any such assertions and key to this is the relationship of increasing trust created between the Foundation directors, members, ourselves and other collaborating partners such a local government.

From the outset our negotiations have been on an equal footing. Our work has not been 'subservient' to the foundation or business interests, nor has the foundation's work been subservient to our creative practice or academic research interests. There has been time and process enough for us all to ask what Taylor calls 'the vital question 'what am I doing this work in the service of?' (Taylor and Thellesen in Darsø et al., 2007 p. 30). As trust has built so we have begun to more openly share the principles and values that underpin this question for each of us as appreciative critical friends.

Through working together we have had chance to see the values underpinning foundation's charitable objective of community capacity building in action in seeking resources and support that strengthen the skills and abilities of people and community groups to take effective action and leading roles in the development of their communities. The foundation has had chance to work alongside us, to see our values in action, the potential value of arts-based methods in opening things, making the unseen visible through fictionalising the real, and to provoke, to create space for voices to be heard and through the evocative report, listened directly to.

This does not mean that our values or strategies in acting for the public good are identical; for example the foundation subscribes to the market ideology in seeing individual employment, employability and development of skills as the 'first steps towards a larger life' where as we foreground the act of democratic participation itself with all the underlying emancipatory values. The main point for us is that our relationship is dynamic, open, on-going and can be perplexed, partly because none of us are interested in the dualities of arts and business 'that sets an evil corporate world that is motivated by power and control against the sacred art world that is motivated by personal freedom and exploration' (Taylor and Thellesen in Darsø et al., 2007 p. 30). The reality is much less clear and we are interested in working through the tensions in that.

We have attempted to show how the series of participative group sessions were designed democratically to further produce and enable democracy, and key to this is the notion of creating a space where we can talk about 'how' we are talking, but the degree to which we achieved this was variable. For example, we gave time in each session to briefly introduce how we were aspiring to use this ABI as a means of allowing all voices to be heard and to allow critical stances to be taken without becoming paralysed by the deadlock of intransigent disagreement, not only to listen but also to 'hear' other viewpoints as a means of reflecting on our own. The majority of people in each focus group session said that it 'made a change to discuss things in this way' and a small number thought it was the best way to consult and broker, but there were also a similar small number in each focus group who said they would rather have just talked directly about the issue, even where they admitted they could see what we were trying to accomplish.

Unsurprisingly tensions were high at the public open meeting at which the evocative report was shared (although the need to call the police prior to the meeting, whilst considered, was discounted), and one person rejected the approach outright. A few minutes into the introduction of the ABI process this participant interrupted and demanded to know why his time was being wasted with this talk and that he had no need to watch a film to know what he thought about what should happen with the Goods Shed and that this was a waste of public money. After acknowledging the point and suggesting that the film would allow us to hear many other points of members of the community he grew angry and interrupted again, saying that he wanted to get on and express his views as was his right. At this point one of the directors of the foundation chairing the meeting told him to 'shut up or get out.' The altercation was heated, and the fault lines of the democratic process were exposed when the participant asserted the basic democratic right to speak in a public meeting. The chair responded by saying that this was a meeting run under the auspices of a social enterprise limited company, and that he did not have a right to speak and should leave unless he was prepared to also listen to others. The meeting continued, the angry participant stayed and he came to talk to us after the evocative report. We thanked him for sharing his thoughts and feelings saying that we valued them as we valued all those we had heard and emphasised that we had no expectations or preferences about the outcome of the data collection but that the evocative report was our interpretation of what we heard about the Goods Shed and that we were glad he could respond to these. We were trying to build a bridge for his participation. In a more conciliatory manner he talked about what he perceived as the lack of clarity at the meeting and expressed his distrust of the politics of the procedures.

After this all the participants were invited to share their response to the report in smaller groups and to consider what the next steps forward should be. After an hour and a half the meeting was concluded, having identified a number of working groups who were willing to act, and in what capacity, before business then shifted to the annual general meeting of the foundation. In this particular instance the space to talk about 'how' we were talking was closed down with no recourse to revisit this subject. On one hand, this can be presented as an enforcement of a 'democratic' operation suitable for an annual general meeting, akin to the UK parliamentary system in which opposing viewpoints are expressed as strongly as possible but controlled ultimately by the speaker of the house who does not allow for insult or dominance by one voice. On the other hand, what were the mechanisms in this instance by which the 'way we were talking about what we were talking about' could be challenged? There was no space and time to reflect critically, and this left the question of whether this could have been built more robustly into the process.

In each of the participatory focus groups we intended to create a culture of creativity that involved everybody and not just a select few, and a case for this could be made as evident in the falling silent of the most strident voices as less powerful voices were heard. This occurred particularly in the process of theatrical image discussion, which allowed for comment and questioning of on a concrete level: the comment 'it could be a motor cycle repair shop' was followed by a discussion of the lack of prospects for the unemployed in the town in a group otherwise not focusing on this issue. However, the attempt to be representative in the selection of the nine focus groups was only partially achieved, particularly in terms of attendance. It was noticeable, for example, that the job seekers and unemployed group was attended largely by professionals working with this 'client group'. No one attended the mothers and children drop in session.

We discussed this issue of inclusivity as part of the job seekers and unemployed group meeting. Members of the Foundation said that new strategies were needed for engaging with these and other socially marginalised groups. How to create a space for engagement without further marginalising through the offer was the tricky question. The need to recognise wider systemic and societal factors and issues was also considered. The perplexities being explored here in terms of the disenfranchisement of the unemployed on the individual and organisational levels were being generated at societal and global levels. In other words systemic change is needed at national and regional policy level to address unemployment, whilst also acknowledging that unemployment is a given feature of the global neoliberal project. The Goods Shed had the potential to not only create local employment opportunities but, equally important, a sense of collective belonging in resistance to the individualism of neoliberalism as well.

The forms, styles, purposes, and values of ABIs and the Turn to Learning in organisations are still taking shape, and it is hard to answer many of the questions this raises as fully as they deserve. If we define democracy itself by 'those intermittent acts of political subjectivisation that reconfigure the communal distribution of the sensible' (Rockhill in Rancière, 2004, p. 3) then there is evidence of an emerging shape, made possible through the space and time distortions, playfully created through the aesthetic distance as presented in this case study:

> Quite regularly the path of fiction is chosen to pint out problematic errors in reality. If anything, creativity thereby makes us aware that values, norms and habits within a culture are only relative . . . One has to step outside the stream to look at the daily flow of life form some distance. This pulling up vertically is at the very core of criticism: to take a step back from what seems to be the determining agent in order to escape determination.
> (Gielen, 2013, p. 89)

Our attempt to use the arts to achieve interaction was in this case through democratic processes that we knew beforehand could not entirely succeed as many of the issues are not just local but systematic and global. Yet at the same time we recognised that the process itself has potential to help us and participants collectively question the 'taken-for-granted' and so start to reshape ways of living together that are regulated not only by money and individualism, but the building of community. Viewed in this way the arts can be used as Gielen (2011) suggests, to create one phase of a larger emancipatory development process.

Conclusion
Creative acts, democratic acts

To conclude we return to some of the theories, practices and ideals that we have argued throughout the book were once to considered to be foundational for education: democratic education, education for a just society, and social mobility; ideals that were at the foundation of the welfare states in Western nations, for which creative, imaginative expressions through the arts were once considered to be as essential and as basic as our more modern educational obsessions with entrepreneurial, technocratic knowledge and competition. One of the premises of this book has been the contention that creativity has played, and continues to play, a fundamental role in conceptions of progressive and democratic education and that if creative learning is impoverished, then the concept of education itself may be fundamentally diminished.

We return to these not through a tidy summing up or synthesising and packaging of the big themes of creativity, education and democracy but, in keeping with the spirit of this book, by turning to the little things in our daily practice that allow us to engage with these themes on a human, relational level. It is a conclusion in three acts; the first takes the form of a travel story, back in time, set in the Czech Republic; the second looks forward to the future of creative practices through one of the most contentious media and topics following the Charlie Hebdo massacre in Paris (2015) – the comic medium and the emergence of documentary graphic novels; the final act is a reminder of the decline of democratic education with a call to imagine the future differently.

The liberating beauty of little things: a travel story

In the course of writing this book (2014) our work took us once more to the Czech Republic where we have over the years worked with students, school and university teachers, lecturers, and arts educators. This was the year of the 25th anniversary of Czechoslovakia's 1989 Velvet Revolution, the non-violent uprising that led to a rapid transition to democracy after 40 years of communist rule. A film series, 'The Play's the Thing: Václav Havel, Art and Politics', about Havel (1936–2011), a key figure in that time, was playing worldwide. We were conscious of being in a state whose first president was a dramatist and dissident, imprisoned for his mix of theatre and politics who then went on to become an internationally recognised statesman. We also recalled an encounter prior to our first visit in 2002 with a colleague from the UK who told us of an experience during his first visit to the newly independent state of the Czech Republic in 1993. After a few days of running workshops he noticed that many of the participants had small bells on chains around their necks. When he asked why, they said that this was to remind them and others never again to act like sheep in following any ideology. They were attending the workshop because they saw the arts as a means of exercising criticality, about self, other and the state.

All of the preceding were in our minds as we travelled on a tram to one of the outer districts of Prague. We had left our group of postgraduate students working with other students in a workshop at the Charles University and went on a mission to deliver a bunch of flowers to one of its alumni, Bohuslava Bradbook. The flowers were from our Dean, Anna Sutton, a former student of hers who first told us about the young Bradbrook's remarkable escape from Czechoslovakia across Europe and eventually to England, at the height of the Cold War. In *'The Liberating Beauty of Little Things': Decision, Adversity & Reckoning in a Refugee's Journey from Prague to Cambridge* (2000), Bradbrook documents the politics and history of those years from her viewpoint as a young academic, stating that: 'it was freedom, for which, we thought, it was worth risking our lives' (p. 18).

Unfortunately we did not meet Dr Brabdbook because our 'surprise visit' did not find her at home. We left the flowers with a note outside the door of her apartment and, when back in the UK, received a letter of thanks inviting us back the next time we were in Prague. What we found through our reading on our return was that she had taken the title of the book from the writing of Capek (1890–1938), the Czech novelist and playwright who campaigned for democracy and wrote prolifically about the crisis of democracy in ways that make them highly relevant today (Chamberlaine, 2010). His thinking was informed in part by Dewey, and we made the connection with our practice-based research interests through the way he considers momentous world scale events by focusing on the small things that could so easily remain unnoticed or dismissed as inconsequential. Capek had a 'lifelong commitment to the celebration of the small' (Hester, 2008), challenging the idea that popular and high culture had particular, distinct inherent values, arguing that culture depends on how things are used. It was through little things that he often brought his concern with humanity to bear on the great political, cultural and social issues of his day.

So what is the point we are making here? For us, the discussion about the roles that creativity plays in democratic education practices involves keeping sight of the overarching context in which our practices occur – how the huge themes of creativity, education and democracy are playing out – but through the perspectives that the liberating beauty of small things permits: the momentary events, long-term relationships and the belief that greater social changes are constituted from numerous minor steps into action. The Czech scholars Kasikova and Valenta argue that education has the possibility to influence societal reality not only through instruction practice or curriculum change, but 'when we change the entire conceptualisation of the "educational encounter" (2011, p. 37). The case studies in the book have been presented to share the challenges, uncertainties and questions that emerge when the steps towards reconceptualisation take the form of relational arts practices that value the interdependent interaction of critical creativity.

Comics and graphic novels

Looking to the future of creative practices, one of the interesting developments of the last 25 years has been the emergence of documentary graphic novels (Adams, 2000; 2008a; 2008b). Novels like Sacco's *Palestine* (2001), Delisle's *Jerusalem* (2012) and Spiegelman's *Maus* (2003) are all examples of the utilisation of the comics medium to create documentary works that deal head-on with serious issues such as war, culture and identity. Spiegelman's work is especially significant in this respect, breaking new ground as it did by attempting to represent the unutterable horrors of the Holocaust in a comic book. The freshness of this hybridity, comic book with documentary, gave the topic an unexpected visual poignancy and avoided the sentimentality into which more conventional mass media, such as film, too readily slipped (i.e. Spielberg's film *Schindler's List* [1993], contemporary with *Maus*).

This coming-of-age of the comic book medium with its transformation into the 'graphics novel' is indicative of the search for alternative media in the face of the corporate monopolisation of mainstream media of newspapers and television and increasingly social media. Sacco uses the phrase 'under the radar' to describe the way that this hitherto undeveloped (in a commercial sense) medium provided a vehicle within which artists like him could talk about the ethnic and military tensions in the Middle East in ways which would have been taboo or subject to censorship, had they been presented more conventionally (interview the author, unpublished, September 2000). It is also noticeable that the increasing use of comic books as a documentary medium entails laborious work on the part of the author/artist; it is slow medium, and the labour of the artist is evident on every page, in sharp contrast to the rapidity and speed of social media, which has developed over the same period. Just as the photographic image has become ubiquitous in the extreme, some artists have turned to these much older, slower forms of creativity which demand manual craft and dexterity, and above all, time.

Many of these documentary graphic novels rely heavily on direct personal observations to instill authenticity into their topics (Adams, 2008a). Sacco makes copious handwritten notes as records of interviews with his subjects, and faithfully documents their experiences in situ, frequently in refugee camps or in the makeshift homes of the poverty-stricken. He uses many photographs for topographical and architectural observations, but these are all translated into drawings later. Similarly Delisle adopts a sketchy, caricature style, and yet depicts the impoverished life to which indigenous Palestinians are subjected in East Jerusalem. This is accomplished autobiographically, centred on his direct experience in

Palestine, and are made to seem all the more authentic by the inclusion of day-to-day domestic details, such as how to get utilities mended, or organising childcare.

Guibert, Lefevre and Lemercier's *The Photographer* (2008), a documentary of a photographer accompanying a Médecins Sans Frontieres mission into Afghanistan during the 1980s when under Russian military occupation, combines photography with comic book drawing. Most pages in the graphic novel are a combination of the two media, although the photographs are serialised across the page in comic book panel form, rather like the methods used in popular teenage photo-comic strips of the 1960s and 1970s, such as those serialised in *Jackie*. *The Photographer* depicts the grim realities of carrying out medical care with almost no resources on the periphery of a war zone. Guibert *et al.* depict the brutalising of children's lives by a war from which they can find no sanctuary and the implied perpetuation of conflict through the ideological conditioning of the youngsters. The mixture of drawn images and photographs, with narrative texts written at the side, top or bottom of the image, is an adaptation of the medium that requires the reader to become accustomed to reading the transitions between the panels, because this does not come naturally. This slight discomfort is part of the construction of the reader as the authors capture and engage attention: the constant oscillation between image type is compelling, if tiring as the reader works to maintain the narrative. By these means the uncomfortable and sometimes confrontational experiences of the narrative are imposed on the reader, amplifying the main themes of the narrative: the neglect of health and the abuse of childhood through the toxic combination of militarisation and poverty.

The adaptation of comic books to documentary is significant for education, since the documentary medium has a close association with pedagogy (Adams, 2008b). The pedagogical function of these graphic novels is evident in their authors' insistence on the inclusion of themselves as the narrating 'teacher', directing the reader's attention to those aspects of the cultural life that they believe has most salience; this, in combination with overtly rigorous observation, provides a hallmark of authenticity, and implies documentary 'truth'. Despite the modern associations the medium of comics has with caricature, cartoons and light reading, these new documentary artists are rethinking the medium by drawing on older traditions of political engagement (i.e. 18th-century satirical political cartoons) and thereby offering a creative production which is deliberately unlike modern mass, high-tech media and therefore less prone, at least for the time being, to appropriation. Through these slow and handcrafted autobiographical accounts new educational experiences are forged, providing other ways of thinking about old and enduring cultural conflicts.

Imagining differently

When Herbert Read (1943/1970) was imagining the possibilities of a comprehensive education system through the arts, he devised a curriculum in which the arts dominated and in which expressive and affective learning was foregrounded.

Creative practices in all aspects of school life were seen as fundamental to teaching and learning, and he advocated their employment in all disciplines, not merely the overtly artistic ones. It is no coincidence that this way of thinking about education was conceived during and after the Second World War, in perhaps the greatest leap towards democracy that the UK has ever experienced. Not content with imagining the democratic revolution inherent in his conception of the arts determining wholesale the practices of teachers and pupils in a school, he also rethought the physical spaces of the school to make them commensurate with this artistic vision. This then can be seen as an example of democratic education made manifest in the materiality of the learning environment; literally, the architecture of emancipation. This concept of a school building that expressed democratic ideals is worth reflecting on, because it represents the spaces of democracy: practical, functioning spaces that encourage collaboration, freedom of expression and equality; the buildings are spacious for the practice of acting, dancing or painting, among others, surrounded by green natural spaces for health, and with many communal areas for meeting, collaborating and sharing, with theatre spaces and galleries.

The creation of an education system mirrored by its physical presence in the buildings and spaces it occupies, expresses the democratic revolution in full force, and stands today in total opposition to neoliberal austerity and philistinism; Read's words are in stark contrast to current political rhetoric, and acts as a salient reminder how much the democratic project has been stalled:

> the question of cost is irrelevant: there is land, there are building materials, there is skill and labour. In a rational society, there is only the question of priority, and no services in such a society, save those nourishing and protecting life itself, should have priority over education.
> (1943/1970, p. 301)

Read's valuing of children and education above economic concerns should act as call for current generations to recognise the importance of restoring the long democratic revolution, especially through education, and of how significant creativity and the arts are to this project. It is not a question of merely embellishing education with interesting creative displays, while the 'core' business of learning how to be economic consumers seeking competitive advantage in an unequal society continues as usual. It is about embodying equality through democratic practices and squarely facing the most difficult challenge of all, imagining how to live together justly.

References

Abdel-Fattah (2013) 'Illegal Mourning: The Nakba Law and the Erasure of Palestine'. Retrieved 30 January 2015 from: http://www.abc.net.au/religion/articles/2013/05/17/3761661.htm

Acemoglu, D., Robinson, J. A. and Verdier, T. (2012) 'Can't We All Be More Like Scandinavians? Asymmetric Growth and Institutions in an Interdependent World', 20 August 20, MIT Department of Economics Working Paper No. 12–22. Available from SSRN: http://ssrn.com/abstract-2132939

Adams, J. (2000) 'Working Out Comics', *International Journal of Art and Design Education* Vol. 19, No. 3, pp. 304–312.

Adams, J. (2008a) *Documentary Graphic Novels and Social Realism*. Oxford: Peter Lang.

Adams, J. (2008b) 'The Pedagogy of the Image Text: Nakazawa, Sebald and Spiegelman Recount Social Traumas', *Discourse: Studies in the Cultural Politics of Education* Vol. 29, No. 1, pp. 37–52.

Adams, J. (2010) 'Risky Choices: The Dilemmas of Introducing Contemporary Art Practices into Schools', *British Journal of Sociology of Education* Vol. 31, No. 6, pp. 683–701.

Adams, J. (2011). 'Room 13 and the Contemporary Practice of Artist-Learners'. In J. Sefton-Green, P. Thomson, K. Jones and Bresler, L. (Eds) *The Routledge International Handbook of Creative Learning* (pp. 217–225). London, Routledge.

Adams, J. (2013) 'The Artful Dodger: Creative Resistance to Neo-Liberalism in Education', *Review of Education, Pedagogy and Cultural Studies* Vol. 35, No.4, pp. 242–255.

Adams, J., Worwood, K., Atkinson, D., Dash, P., Herne, S. and Page, T. (2008) *Teaching through Contemporary Art: A Report on Innovative Practices in the Classroom*. London: Tate Publishing.

Adler, N. (2010) 'Arts Reflection and Leadership'. Retrieved 16 January 2015 from: http://www.rh2010.com/bilan2010/pdf/14a17_Adler_v13n4-en.pdf

Aitken, V., Fraser, D. and Price, G. (2007) Negotiating the Spaces: Relational Pedagogy and Power in Drama Teaching, *International Journal of Education & the Arts* Vol. 8. No. 4, pp. 42–52.

Al Jazeera (2011) 'South Korea's Exam Suicides'. Retrieved 30 January 2015 from: http://www.youtube.com/watch?v=8o0tcZ4mru8

Al Yamani, H. (2004) *The Role of Drama in Initial Teacher Education: A Study of Drama's Use in Early Childhood Teacher Education Programmes at Bethlehem University, Palestine*, PhD thesis, University of Exeter, unpublished.

Allen, D. (2014) *Gypsy, Roma Traveller Communities: A Lived Experience*, Forum for Equality and Diversity Public Lecture, Law School, University of Chester, 14 May.

Alvesson, M. and Willmott, H. (1992) 'On the Idea of Emancipation in Management and Organisational Studies', *Academy of Management Review* Vol. 17, No. 3, pp. 432–464.

Angelou, M. (1969) *I Know Why the Caged Bird Sings*. New York: Virago.

Antonacopoulou, E. (2010) 'Making the Business School More 'Critical': Reflexive Critique Based on Phronesis as a Foundation for Impact', *British Journal of Management* Vol. 21, pp. 6–25.

Anthony, T. (2005) *Da Kink in My Hair*. Toronto: Playwrights Canada Press.

Apple, M. (2013) 'Teacher Education'. Symposium on Teacher Education, Society for Education Studies, University of Manchester, 28 June, unpublished, author's notes.

Atkinson, D. (2011) *Art, Equality and Learning: Pedagogies against the State*. Rotterdam: Sense Publishers.

Badiou, A. (2006) 'Democracy, Politics and Philosophy', lecture at the European Graduate School EGS, Saas Fee, Switzerland. Retrieved 30 January 2015 from: http://www.egs.edu/faculty/alain-badiou/articles/democracy-politics-and-philosophy/; video lecture, retrieved 30 January 2015 from: http://www.egs.edu/faculty/alain-badiou/videos/the-event-as-creative-novelty/

Badiou, A. (2009) 'The Event as Creative Novelty' (The European Graduate School). Retrieved 30 April 2014 from: https://www.youtube.com/watch?v=ZekT_HQmYo8

Bandura, A. (1986). *Social Foundations of Thought and Action: A Social Cognitive Theory*. Englewood Cliffs, NJ: Prentice Hall.

Barakat, H. (1993). *The Arab World: Society, Culture and State*. Berkeley: University of California Press.

Barakat, H. (1995). *Aldimocratiyya Wal-Adala Al-Ijtimaiyya* [*Democracy and Social Justice*] (in Arabic). Ramallah: MUWTIN, The Palestinian Institute For the Study of Democracy.

Barakat, H. (2000). *Mujtama ' al-'Arabi Fi al-qarn al-'ishrin, bahth fi taghyir al-ahwal wa-al-'alaqat* [*Arab Society in the Twentieth Century*] (in Arabic). Beirut: Center for Arab Unity Studies.

Barry, D. (2006) 'The Art of . . .'. In D. Barry and H. Hansen (Eds) *The SAGE Handbook of New Approaches in Management and Organization* (pp. 31–41). London: Sage.

Barry, D. and Meisiek, S. (2010) 'Seeing More and Seeing Differently: Sensemaking, Mindfulness, and the Workarts', *Organisation Studies* Vol. 31, No.11, pp. 1505–1530.

Bauman, Z. (2001). *Community: Seeking Safety in an Insecure World*. Oxford: Polity Press.

Bauman, Z. (2002). *Society under Siege*. Oxford: Polity.

Bauman, Z. (2004). *Identity: Conversations with Benedetto Vecchi*. Cambridge, UK: Polity Press.

Bauman, Z. (2011). 'Bauman Talks about Democracy, Facebook and Other Contemporary Issues in a 30 Minute Interview'. Retrieved 30 January 2015 from: http://vimeo.com/27702137

Bernstein, B. (1966/2000). *Pedagogy, Symbolic Control and Identity: Theory, Research, Critique*. Lanham, MD: Rowman and Littlefield.

Berthoin Antal, A. (2009). *Research Report: Research Framework for Evaluating the Effects of Artistic Interventions in Organisations.* Gothenburg: TILLT Europe.
Bhabha, H. (1994). *The Location of Culture*. London: Routledge
Bhabha, H. (2003). 'On Writing Rights'. In M. Gibney (Ed.) *Globalising Rights* (pp. 162–183). Oxford: Oxford University Press.
Bishop, C. (2004) 'Antagonism and Relational Aesthetics', October 110, Fall, pp. 51–79. Retrieved 30 January 2015 from: http://www.teamgal.com/production/1701/SS04October.pdf
Boal, A. (1979). *Theatre of the Oppressed* (Trans. Leal McBride). London: Pluto Press.
Boal, A. (1995) *The Rainbow of Desire: The Boal Method of Theatre and Therapy*. London: Routledge.
Boal, A. (2002) *Games for Actors and Non-Actors*. London: Routledge.
Boal, A. (2005) 'Interview with Juan Gonzalez', *Democracy Now*, 3 June. Retrieved 10 January 2014 from: http://www.democracynow.org/2005/6/3/famed_brazilian_artist_augusto_boal_on
Boje, D. M., Luhman, J. T. and Cunliffe A. L. (2003) 'A Dialectic Perspective on the Organisation Theatre Metaphor', *American Communication Journal* Vol. 6, No. 2, pp. 1–16.
Bolton, G. (1998). *Acting in Classroom Drama: A Critical Analysis*. Birmingham: Trentham Books.
Bourdieu, P. (1986) *Forms of Capital*. Retrieved 30 January 2015 from: https://www.marxists.org/reference/subject/philosophy/works/fr/bourdieu-forms-capital.htm
Bourdieu, P. and Passeron, J. (1990) *Reproduction in Education, Society and Culture*. London: Sage.
Bourriaud, N. (2002). *Relational Aesthetics* (Trans. Simon Pleasance and Fronza Woods). Paris: Les presses du réel.
Bourriaud, N. (2009) *Altermodern, Tate Triennial*. London: Tate Publishing.
Bradbrook, B. (2000) *'The Liberating Beauty of Little Things': Decision, Adversity & Reckoning in a Refugee's Journey from Prague to Cambridge*. London: Alpha Press.
Brecht, B. (1936/1964), *Brecht on Theatre* (Trans. John Willet). London: Methuen.
Bresler, L. (2013) 'Creative Approaches to Research', *Association for Qualitative Research* Vol. 6. no.1, pp. 4–5.
Bresler, L. (2007). *The International Handbook of Research in Arts Education*. Dordrecht: Springer.
Britzman, D. (2003). *Practice Makes Practice: A Critical Study of Learning to Teach*. New York: State University of New York Press.
Butler, J. (1990) *Gender Trouble*. London: Routledge.
Carr, W. and Hartnett, A. (2010) *Education and the Struggle for Democracy: The Politics of Educational Ideas*. Berkshire: Open University Press.
Chamberlain, O. (2014) *The Frodsham Goods Shed: An Evocative Report*, part submission for Master's Thesis, University of Chester, blurb.
Chamberlaine, L. (2010) Karel Capek, *New Statesman*, 14 October. Retrieved 26 January 2015 from: http://www.newstatesman.com/books/2010/10/karel-capek-world-life-czech
Chomsky, N. and Pappe, I. (2010) *Gaza in Crisis: Reflections on Israel's War against Palestine*. London: Hamish Hamilton.

Clark, T. (2008) 'Performing the Organization'. In D. Barry and H. Hansen (Eds) *New Approaches in Management and Organization* (pp. 401–411). London: Sage.

Clark, T. and Mangham, I. (2004a) 'From Dramaturgy to Theatre as Technology: The Case of Corporate Theatre', *Journal of Management Studies* Vol. 41, No. 1, pp. 37–59.

Clark, T. and Mangham, I. (2004b) 'Stripping to the Undercoat: A Review and Reflections on a Piece of Organization Theatre', *Organization Studies* Vol. 25, No. 5, pp. 841–851.

Combatants for Peace (2010) 'Theatre Protest at Shufa', 2 July. Retrieved from: https://www.youtube.com/watch?v=BA5tSkXg2G4

Council of Europe (2011) 'Annual Activity Report: Thomas Hammarberg, Commissioner for Human Rights of the Council of Europe'. Retrieved 4 November 2014 from: https://wcd.coe.int/ViewDoc.jsp?id=1895365

Craft, A. (2001) *Analysis of Research and Literature on Creativity in Education*. London: NACCCE.

Craft, A. and Jeffrey, B. (2008). 'Creativity and Performativity in Teaching and Learning: Tensions, Dilemmas, Constraints, Accommodations and Synthesis', *British Educational Research Journal* Vol. 34, No. 5, pp. 577–584.

Curtis, T. (2012) 'Toward an Ideology Critique of Social Entrepreneurship', *Academia.edu*. Retrieved 5 October 2014 from: http://www.academia.edu/2447125/Toward_an_Ideology_Critique_of_Social_Entrepreneurship.docx

Darsø, L., Meisiek, S. and Boje, D. (Eds) (2007) *Thin Book: Organisational Theatre, Learning Lab*. Frederiksberg: The Danish University of Education. Retrieved 5 January 2015 from: www.dpu.dk/thinbook

Delisle, G. (2012) *Jerusalem: Chronicles from the Holy City*. London: Jonathan Cape.

Department for Education. (2010) 'Improving the Outcomes for Gypsy, Roma and Traveller Pupils: Final Report'. Retrieved 30 April 2015 from: https://www.gov.uk/government/uploads/system/uploads/attachment_data/file/181669/DFE-RR043.pdf

Dewey, J. (1899/2008) *The School and Society*. New York: Cosimo Classics.

Dewey, J. (1916/1966) *Democracy and Education. An Introduction to the Philosophy of Education*. New York: Free Press.

Dewey, J. (1934) *Art as Experience*. Retrieved 30 January 2015 from: http://thenewschoolhistory.org/wp-content/uploads/2013/09/Dewey-ArtasExperience.pdf

Dewey, J. (1938/1969) *Experience and Education*. London: Collier-Macmillan.

Dostal, R. (2002) *The Cambridge Companion to Gadamer*. Cambridge: Cambridge University Press.

Drain, R. (Ed.) (1995). *Twentieth Century Theatre: A Source Book*. London: Routledge.

DTI (Department of Trade and Industry) (2002) *Social Enterprise: A Strategy for Success*. London: UK Department of Trade and Industry. Retrieved 30 January 2015 from: http://www.seeewiki.co.uk/~wiki/images/5/5a/SE_Strategy_for_success.pdf

Dunbar, P. L. (1899) 'Sympathy'. Retrieved 30 April 2015 from: http://www.potw.org/archive/potw219.html

Eakin, E. (2001). *Homi Bhabha: Harvard's Prize Catch*, 17 November. Retrieved 30 January 2015 from: http://www.csudh.edu/dearhabermas/bhabhabk01.htm

Eriksson, S. (2014) 'Exploring Distancing in the Work of Dorothy Heathcote: Estrangement as Poetic Distortion', *Drama Research: International Journal of Drama in*

Education Vol 5, No. 1. Retrieved 15 January 2015 from: http://www.dramaresearch.co.uk/journal/index.cfm/linkservid/13E4023A-CC8B-8A1F-12B229BC1B8D28D0/showMeta/0/

Evans, B., Richmond, T. and Shields, J. (2005) 'Structuring Neoliberal Governance: The Nonprofit Sector, Emerging New Modes of Control and the Marketization of Service Delivery', *Policy and Society* Vol. 24, No. 1, pp. 73–97. Retrieved 15 January 2015 from: http://www.sciencedirect.com/science/article/pii/S1449403505700503

Fannes, P. (2013) 'The Concept of Creativity in Education Discourse: A Historical Approach', conference paper, European Conference for Education Research (ECER), September, Istanbul, paper 804.

Fleming, M. (2001). *Teaching Drama in Primary and Secondary Schools*. London: David Fulton Publishers.

Foucault, M. (1967/2002). *Madness and Civilisation: A History of Insanity in the Age of Reason* (Trans. R. Howard). London: Routledge.

Freedom Theatre (2015) *Freedom Theatre, Jenin: Our Mission*. Retrieved 23 January 2015 from: http://www.thefreedomtheatre.org/who-we-are/mission/

Freire, P. (1970/2006) *Pedagogy of the Oppressed* (Trans. Myra Bergman Ramos). London: Continuum.

Freire, P. (1998). *Teachers as Cultural Workers* (Trans. D. Macedo). Oxford: Westview Press.

Gallagher, K. (2000). *Drama Education in the Lives of Girls: Imagining Possibilities*. Toronto: University of Toronto Press.

Gallagher, K. & Ntelioglou B.Y. (2013) 'On the Pedagogical Importance of (not) Knowing the Other: Listening, Risk, Drama and Difference'. In M. Anderson and J. Dunn (Eds) *How Drama Activates Learning: Contemporary Research and Practice* (pp. 94–108). London: Continuum, Bloomsbury Academic.

Gallagher, K. and Rivierre, D. (2007). 'When Drama praxis Rocks the Boat: Struggles of Subjectivity, Audience and Performance', *Research in Drama Education* Vol.12, No. 3, pp 319–330.

Garratt, D. and Piper H. (2008) *Citizenship Education, Identity and Nationhood – Contradictions in Practice*. London: Continuum.

Geertz, C. (2000). *Local Knowledge: Further Essays in Interpretive Anthropology*, 3rd edn. New York: Basic Books

Gergen, K. (2009) *Relational Being*. New York: Oxford University Press.

Gibb, C. (2012) 'Room 13: The Movement and International Network', *International Journal of Art and Design Education* Vol. 31, No. 3, pp. 237–244.

Gibson, L. and Stevenson, D. (Eds) (2004) 'Special Issue: Urban Space and the Uses of Culture', *International Journal of Cultural Policy* Vol. 10, No. 1.

Giddens, A. (2000) *The Third Way and its Critics*. London: Polity.

Gielen, P. (2011) *Mapping Community Arts: Subversion, Repressive Tolerance and Pastoral Power*, Public Lecture, 8 November, New York. Retrieved 12 Jan 2015 from: https://soundcloud.com/newgray/pascal-gielen-public-lecture-8;

Gielen, P. (2013) *Creativity and other Fundamentalisms*. Heijningen: Japan Books.

Gielen, P. and De Bruyne, P. (2012) 'A Plea for Communalist Teaching: An Interview with Richard Sennett'. In P. Gielen and P. De Bruyne (Eds), *Teaching Art in the Neoliberal Realm* (pp. 33–47). Amsterdam: Antennae Valiz.

Giroux, H. (2014a) *Neoliberalism and the Machinery of Disposability*. Retrieved 12 January 2015 from: http://philosophersforchange.org/2014/04/15/neoliberalism-and-the-machinery-of-disposability/

Giroux, H. (2014b) *Neoliberalism's War on Democracy*. Retrieved 12 January 2015 from: http://www.truth-out.org/opinion/item/23306-neoliberalisms-war-on-democracy

Gluck, C. and Sharpe, M. (Eds) (1998). *Asia in Western and World History: A Guide for Teaching*. New York: Sharpe.

Goffman, E. (1974) *Frame Analysis: An Essay on the Organization of Experience*, London: Harper and Row.

Gonnami, T. (1998). *Images of Foreigners in Edo Period Maps and Prints*. Retrieved 4 October 2005 from: Patriot.lib.byu.edu/ERastAsianLibraries/image/6713152132008_1266224

Gray, N. (1991). 'The Kaleidoscope: Shake, Rattle, and Roll', *The Australian Journal of Media and Culture* Vol. 6, No. 2, pp. 317–320. Retrieved 30 January 2015 from: http//wwwmcc.murdoch.edu.au/Reading

Greenberg, C. (1960) *Modernist Painting*. Retrieved 12 January 2015 from: http://cas.uchicago.edu/workshops/wittgenstein/files/2007/10/Greenbergmodpaint.pdf

Grenfell, M. and Hardy, C. (2007) *Art Rules: Pierre Bourdieu and the Visual Arts*. Oxford: Berg.

Guibert, E., Lefevre, D. and Lemercier, F. (2008) *The Photographer*. London: First Second.

Hall, S. (2011) 'The Neo-Liberal Revolution', *Cultural Studies* Vol. 25, No. 6, pp. 705–728.

Hester, J. T. (2008) *Karel Capek, Author of the Apocryphal Tales: A Study of Genre and the Capekian*, MA thesis, North Carolina State University.

Hewitt, A. (2011) 'Privatizing the Public: Three Rhetorics of Art's Public Good in "Third Way" Cultural Policy'. *Art and the Public Sphere* Vol. 1, No. 1, pp. 19–36.

Hewitt, A. (2012) *Art and Counter-Publics in Third Way Cultural Policy*, PhD thesis, University of the Arts London. Retrieved 12 Jan 2015 from: http://ualresearchonline.arts.ac.uk/5679/

Holtham, C., Ward, V. and Owens, A. (2010). *Slow Knowledge Work – Designing Space and Learning*. Retrieved 10 January 2015 from: http://www.sparknow.net/pace-publications.html

hooks, b. (1994). *Outlaw Culture: Resisting Representations*. New York: Routledge.

H. M. Government (2012) *Challenge it, Report it, Stop it: The Government's Plan to Tackle Hate Crime*. Retrieved 30 April 2015 from: https://www.gov.uk/government/uploads/system/uploads/attachment_data/file/97849/action-plan.pdf

Huizinga, J. (1944/1949). *Homo ludens; a Study of the Play-Element in Culture*. Retrieved 12 January 2015 from: http://art.yale.edu/file_columns/0000/1474/homo_ludens_johan_huizinga_routledge_1949_.pdf

Inglis, F. (2005). *Methods and Morality: How to Keep the Human in the Human Science*. London: Sage.

Jackson, T. and Vine, C. (2013) *Learning through Theatre: The Changing Face of Theatre in Education*. Oxford: Routledge.

jagodzinski, j. (2010) *Visual Art and Designer Education in an Era of Designer Capitalism: Deconstructing the Oral Eye*. New York: Palgrave Macmillan.

Jewish Voice for Peace (2015) 'The Incredible Shrinking Palestine: A Brief History', *Jewish Voice for Peace-Chicago*. Retrieved 22 January 2015 from: http://jvpchicago.org/resources/brief-history

Johnson, D. (2014) 'His Sin? Wanting to Make Children Learn', *Daily Mail Online*, 15 July. Retrieved 30 January 2015 from: http://www.dailymail.co.uk/news/article-2693678/DANIEL-JOHNSON-His-sin-wanting-make-children-learn.html

Johnstone, W. (1941) *Child Art to Man Art*. London: Macmillan.

Jones, K. (2009) *Culture and Creative Learning*. London: Arts Council England, Creative Partnerships Literature Reviews.

Jones, K. (2012) 'Power, Democracy – and Democracy in Education', *Forum* Vol. 54, No. 2, pp. 205–214.

Kasikova, H. and Valenta, J. (2011) 'Educational Strategies Based on Conflict in Intercultural Education', *PEDAGOGIJSKA istrazivanja* Vol. 8, No. 1, pp. 37–51.

Kellman, D. (2009) *Stories of Significance: An Investigation in to the Construction of Social Meaning in Young People's Dramatized Stories*, PhD Thesis, University of Melbourne, unpublished.

Kenworthy, L. (2014) 'America's Social Democratic Future: The Arc of Policy Is Long but Bends toward Justice', *Foreign Affairs* Vol. 93, No. 1. Retrieved on 14 January 2015 from: http://www.foreignaffairs.com/articles/140345/lane-kenworthy/americas-social-democratic-future

Kershaw, B. (1992) *The Politics of Performance: Radical Theatre as Cultural Intervention*. Oxford: Routledge.

Khalidi, I. and Marlowe, J. (2011) 'Remembering Juliano Mer-Khamis', *The Nation*, 11 April. Retrieved 30 Jan 2015 from: http://www.thenation.com/article/159842/remembering-juliano-mer-khamis

Korhonen, J. (2012) 'The crumbling of Finland's consensus culture: silence into rumpus', *Open Democracy*, 30th November. Retrieved 12 January 2015 from https://www.opendemocracy.net/johanna-korhonen/crumbling-of-finland%E2%80%99s-consensus-culture-silence-into-rumpus

Korhonen, P. and Airaksinen, R. (Eds) (2014) *Hyva Hankaus 2.0*. Helsinki: Draamatayo.

Lakoff, G. and Johnson, M. (2003). *Metaphors We Live By*. Chicago: University of Chicago Press.

Landy, C. (2015) Creative Cities. Retrieved 15 June 2015 from: http://charleslandry.com/themes/making-great-cities/

Lave, J. and Wenger, E. (1991). *Situated Learning: Legitimate Peripheral Participation*. Cambridge: Cambridge University Press.

Lehikoinen, K. (2013). 'Artistic Interventions as a Strand of Artistic Research', *The Impact of Performance as Research: CARPA3 Proceedings*. Retrieved 20 January 2015 from: http://nivel.teak.fi/carpa/artistic-interventions-as-a-strand-of-artistic-research

Lemov, D. (2010) *Teach Like a Champion: 49 Techniques that Put Students on the Path to College*. San Francisco, CA: Jossey-Bass. Retrieved 14 October 2014 from: https://dese.mo.gov/sites/default/files/11-Research-ProvenPracticesTLAC.pdf

Lingis, A. (1994). *The Community of Those Who Have Nothing in Common*. Bloomington: Indiana University Press.

Lingis, A. (1995) *Abuses*. Berkeley: University of California Press.

Liverpool Biennial (2012). Retrieved 30 January 2015 from: http://liverpoolbiennial.co.uk/whatson/current/all/528/oslo-palestinian-embassy/

MacDonald, L. (2015) *Curriculum Reform in Japan: Reflections of Cultural Change via the Integrated Curriculum.* Retrieved 15 June 2015 from: http://www.p.u-tokyo.ac.jp/coe/workingpaper/Vol.18.pdf

Mannermaa, M. (2007) *Democracy in the Turmoil of the Future: Societal Influence within a New Frame of Reference*, Committee for the Future, Eduskunta, Parliament of Finland (Original work in Finnish: *Demokratia tulevaisuuden myllerryksessä*). Retrieved 13 January 2015 from: http://web.eduskunta.fi/dman/Document.phx?documentId=rs17607151840242

Matthews, J. (2003) *Drawing and Painting: Children and Visual Representation.* London: Paul Chapman.

McCaughrean, G. (2001) *The Kite Rider.* Oxford: Oxford University Press.

McDonnell, J. (2014) 'Reimagining the Role of Art in the Relationship between Democracy and Education', *Educational Philosophy and Theory* Vol. 46, No. 1, pp. 46–58.

Meisiek, S. (2002) 'Situation Drama in Change Management: Types and Effects of a New Managerial Tool', *International Journal of Arts Management* Vol. 4, pp. 48–55.

Meisiek, S. (2004) 'Which Catharsis Do They Mean? Aristotle, Moreno, Boal and Organizational Theatre', *Organization Studies* Vol. 25, No. 5, pp. 797–816.

Meisiek, S. and Barry, D. (2007) 'Through the Looking Glass of Organizational Theatre: Analogically Mediated Inquiry in Organizations', *Organization Studies* Vol. 28, pp. 1805–1827.

Meisiek, S. and Barry, D. (2014) 'Theorizing the Field of Arts and Management', *Scandinavian Journal of Management* Vol. 30, No. 1, pp. 83–85.

Melkas, H. and Haarmaakorpi, V. (2012) *Practise-Based Innovation: Insights, Applications and Policy Implications.* Heidelberg: Springer Press.

Meyer, H. and Benavot, A. (Eds) (2013) *PISA, Power, and Policy.* Oxford: Symposium.

Mill, J.S. (1859) *On Liberty.* London: John W. Parker & Son.

MEC (Ministry of Education and Culture) (2010) *Ministry of Education and Culture Strategy 2020.* Helsinki: Ministry of Education and Culture Publications. Retrieved on 12 January 2015 from: http://www.minedu.fi/export/sites/default/OPM/Julkaisut/2010/liitteet/EDU06.pdf?lang=en

MEC (Ministry of Education and Culture Finland) (2014) 'Art and Culture for Well-Being – Proposal for and Action Program'. Retrieved 12 January 2015 from: http://culture360.asef.org/organisation/ministry-of-education-and-culture-finland/

Ministry of Education, Culture, Sport, Science and Technology (2005) *Japan's Education at a Glance.* Retrieved 30 January 2015 from: http://www.mext.go.jp/english/statist/05101901.htm

Ministry of Education and Higher Education. (2014) *A Learning Nation, Summary of Education Development Strategic Plan 2014–2019*, Directorate General of Planning, Ministry of Education and Higher Education Palestine. Retrieved 15 December 2014 from: http://planipolis.iiep.unesco.org/upload/Palestine/Palestine_Education_development_strategic_plan_2014_2019_summary.pdf

Mouffe, C. (2005) *The Return of the Political.* London: Verso

Mouffe, C. (2007) 'Artistic Activism and Agonistic Spaces', *Art and Research* Vol. 1, No. 2. Retrieved 13 January 2015 from http://www.artandresearch.org.uk/v1n2/mouffe.html

Mouffe, C. (2009) *The Democratic Paradox*. New York: Verso
NACCCE (National Advisory Committee on Creative and Cultural Education) (1999) *All our Futures: Culture, Creativity and Education*. Suffolk: DfES.
National Centre for Culture and Arts (2015) National Centre for Culture and the Arts, King Hussein Foundation, Jordan. Retrieved 30 January 2015 from: http://www.kinghusseinfoundation.org/index.php?pager=end&task=view&type=content&pageid=40
Nealon, J. T. (2004) *Foucault Beyond Foucault: Power and its Intensifications Since 1984*. Stanford, CA: Stanford University Press.
Neelands, J. (1990). *Structuring Drama Work: A Handbook of Available Forms in Theatre and Drama*. Cambridge: Cambridge University Press.
Neelands, J. (1992) *Learning through Imagined Experience*. London: Hodder & Stoughton.
Neelands, J. (2002) '11/09: The Space in our Hearts', *Drama Magazine*, Summer, pp. 4–11.
Neelands, J. (2004). 'Miracles Are Happening: Beyond the Rhetoric of Transformation in the Western Traditions of Drama Education', *Research in Drama Education* Vol. 9, No. 1, pp. 47–56.
Neelands, J. (2009) 'Acting Together: Ensemble as a Democratic Process in Art and Life', *Research in Drama Education: The Journal of Applied Theatre and Performance* Vol. 14, No. 2, pp. 173–189.
Neill, A. S. (1962/1976). *Summerhill*. Middlesex: Penguin.
Nelson, C. (2013) 'Creativity, Genealogy, Capitalism', conference paper, European Conference for Education Research (ECER), September, Istanbul, paper no. 2751.
Nicholson, H. (2005). *Applied Drama: The Gift of Theatre*. Basingstoke: Palgrave Macmillan.
Oldenburg, R. (1989) *The Great Good Place: Cafes, Coffee Shops, Community Centers, Beauty Parlors, General Stores, Bars, Hangouts, and How They Get You through the Day*. New York: Paragon House.
Olsson, G. (2007) *Abysmal: A Critique of Cartographic Reason*. Chicago: University of Chicago Press.
O'Neill, C. (1995). *Drama Worlds*. Portsmouth: Heinemann.
Ostern, A. L. (2001). 'Drama and Theatre as Arts Education'. In H. Aaaltonen and A. L. Ostern (Eds) *Organising Young People's Dramatic Practices* (pp. 11–25). Jyvaskyla: Jyvaskylan Yliopistopaino Press.
Owens, A. (1997). *Report on the Development of Children's Thinking Skills through Drama*, Palestinian National Authority DFID Education Project, The British Council. ISO9002.
Owens, A. (2005) 'Planning for the Possibilities of Dissensus'. In P. Korhonen and R. Airaksinen (Eds) *Hyva Hankaus* (pp. 9–15). Helsinki: Draamatayo.
Owens, A. (2014) 'Translating and Understanding: Pre-Text Based Drama'. In P. Korhonen and R. Airaksinen (Eds) *Hyva Hankaus 2.0* (pp. 45–68). Helsinki: Draamatayo.
Owens, A. and Al Yamani, H. (2010) 'Returning to Haifa: Using Pre-Text Based Drama to Understand Self and Other'. In J. Freeman (Ed.) *Blood Sweat and Theory: Research through Practice in Performance* (pp. 9–22). Middlesex: Libri.
Owens, A. and Green, N. (2010). *Applied Drama: Communication through Pre-Texts*. Tokyo: Toshabunka.

Owens, A. and Pickford, B. (2014) *Developing Understandings of Gypsy Traveller Culture*, (DVD/CD-ROM) Chester: University of Chester Press.

Oxford English Dictionary (1998) Vol. 7. Oxford: Clarendon Press.

Pappe, I. (2007) *The Ethnic Cleansing of Palestine*, Oxford: Oneworld Publications.

Pappe, I. (2014) 'Interview with Ilan Pappe – Dag Holmboe,' *The White Review*, 21 July, Arts Council England. Retrieved 5 January 2015 from: http://www.thewhitereview.org/poetry/interview/interview-with-ilan-pappe/

Pappe, I. (2015) *The Biggest Prison on Earth: A History of the Occupied Territories*. Oxford: Oneworld.

Pässilä, A. (2012) *Reflexive Model of Research-Based Theatre – Processing Innovation at the Crossroads of Theatre, Reflection and Practice-Based Innovation Activities*, Acta Universitatis Lappeenrantaensis 492. Lappeenranta: Lappeenranta University Press. Retrieved 30 January 2015 from: http://www.doria.fi/bitstream/handle/10024/86216/isbn%209789522653222.pdf

Pässilä, A. and Oikarinen, T. (2014) 'Research-Based Theatre as a Facilitator for Organisational Learning'. In P. Meusburger, A. Berthoin Antal and L. Suarsana (Eds), *Learning Organizations: Extending the Field* (pp. 203–221). Dordrecht: Springer Verlag.

Pässilä, A. Oikarinen, T. and Harmmkorpi, V. (2013) 'Collective Voicing as a Reflexive Practice'. *Management Learning* Vol. 44, No. 4, pp. 42–52.

Pässilä, A., Oikarinen, T. and Kallio, A. (2013) 'Creating Dialogue by Storytelling', *Journal of Workplace Learning* Vol. 25, No. 3, pp. 159–177.

Pässilä, A., Oikarinen, T. and Harmaakorpi, V. (2013) 'Collective Voicing as Reflexive Practice', *Management Learning* Vol. 44, No. 5, pp. 1–20. Retrieved 9 January 2015 from http://mlq.sagepub.com/content/early/2013/06/26/1350507613488310

Pässilä, A., Oikarinen, T., Parjanen, S. and Harmaakorpi, V. (2013) 'Interpretative Dimension of User-Driven Service Innovation: Forum Theatre in Facilitating Renewal in Finnish Public Health Care', *Baltic Journal of Management* Vol. 8 No. 2, pp. 166–182.

Pässilä, A., Owens, A. and Chamberlain, O. (2014) *Evocative Report: Goods Shed* (film). Retrieved 30 January 2015 from: https://www.youtube.com/watch?v=QTCjLFUowww&feature=youtu.be

Paterson, K. (1989). *The Spying Heart: More Thoughts on Reading and Writing Books for Children*. New York: Dutton.

Perry, G. (2014) 'In the Best Possible Taste', Channel 4. Retrieved 11 January 2015 from: http://www.channel4.com/programmes/in-the-best-possible-taste-grayson-perry

PNN (2014) *Alrowwad Center Offers Alternative Education to the Children Affected by the UNRWA Strike*, Palestinian News Network. Retrieved 6 February 2014 from: http://english.pnn.ps/index.php/tv/6844-alrowwad-center-offers-alternative-education-to-the-children-affected-by-the-unrwa-strike

Rancière, J. (1991) *The Ignorant Schoolmaster: Five Lessons in Intellectual Emancipation* (Trans. Kristin Ross). Stanford, CA: Stanford University Press.

Rancière, J. (2004) *The Politics of Aesthetics: The Distribution of the Sensible* (Trans. Gabriel Rockhill). London: Continuum.

Rancière, J. (2010a) 'On Ignorant Schoolmasters', In C. Bingham and G. Biesta (Eds) *Jacques Rancière, Education, Truth, Emancipation* (pp. 1–24). London: Continuum.

Rancière, J. (2010b) *The Emancipated Spectator*. London: Verso.
Rancière, J. (2011) *Dissensus: On Politics and Aesthetics*. London: Continuum.
Rania, J. (2013) *Theatre Encounters: A Politics of Performance in Palestine*. PQTD Open, New York University, 280; 3557005. Retrieved 30 January 2015 from: http://pqdtopen.proquest.com/pqdtopen/doc/1334957153.html?FMT=ABS
Read, H. (1943/1970) *Education through Art*. London: Faber & Faber.
Richardson, J. and Ryder, A. (2012) *Gypsies and Travellers: Empowerment and Inclusion in British Society*. Bristol: Policy Press.
Ricoeur, P. (2003). *The Rule of Metaphor. The Creation of Meaning in Language* (Trans. R. Czerny, K. McLauglin and S. Coatello). London: Routledge.
Roberts, T. (2008) 'What's Going On in Room 13?', *Art Education* Vol. 61, No. 5, pp. 19–24.
Robinson, K. (2011) *Out of Our Minds: Learning to be Creative*. Chichester: Capstone.
Room 13 (2015) *Room 13 International Community of Creatives*. Retrieved 30 January 2015 from http://room13international.org/
Room13/ZCZ Films for Channel 4 (2004). *What Age Can You Start Being an Artist?*, January. UK: Channel 4 Television.
RSA (2014) 'Mission'. Retrieved 30 January 2015 from: http://www.thersa.org/about-us/mission
Sacco, Joe (2001) *Palestine*. Seattle, WA: Fantagraphics Books.
Said, E. (1978) *Orientalism*. New York: Vintage.
Said, E. (1993) *Edward Said: Representation of the Intellectual*, Reith Lectures 2013, BBC Radio 4. Retrieved 30 January 2015 from: http://www.bbc.co.uk/podcasts/series/rla76/all
Saito, N. and Imai, Y. (2004). 'In Search of the Public and the Private: Philosophy of Education in Post-War Japan', *Comparative Education* Vol. 40, No. 4, pp. 583–594.
Sauter, W. (2000) *The Theatrical Event: Dynamics of Performance and Perception*. Des Moines: University of Iowa Press.
Schechner, R. (2002) *Performance Studies: An Introduction*. London: Routledge.
Scheyogg, G. and Hopfl, H. (2004) Special Issue. *Theatre and Organization Studies* Vol. 15, No. 5, pp. 42–52.
Schiuma, G. (2011) *The Value of Arts for Business*. Cambridge: Cambridge University Press.
Schratz, M. and Walker, R. (1995) *Research as Social Change*. London: Routledge.
Segal, R. and Weizman, E. 2003. *A Civilian Occupation: The Politics of Israeli Architecture*. Tel Aviv: Babel/Verso.
Sennett, R. (1998) *The Corrosion of Character: The Personal Consequences of Work in the New Capitalism*. New York: W.W. Norton.
Sherwood, H. (2013) 'Israeli and Palestinian Textbooks Omit Borders: Schoolchildren Grow Up Believing One Homeland Does Not Include the Other as Majority of Maps Erase Dividing Lines', *The Guardian*, 4 February. Retrieved on 10 January 2015 from: http://www.theguardian.com/world/2013/feb/04/israeli-palestinian-textbooks-borders
Simons, M. and Masschelein, J. (2012) 'School – a Matter of Form'. In P. Gielen and P. De Bruyne (Eds) *Teaching Art in the Neoliberal Realm* (pp. 69–83). Amsterdam: Antennae Valiz.

Smith, R. (2011) 'Interview: Raja Khalidi on the Neoliberal Consensus in Palestine', *Electroni Intifada*. Retrieved 30 January 2015 from: http://electronicintifada.net/content/interview-raja-khalidi-neoliberal-consensus-palestine/9870

Smyth, J. (2004) 'Social Capital and the "Socially Just School"', *British Journal of Sociology of Education* Vol. 25, No. 1, pp. 19–33.

Spiegelman, A. (2003) *The Complete Maus*. New York: Penguin.

Sproedt, H. (2012) *Play, Learn and Innovate*. Kolding: Books on Demand.

Stake, R. (1995) *The Art of Case Study Research*. Thousand Oaks, CA: Sage.

Steiner, G. (1998). *After Babel: Aspects of Language and Translation*, 3rd edn. Oxford: Oxford University Press.

Tamari, V. (2005) Interview, Wednesday, May 11. Retrieved 1 November 2014 from: http://www.motherjones.com/media/2005/05/interview-vera-tamari

Taylor, M. (2014) 'There Is Now Space for Future Narratives', *RSA Journal* Vol. 2, pp. 42–52.

Taylor, S.S. and Ladkin, D. (2009) 'Understanding Arts-Based Methods in Managerial Development', *Academy of Management Learning and Education* Vol. 8, No. 1, pp. 55–69.

Teasdale, S. (2011) 'What's in a Name? Making Sense of Social Enterprise Discourses', Working Paper 46, 6 September 2010, Third Sector Research Centre. Retrieved 23 January 2015 from: http://www.birmingham.ac.uk/generic/tsrc/documents/tsrc/working-papers/working-paper-46.pdf

Theatre Pa'tothom (2015) *Amina's Looking for a Job (Amina busca feina)*. Retrieved from http://dspace.mah.se/bitstream/handle/2043/8618/?sequence=1

Thompson, J. and Schechner, R. (2004) 'Why Social Theatre?', *The Drama Review* Vol. 48, No. 3, pp. 11–16.

Tolan, S. (2006) 'The Incredible Shrinking Palestine', *Los Angeles Times*, 21 May. Retrieved 22 January 2015 from: http://articles.latimes.com/2006/may/21/opinion/op-tolan21

Tomlinson, B. and Lipsitz, G. (2013) 'Insubordinate Spaces for Intemperate Times: Countering the Pedagogies of Neoliberalism', *The Review of Education, Pedagogy, and Cultural Studies* Vol. 35, No. 3, pp. 3–26.

Tyler, I. (2013) *Revolting Subjects: Social Abjection and Resistance in Neoliberal Britain*. London: Zed Books.

Valentine, G. and McDonald, I. (2003) *Understanding Prejudice: Attitudes towards Minorities*. London: Stonewall. Retrieved on 10 December 2014 from: http://www.stonewall.org.uk/documents/pdf_cover__content.pdf

Verhaeghe, P. (2014) 'Neoliberalism Has Brought Out the Worst in Us: An Economic System that Rewards Psychopathic Personality Traits Has Changed Our Ethics and Our Personalities', *The Guardian*, 29 September. Retrieved 30 January 2015 from: http://www.theguardian.com/commentisfree/2014/sep/29/neoliberalism-economic-system-ethics-personality-psychopathicsthic

Vygotsky, L. (1933) *Play and its Role in the Mental Development of the Child*. Retrieved 30 January 2015 from: http://www.marxists.org/archive/vygotsky/works/1933/play.htm

Vygotsky, L.S. (1930/2014) 'Imagination and Creativity in Childhood' (Trans. M.E. Sharpe), *Journal of Russian and East European Psychology* Vol. 42, No. 1, pp. 7–97. Retrieved 30 January 2015 from: http://lchc.ucsd.edu/mca/Mail/xmcamail.2007_08.dir/att-0149/LSV__1967_2004_._Imagination_and_creativity_in_childhood.pdf

Weale, S. (2014) 'One to Watch: American Who Wrote the Latest Classroom Bible', *The Guardian*, 13 October, p. 12.
Wenger, E. (2005) *Communities of Practice: Learning Meaning and Identity*. Cambridge: Cambridge University Press.
Western Edge Youth Arts (2008) *The Government Project: A Research Report in to a Western Edge, Youth Arts Project at Kensington Primary School, 2008*. Retrieved 13 January 2015 from: http://www.westernedge.org.au/WEYA-at-school/
Willet, J. (2001) (Ed.) *Brecht on Theatre: The Development of an Aesthetic*. Berkshire: Methuen.
Williams, R. (1961) *The Long Revolution*. London: Pelican.
Williams, R. (1976/1984) *Keywords*. London: Fontana.
Williams, R. (1983) *Towards 2000*. London: Chatto and Windus.
Willis, P. E. (1977). *Learning to Labour. How Working Class Kids Get Working Class Jobs*. Guildford: Gower Publishing.
Winner, E., Goldstein, T. and Vincent-Lacrin, S. (2013) *Art for Arts Sake: The Impact of Arts Education*, Centre for Educational Research and Innovation: OECD. Retrieved 16 January 2015 from http://www.keepeek.com/Digital-Asset-Management/oecd/education/art-for-art-s-sake_9789264180789-en#page8
Wolfwoo, T. (2014) *Together for the One Democratic State*, ODS Report. Retrieved 30 January 2015 from: http://www.bbcf.ca/_articles/together_odg.pdf
World Data on Education V11 Edition (2011), Palestine, ESCO, United Nations, BE/2011/CP/WDE/PS. Retrieved 30 January 2015 from: http://www.ibe.unesco.org/fileadmin/user_upload/Publications/WDE/2010/pdf-versions/Palestine.pdf
Zizek, S. (1999) *The Thing from Inner Space*. Retrieved 30 January 2015 from: http://www.lacan.com/zizekthing.htm
Zizek, S. (2007) 'Tolerance as an Ideological Category', *Critical Inquiry*, Autumn. Retrieved 30 January 2015 from: http://www.lacan.com/zizek-inquiry.html#_ftnref13
Zizek, S. (2013) 'Trouble in Paradise', *London Review of Books* Vol. 35, No. 14, pp. 11–12.

Index

Acemoglu, D. 112
Adams, J. 34; Teaching through Contemporary Art project 32
aesthetics 34; Boalian theatre technique 37; and formalism 23, 25; process drama 38
agonism/antagonism 3, 10–2, 20, 39, 82, 113
Aida refugee camp 18, 49
Aitkin, V. 59
Al Hara Theatre 50
Al Rowwad Cultural and Theatre Society 18, 49, 50
Al Yamani, H. 44, 50; equality 46; traditional 45; value of education 46–7
'Amina's Looking for a Job' 30
Angelou, M.: *I Know Why the Caged Bird Sings* 55
Anthony, T.: 'Da Kink in My Hair' 36
Apple, M. 15
applied drama in Japan 81–7
Arena Theatre 26
arts-based initiatives in organisations in Finland and the UK 109–19; Anglo-Finnish cultural and political context 112–14; arts 115–16; case study 119–34; fictionalising the real 118–19; innovation and creativity 110–2; turn to learning 114–15
arts education 13, 62, 63, 70, 79
arts in organisations: and business 115–16; claims and critique 116–18
Ashtar Theatre 50
Atkinson, D. 79; Teaching through Contemporary Art project 32
Australia 36, 38
Az Theatre 50

Bab al Shams 6, 29
balance 39
Banksy 33
Barakat, H. 46
Bauman, Z. 81–2, 96
beauty, liberating 135–7
Bedouins 46–7, 97, 98
Benavot, A. 13
Benetton 6
Bernstein, B. 79–80
Bhabha, H. 61; fixity 91; quilts of confluences and influences 100; right to narrate 52; Third Space 37–8, 108
'The Bird in the Cage' 53
Bishop, C. 26
Boal, A. 26, 37, 51, 107
Bolton, G. 51
Bourdieu, P.: artwork 79; inequalities 8; habitus 63, 65
Bourriaud, N. 22, 25–6, 32; *Relational Aesthetics* 24
Bradbook, B.: *The Liberating Beauty of Little Things* 136
Brecht, B. 57, 102, 119
Brewster, D. 102
British Academy 45
Butler, J. 31

Canada 38
Caol Primary School 67, 70, 71, 72
Carr, W. 9, 18
CfP 30
Chamberlain, O. 123
collaboration 2, 3, 32, 33, 45, 50, 71–2, 74, 111, 131; process and research methods 121–3
'Combatants for Peace' 30
comics and graphic novels 137–9

conformist education systems 16–21; critical creativity 19–21
contemporary art 3, 12, 22–3, 24, 25, 32, 62, 67, 70; teaching through 32–6
conversation 75, 76, 80; dialogic 32
Craft, A. 5–6
creative interventions 97–108; drama education, identity and democracy 100–6; Gypsy Roma Traveller culture 97–9; metaphor of the kaleidoscope 101–3; Michael's story 106–8; pretext and process drama research methodologies 103–5; pretext-based process drama 100–1; translating and understanding in action 105–6
creative pedagogies 41–61; dangerous and domesticated practice of creativity and democracy 47–52; drama pretext 52–61; dramaturgical form in case study 51–2; dramaturgy in non-formal and formal education 49–51; educational and cultural context 45–7; political context 41–7; present and future 61
creative pedagogies, contemporary 81–96; applied drama in Japan 81–7; creativity 81–3; dreamer case study 87–96; dreamer pretext 88–9; dreamer synopsis 89–90; emancipation and the dramaturgical form: applied drama 86–7; emergent issues 90–5; Japanese context: relationship between education and creativity 83–5; relationship between art and politics 85–6
creativity: definition 5
creativity and democratic education theories 5–21; democracy and equality in education 7–9; disruptive democracy 9–13; measuring, calibrating, and segregating 13–16; tensions in conformist education systems 16–21; themes of creativity and democracy 5–9
critical creativity 19–21, 61, 137
critical education see Giroux
cultural traditions 53
cultural: understanding 3, 51, 82, 93, 97–100, 102, 104–5, 109; difference 20
culture 12, 20, 74, 136; Arab 51; audit 15; consensus 113; contemporary 62; creativity 111, 133; Gypsy Roma Traveller culture 97–9, 100, 107; institutional 79; itinerant 98; marginalised 25, 103; micro- 7, 49; organisational 110; relationships between teaches and students 37; secular 23; students 66, 67; studio 73; sub- 67; traditional 85, 90; UK 35, 82, 112; whole 82
Curtis, T. 121
Czech Republic 135–7

Darsø, L. 116–17, 132
Dash, P.: Teaching through Contemporary Art project 32
Deleuze, G. 6
Delisle, G.: *Jerusalem* 137
democratic education 5–21; Dewey experience 62–5; forms of 62–7; learning 62–80; learning through art practice: Room 13 67–72; pedagogy 72–5, 75–80; progressive 3, 21, 62–5, 67, 70, 109, 112
democratic practices 3, 4, 14, 39, 51, 65, 139
democratic revolution 2, 139
democratic society 17, 65, 98
democratic space 66
democratic thinking 3
democratic trends in the politics of creativity and innovation 109–34; arts-based initiatives in organisations in Finland and the UK 109–19
Department for International Development (DfID) 45
Dewey, J. 2, 136; democratic and progressive education 3, 21, 62–5, 67, 70, 109, 112; education resemble democracy 21; experience 62–5, 75, 77; *Experience and Education* 63; habits 65–6, 77
dialogue 26, 37
Dijkstra, R. 36
disruptive democracy 9–13; creativity under the global governance of education 12–13
Dunbar, P. L.: 'Sympathy' 55
drama pretext 7, 31, 52, 55–6, 59, 87–90, 94–5, 97–108

educational practices 2–3; dangerous and domesticated practice of creativity and democracy 47–52; democratic

learning through art: Room 13 67–72; relational creativity 27–31; socially engaged art 117–18
educational research: pretext and process drama methodologies 103–5; process and research methods 121–3
emancipation 9, 86–7
equality 6, 7–9, 17, 21, 31, 35, 139; Al Yamani 46; identity 82; intellectual 85; learning space questions 37; Rancière 7, 46, 71, 80, 85, 100; Smith 48; socialist 113; *see also* inequality
Evans, B. 120
evocative reporting 122, 123–6, 127, 128, 130, 131, 132
experiential democratic learning 68

Fairley, Rob 68, 69, 70, 71, 72–3
Fanon, F. 37–8
Finland 121; Anglo-Finnish cultural and political context 112–14; arts-based initiatives in organisations 109–19; Goods Shed 109–10; liberal democracy 109
fixity 91, 93–4
Fleming, M. 51
Folk High Schools 68
formalism 24; aesthetics 23, 25
Forn de Teatre Pa'tothom 30
Freedom Theatre 49, 50
Freire, P. 26, 85–6
Frodsham Foundation 119–20

Gadamer, H-G. 105, 108
Gallagher, K. 36, 37
Garratt, D. 99
Gaza 41, 42, 43–4, 47, 48, 49, 53–5; Az Theatre 50; Theatre for Everybody 50
Geertz, C. 91
Gibb, C. 69–70, 73, 74
Giddens, A. 82, 89, 94; *see also* Third Way politics
Gielen, P. 134; horizontal or flat world 15; organisational restructurings 16; socially engaged art practices 117–18; vertical creation 19–20
Giroux, H. 9, 60
Gluck, C. 82
Goffman, E. 101
Goksøyr, T.: 'Palestinian Embassy' 27, 28, 29
Goldstein, T.: *Art for Arts Sake* 13

Goods Shed project 109–11, 113, 118–33
graphics novels 135, 137–8
Gray, N. 102
Greenberg, C. 24
Gibert, E.: *The Photographer* 138
Gypsy Roma Traveller culture 97–9, 107–8; wider context 98–9; UK 99, 100; *see also* non-Travellers

Harmaakorpi, V. 111
Hartnett, A. 9, 18
Havel, V. 135
Heathcote, D. 51, 53
Hebdo, C. 135
Herne, S.: Teaching through Contemporary Art project 32

ignorance/ignorant 8, 86; *see also* Rancière
imagination, creative 19, 20, 61, 101, 110, 111
Imai, Y. 85
independent and democratic learning 62–80; democratic learning through art practice: Room 13 67–72; Dewey experience 62–5; forms of democratic education 62–7; habits of democratic experience 65–6; institutional conditions for creative learning 66–7; pedagogical methods 75–80; Room 13 pedagogy 72–5
inequality 126; maintenance 8; Perry 31; Rancière 8; *see also* equality
innovation and creativity 6, 24, 110–2, 120, 121; economic growth 13; *see also* democratic trends in the politics of creativity and innovation
intifada 45, 49

jagodzinski, j. 6, 17
Japan: applied drama 81–92; relationship between education and creativity 83–5
Japanese Ministry of Education, Culture, Sports, Science and Technology 84
Johnson, M. 108
Johnstone, W. 68
Jones, K., 6, 10, 108

Kasikova, H. 136–7
Kellman, D. 38

Khoury, E. 29
knowledge 8–9, 14, 45–6, 64–5, 79, 85–6, 102, 105, 107; emotive 115; technical 114

Lakoff, G. 108
Lave, J. 63, 70
learning: arts based 114–15; democratic education 62–80; experiential democratic 68; habitual 64; independent and democratic 62–80; institutional conditions for creative 66–7; lifelong 3, 63, 109; social 1, 22, 113
Lefevre, D.: *The Photographer* 138
Lemercier, F.: *The Photographer* 138
Lemov, D. 13–14, 15
liberal democracy: Finland 109; UK 109
lifelong learning 3, 63, 109
Lipsitz, G. 14–15
Liverpool Biennial 27, 28
long revolution 2

managerialism 15, 16, 114, 115
Martens, C.: 'Palestinian Embassy' 27, 28, 29
Masschelein, J. 66
Matthews, J. 75–6, 80
McCaughrean, G.: *The Kite Rider* 88–9
McDonnell, J. 12
Meisiek, S. 115, 117
Melkas, H. 111
Mellanen, L. 122, 123
Mer-Khemis, J. 50
metaphor of the kaleidoscope 101–3
Meyer, H. 13
Mill, J. S. 91
Mori 99
Mouffe, C. 3, 96; agonism/antagonism 3, 10–2, 20, 26, 82, 95; democracy is a contest 9; neoliberalism 9; opposing views never settled 61

National Centre for Culture and Arts 50
National Children's Theatre Association 81
Neelands, J. 38, 39
neoliberalism 2, 3, 6, 7, 9, 10, 14, 15, 16, 20, 27, 32, 44, 82, 109, 113, 115, 119, 133
New Public Management era 120

non-governmental organisations (NGOs) 41–2
non-Travellers 98, 104

Occupied Palestinian Territories (OPT) 41, 42
OECD (Organisation for Economic Cooperation and Development) 83; Centre for Educational Research 13
O'Neill, C. 51
OPT *see* Occupied Palestinian Territories
Organisation for Economic Cooperation and Development *see* OECD
Other 51, 101
Othering 51
Owens, A.: Michael's Story 104; performed research 103; slow knowledge work 111

Page, T.: Teaching through Contemporary Art project 32
Palestine 27, 28, 30, 41–61, 98, 138; dangerous and domesticated practice of creativity and democracy 47–52; drama pretext 52–61; dramaturgical form in case study 51–2; dramaturgy in non-formal and formal education 49–51; educational and cultural context 45–7; political context 41–7; present and future 61
Palestinian Ministry of Education: Center for Research into Education, Creativity and the Arts through Practice 41, 109, 119
Palestinian National Authority Ministry of Education (PNAME) 45, 61
Pappe, I. 55; *The Biggest Prison on Earth* 44; *The Ethnic Cleansing of Palestine* 44
Passeron, J. 8, 79
Pässilä, A. 103, 109, 112, 122; aesthetic distancing 118; definition of innovation activities 130; evocative reporting 123; innovation 110–1; management 115
pedagogies 41–61, 81–96; applied drama in Japan 81–7; creativity 81–3; dangerous and domesticated practice of creativity and democracy 47–52; drama pretext 52–61; dramaturgical form in case study 51–2; dramaturgy in non-formal and formal education 49–51; dreamer case study 87–96;

dreamer pretext 88–9; dreamer synopsis 89–90; educational and cultural context 45–7; emancipation and the dramaturgical form: applied drama 86–7; emergent issues 90–5; Japanese context: relationship between education and creativity 83–5; political context 41–7; present and future 61; relationship between art and politics 85–6
performance 1, 3, 14, 15, 22, 23–5, 27, 31, 33, 34, 38, 74, 76, 87; -based curriculum 6; collaborative 35; participative 52; public 34, 37; Western
Perry, G.: 'The Vanity of Small Differences' 30–1
Piper, A. 99; 'Catalysis III' 35
PISA (Programme for International Student Assessment) 12–13
Plato 85
'The Play's the Thing: Václav Havel, Art and Politics' 135
PNAME see Palestinian National Authority Ministry of Education
politics: democratic 12, 39, 61; global 47; of mainstream education 2; proper 10, 11; of taste 31
practice 2–3; dangerous and domesticated practice of creativity and democracy 47–52; democratic learning through art: Room 13 67–72; relational creativity 27–31; socially engaged art 117–18
process drama 38, 87–8, 97; pretext-based 100–3; 106
professional: values 114
Programme for International Student Assessment see PISA

Queen Noor Centre 50

Race Hate Crime UK 97
Ramallah 28, 29; Safar Theatre 50
Rancière, 2, 3, 96, 98–9, 101; art and politics 40; distribution of the sensible 100; *The Emancipated Spectator* 85; equality 7–8, 21, 46, 71, 80, 85, 100; *The Ignorant Schoolmaster* 8, 80, 85, 86; inequality visible 8–9; parallels between models of democracy and models of art 12; real 118; sensible order 119, 126; theatre 86; understanding 8, 105
Rania, J. 49
Read, H. 138, 139
real: fictionalised 118–19
RECAP see Palestinian Ministry of Education: Center for Research into Education, Creativity and the Arts through Practice
relational creativity 23–6; drama in education as a living process 36–9; in education 31–40; politics 39–40; in practice 27–31; teaching through contemporary art project 32–6
relational practices 3, 22–6, 27; politics 39–40
research: -based applied drama 97; -based drama 104; process 82, 91, 96, 98, 99, 111
resistance 10, 15–16, 18, 29–30, 41, 45, 47, 49–50, 55, 89, 93, 133
revolution, democratic 2, 139
Richardson, J. 99
Richmond, T. 120
Rivierre, D. 36, 37
Robinson, J. A. 112
Robinson, K. 110–1
Room 13 62, 65, 67–72, 75; pedagogy 72–4; *What Age Can You Start Being an Artist* 69
Ryder, A. 99

Sacco, J. *Palestine* 137
Safar Theatre 50
Said, E. 18, 44, 51–2
Saito, N. 85
Sauter, W. 101
Schechner, R. 25, 87
Schiuma, G. 114, 115
Schmitt, C. 11
self 41, 48, 51, 56, 59, 61, 82–3, 136; altered 83, 93; value 116
self-criticism 20, 24
self-identity 82, 83, 96, 100
self-Other imagining 51, 101
self-reflection 20, 96, 117, 131
Sennett, R. 32, 118
Sharpe, M. 82
Sherman, C. 36
Shields, J. 120
shockvertising 6
Simons, M. 66
Smith, R. 48

Smyth, J. 66–7
social: change 1, 2, 9, 25, 49, 50, 83, 94, 116, 120, 136; divisions 10; encounter 23, 25; engagement 12, 23, 33, 131; exchange 25; responsibilities 90; structure 91, 121
social enterprise 109, 111, 120–1, 131, 132
social justice 2, 61
social media 12, 16, 23, 137
socially engaged practices 7, 109, 117
society: British 31; civil 46, 50; and culture 20; democratic 17, 65, 98; multicultural 12
space 39, 47, 49, 52, 53, 72, 84, 86, 89, 96–7, 98, 100, 102, 104, 127, 133; community 130; create 81, 82, 83, 111, 131, 132; defining 57; democratic 66; discursive 30; learning 37; personal 59; physical 139; pictorial 24, 78; private symbolic 32; public 18, 25, 113, 126; temporal 74; theatre 139; third 38, 108; transgressive 121
Spiegelman, A.: *Maus* 137
Spielberg, S.: *Schindler's List* 137
Stonewall 99
Summerhill 68
Sunderland 31

Tamari, V.: 'Crushed Cars' 28–9
Tan, Shaun: *The Arrival* 38–9
Taylor, S. S. 116, 131
TCA *see* Teaching through Contemporary Art project
teacher-in-role 58, 59–60
Teaching through Contemporary Art (TCA) project 32, 33, 34, 35, 39
Teatro Sociale 25, 27
Theatre for Everybody 50
Theatre in Education 50
Theatre Pa'tothom: 'Amina's Looking for a Job' 30
third space 38, 108
Third Way politics 10, 109, 113, 121
Thompson, J. 25, 87
Tokyo 83, 87–8

Tomlinson, B. 14–15
translating and understanding in action 105–6

UK 53, 62, 109–10, 111, 113, 133, 139; creativity 47, 48; culture 35, 82, 112; data 13; Department of Trade and Industry 121; education and culture 45; globalization 81; mass secondary education 10, 84, 87–96; Room 13 67, 74; social enterprise 120–1 *see also* Gypsy Roma Traveller culture
understanding 8, 28, 36, 45–6, 50, 65, 66, 74, 76, 79, 80, 119; in action 105–8; adaptive 103; adult 75; 'as agreement' 108; 'application and translation' 108; deficit 86; 'intellectual grasp/I get it' 107–8; political 44; 'practical know-how' 108; skills 117
United Nations 41
UNRWA 49

Valenta, J. 136–7
Verdier, T. 112
Vincent-Lacrin, S.: *Art for Arts Sake* 13

Wenger, E. 63, 70–1
West Bank 6, 28–30, 41, 42, 44, 47, 49, 50; C areas 48
Western Edge Youth Arts; 'Government Project' 38
Williams, 2; definition of creativity 5; participation 7–8, 21
Willis, P. E. 67
Winner, E.: *Art for Arts Sake* 13
Wittgenstein, L.: *Philosophical Investigations* 10–1
World Bank 45, 48
Worwood, K.: Teaching through Contemporary Art project 32

Yes Theatre 50

Zizek, S. 7, 17–18